Her St

Dr Deepti Priya Mehrotra is a political scientist, with cross-disciplinary interests. Her ground-breaking books include *Home Truths: Stories of Single Mothers, Burning Bright: Irom Sharmila and the Struggle for Peace in Manipur, A Passion for Freedom: The Story of Kisanin Jaggi Devi, Gulab Bai: The Queen of Nautanki Theatre* and *Bhartiya Mahila Andolan: Kal, Aaj aur Kal.* She advises civil society organizations on gender and education issues, taught social science at Delhi University, Dayalbagh Educational Institute (DEI), Agra, and Tata Institute of Social Sciences (TISS), Mumbai, and designed curriculum for the Indira Gandhi National Open University (IGNOU). She is recipient of fellowships by Indian Council for Philosophical Research, MacArthur Foundation and Nehru Memorial Museum and Library.

Her Stories
Indian Women Down the Ages
Thinkers, Workers, Rebels, Queens

Deepti Priya Mehrotra

RUPA

Published by
Rupa Publications India Pvt. Ltd 2022
7/16, Ansari Road, Daryaganj
New Delhi 110002

Sales Centres:
Allahabad Bengaluru Chennai
Hyderabad Jaipur Kathmandu
Kolkata Mumbai

ISBN: 978-93-5520-203-1

Third impression 2022

10 9 8 7 6 5 4 3

The moral right of the author has been asserted.

Printed in India

Contents

Introduction
Stories of Incredible Women

The more I read history, the less, it seemed, I knew about women. Conventional histories told us about kings and wars, relegating women to the margins—whether queens or commoners, poets or saints; stray images of wives and daughters lurked in the shadows. Wouldn't it be wonderful, I asked myself, to shine a light on these barely visible figures, and try to understand the past through their eyes? Over many years, I kept squirreling away interesting material wherever I found it, on little-known, but clearly fascinating, women.

As I researched for this book, entire worlds opened up. Forgotten figures took shape, history took on new contours. Each woman profiled here was a protagonist in her times, and helped shape the world in special ways. Some were celebrated, others vilified, or simply casually neglected, victims of collective amnesia. It is testimony to the sheer power of their personae, that somebody somewhere preserved their memory—through folklore, legend, biographical fragment, coin, sculpture, article, official memo, a stamp, a film, a paper, a chapter in a book. I delved into available sources to reconstruct their lives and times. The most evocative sources were their own writings—often poetry, sprinkled with autobiographical minutiae, speaking of rich inner life and multilayered journeys. Other works, such as architectural and philanthropic, also carry authorial signatures, revealing some of the complex emotions and ambitions that constituted these women.

Stories and sheer drama may lie concealed beneath the surface of bland texts. Where mainstream histories display yawning gaps, feminist scholarship, and Dalit, subaltern and gender studies have gradually unearthed rich data, and made analytical advances. Some gaps persist, for historical sources are inevitably limited. One needs to sift through document, legend, myth and hagiography, to arrive at the most plausible truth. While remaining true to evidence, through empathy and imagination facts grow wings, and characters come alive.

Critical feminist subaltern historiography asks new questions and makes fresh interpretations. The move away from androcentric elite history breaks down walls, releasing a surging ocean of human beings, who have much to tell. Women characters emerge from nooks and crannies; each different, in varied circumstances, yet each labouring against the grain of patriarchy, in some or the other aspect of her life. For centuries, patriarchy has defined and limited, reserved the public sphere for men and assigned subsidiary roles in the private domain to women. Mainstream— 'malestream'—history has colluded with these constructions, naturalizing women as stereotypical daughters, wives, mothers— symbols of domesticity, rather than active human beings. Dalit and working-class women have been, additionally, naturalized as workers whose labour belongs to the elite.

When we look with curiosity and awareness of the hidden agency of the oppressed, we find not only subjugation, but also protest, creativity, resistance and achievement. Lives of ordinary people are at least as interesting as the lives of kings and emperors. Women have been thinkers, doers, movers and shakers, subverting hierarchies, bringing peace out of chaos, surviving despite routine devaluation.

Many of our foremothers emerge as gutsy, often startling in their originality, independence and derring-do. Their multifaceted contributions indicate that women were not just victims, but makers of history—and of literature, philosophy, law, medicine, science, art, architecture, music and religion. Their poems and prose often contained pithy wisdom; they acted upon adverse circumstances with will and courage. It is overwhelming just how much women managed to do, despite pervasive controls, violence and suppression.

Objectively appreciating their struggles goes along with noticing women's flaws, shortcomings and failures. One steers clear of hagiography. One tries to understand the living, breathing human being, who may have lived hundreds or thousands of years ago. You put yourself in her skin, her context, examine her words and deeds (as much as we know), to understand what formed her, her challenges, motivations, emotional–mental make-up. One reinterprets from this position: for instance, if a queen such as Didda or Baiza Bai, after years of experience as regent, did not want to hand over to a raw young man, privileged over her by virtue of gender, she was not 'lusting for power' (as male commentators have long insisted); rather, she was staking a just claim.

∽

I have attempted to source stories from as many regions of India as I could manage, over a span of three millennia. There are several clusters of stories—Buddhist women of ancient India; Bhakti movement poet-saints of medieval India; women of the Mughal court; and freedom fighters of the eighteenth and nineteenth centuries.

From ancient India, Sulabha and Lopamudra—philosopher-teachers of the second millennium BCE—hold sway. From Jain literature, I retell the story of Chandana. The next 11 stories—from Gautami to Sanghamitra—are about Buddhist women; rich details of their lives and compositions survive in the *Therigatha* (Hymns of the Elders/Senior Nuns), the world's oldest collection of women's poetry. They carved out their own space within Buddhism, a counterculture that allowed dignity and self-expression. Some Buddhist women were queens or princesses (of Magadha, Kosala and the Mauryan empire), or wealthy benefactor-patrons, like Visakha.

Royal women, though frequently pawns in games played by kings, exercised a measure of power. They conveyed information, beliefs, ideas from one culture to another; intervened in the administration to push different agendas, often mitigating effects of violent statecraft. Queens profiled here include Prabhavatigupta of the Vakataka, Naganika of the Satavahana and Leima Laisna of the Ningthouja dynasties in ancient India; in medieval and modern India, Didda of Kashmir, Razia of Delhi, Umayamma of Travancore, Ahilyabai of Indore; Begums of Bhopal; and Joanna (Begum Samru) of Sardhana.

From a surprisingly little-known galaxy of feisty Mughal women, we have here: Gulbadan the historian; Bega, creator of magnificent architecture; Maham Anaga, diligent child-nurse and royal advisor; Harkha, known to history as Maryam-uz-Zamani; Jahanara, the wealthy Sufi fakira-princess; and the 'hidden' poet Zebunissa.

From medieval India, we have a clutch of women poet-mystics. The stories foreground their own writings: Andal the Vaishnavite; Karaikkal Ammaiyar the Shaivite; Akkamahadevi the Virashaivite; Lalla from Kashmir; Janabai and Kanhopatra from Maharashtra; Rami from Bengal; and Meera from Rajasthan. They blazed paths off the beaten track, to stunning effect, their lifestories and literary contributions extraordinarily diverse. Rejecting religious and social orthodoxies, they claimed legitimacy for bhakti—personal devotion—directly communing with the divine, accessible to all social strata. Their writings are realistic, frank, colourful, speaking of personal experience in ways male poet-saints seldom do. Several were from working-class, Dalit backgrounds—including Janabai (maidservant), Kanhopatra (devadasi or ganika) and Rami (washerwoman). Women, such as these, brought God out of the temple and monastery, into the home and kitchen; making spiritual succour accessible to a far wider swathe of humanity.

Khivi institutionalized langar—food offered to all by Sikh congregations—a unique contribution to human imagination of inclusive community. Other poets in the collection include Auvaiyar the Sangama poet (1–3 CE); Khona the scientist-poet; the tawaifs Muddupalani (who wrote an 'erotic epic'), Molla (who wrote a Ramayana) and Mahlaqa Bai Chanda (arguably the first woman writer of Urdu ghazals).

Women warriors, freedom fighters and revolutionaries included the indefatigable queens Rudrama of Telangana, Durgavati of Gondwana, Abbakka of Tulu Nadu, Velu Nachiyar of Shivagangai, Chenamma of Kittur, Baiza Bai of Gwalior, Jind Kaur of Punjab, Avanti Bai Lodhi, Lakshmibai, and Begum Hazrat Mahal. Some of their stories importantly include more than one central character: thus, we have Kuyili and Udaiyal, who fought along with Velu Nachiyar; Jhalkari Bai of Jhansi (Dalit 'twin' of Lakshmibai); Uda Pasi, the 'sharpshooter' of Lucknow, in Hazrat Mahal's resistance army.

Some other important dalit icons: Unniyarcha, martial artiste, battled the harassment of women in north Kerala; Nangeli opposed the exploitative 'breast-tax' in Travancore; Onake Obavva single-handedly defended the Chitradurga Fort, Karnataka. And finally, there is a band of activist-teacher-writers who battled to educate girls of vulnerable castes and communities—Savitribai, Sagunabai, Fatima Sheikh, Mukta Salve and Tarabai Shinde—

leading the way into the future.

The stories are presented in chronological order: second millennium BCE, to the nineteenth century CE. This book winds up somewhere in the nineteenth century; more figures from the late nineteenth, as well as plenty from the twentieth and early twenty-first centuries, will be covered in my next book.

∽

All the women profiled here negotiated minefields of prejudice and stigma: their stories hold betrayal, suffering, loss and grief. Each one strove bravely to make a better life: to reimagine the world. They made their voices heard, in modes that have somehow survived.

We find that many—perhaps most—women who played a visible role in history were single, by choice or circumstance; to wit, Jain and Buddhist *bhikkhunis* (female monks); Bhakti movement poet-saints; royal women such as Jahanara, Zebunissa, Didda, Durgavati, Rudrama and Lakshmibai; and 'public women' such as Amrapali, Muddupalani, Chanda and Kanhopatra. Many nonconformist women asserted and articulated sharp critiques of marital servitude and male duplicity and an intense desire for autonomy. Chandana, Sumangalamata, Kundalakesi, Mahadeviakka, Lalla, Meera, Janabai, Kanhopatra and several others confronted violence in personal life; their rejection of conventional norms was at the same time a struggle for sheer survival. Many critiques were intersectional: the struggle for dignity was a war against multiple violations, articulated by working and Dalit women.

The stories in this book describe desperate situations, ingenious strategies, hard struggles and brilliant sparks of feminist consciousness. Far from being accounts of isolated heroines or 'great women', these her-stories place at their centre the ordinary woman, in all her splendid diversity, multifaceted struggle and achievement. The women profiled were generally encouraged or supported by other women in their lives; their achievements represent the aspirations of many in the past, and provide inspiration for us in the present.

The joy of writing has been in the discovery of these inspiring stories, and retelling them, to share with you. Each her-story is unique. I personally found the saga of Maharani Jind Kaur the most searing; that I had never heard of her earlier was inexplicable, considering I have family roots in Punjab. But *all* the stories were deeply moving; so much intelligent action, virtually erased from public memory. To reclaim our past, we remember and celebrate these remarkable women: our common heritage. Even as we read, may our powers grow! We need all the power we can muster, to continue the good fight—for voice, dignity, autonomy and independence—in a country that continues to torment its girls and women.[1]

1 | Sulabha: Peripatetic Philosopher

Second Millennium BCE

S ulabha was an independent, peripatetic philosopher. She set her own course in life, belonged to no organized order and went from place to place holding discussions on ethics and metaphysics. Autonomous and self-confident, she had opted out of marriage, caste and community. Sulabha was single, and singular. Her debate with the famous King Janaka indicates her depth and intellectual genius.

One day, Sulabha arrived at Janaka's court, having heard that he was devoted to understanding emancipation. Janaka received her with honour. Both took their seats in court, scholars gathered to listen. Sulabha used yogic powers to enter and examine his state of consciousness. The king meanwhile asked who she was, and whose, and where she had come from. He asserted that he, though a king and householder, was a liberated soul; while she, being a beautiful young woman, was full of attachment and desire. He accused her of entering him through yogic powers: wrong because they were of different castes and ways of life (she ascetic, he householder). Disdainfully he noted that she was 'thoroughly independent or unrestrained' and 'evil', for trying to display superiority over him. He speculated that a rival king may have sent Sulabha as a spy; and insisted that the power of a king lay in sovereignty, while the power of women was their beauty.

Sulabha replied with dignity, unfazed by Jananka's aggressive diatribe. She described the inappropriateness of speaking in anger, and calmly exposed Janaka's prejudices. She described the nature of the body: pure consciousness or Purusha, when moved by the active principle, Prakriti, differentiates to form multiple objects. The same primal material and consciousness permeates all: 'As lac and wood, as grains of dust and drops of water exist commingled when brought together, even so are the existences of all creatures.' Since all bodies are composed of the same elements in constant flux, there is no stable 'person', and the notion of individual identity is an illusion: 'Myself, thyself, O monarch, and all others that are endued with body are the result of that Prakriti.'

She asked Janaka why he was so interested in individual identity: 'As thou seest thy own body in thy body and as thou seest thy soul in thy own soul, why is it that thou dost not see thy body and thy soul in the bodies and souls of others? If it is true that thou seest an identity with thyself and others, why then didst thou ask me who I am and whose? If it is true that thou hast, O king, been freed from the knowledge of duality that (erroneously) says—this is mine and this other is not mine—then what use is there with such questions as 'Who art thou, whose art thou and whence dost thou come?' The logic was powerful and flawless; everybody in court was awestruck.

Sulabha asked: 'What harm have I done thee by entering thy person with only my intellect? I have not touched thee, O King, with my hands, or arms, or feet, or thighs, or with any other part of the body.' She had examined his Atman, but Janaka confused body with Atman. Also, he had assumed she was Brahmin, but in fact she was born in a royal household and thus Kshatriya.

Sulabha pointed out that attaching too much significance to a person being woman or man, as Janaka did, was a grave mistake. She described how at some point, the fetus acquires sexual characteristics, and after birth, 'its sex being known, it comes to be called a boy or girl.' Gender is a fluid construct, and what seems fixed is actually in flux: 'Particles of the body are constantly born and constantly die, but these changes are so minute that they cannot be observed, just as one cannot perceive the changes in the flame of a lamp.'

Viewing her as a woman, Janaka assumed she was inferior to men, betraying gross prejudice. His notion that a woman must belong to a man was wrong thinking. She explained that she was single: 'No husband could be obtained for me that would be fit for me. Instructed then in the religion of Emancipation, I wander over the Earth alone, observant of the practices of asceticism. I practise no hypocrisy in the matter of the life of Renunciation... I am firm and steady in my vows.'

Janaka, on the other hand, was far from emancipation: 'Thy endeavour to attain Emancipation when thou hast so many faults is like the use of medicine by a patient who indulges in all kinds of forbidden food and practices.' A king 'is attached to the duties of rewarding and punishing,' as are householders: '...all men in their own houses chastise and reward.' Sulabha asked why Janaka wished to remain king: 'If thou hast prevailed over all thy bonds and freed thyself from all attachments, may I ask thee, O King, why thou preservest thy connections still with this umbrella and these other appendages of royalty? I think that thou hast not listened to the scriptures, or, thou hast listened to them without any advantage.' A kingdom 'is as unsubstantial as burning flames fed by straw or the bubbles of froth seen on the surface of water. Who is there that would like to obtain sovereignty, or having acquired sovereignty can hope to win tranquility?'

Aware and self-assured, Sulabha confirmed that she herself was tranquil and detatched. She desired only to explore the truth: 'impelled by sincerity only', not interested 'in that intellectual gladiatorship which is implied by a dialectical disputation for the sake of victory.'

The Sulabha–Janaka dialogue was reported by Bhishma, in the Mahabharata's Shanti Parva.[2] Bhishma concluded: 'Hearing these words fraught with excellent sense and reason, King Janaka failed to return any answer thereto.' Sulabha's intelligence and genuine quest for truth won the day.

The Sulabha-Janaka dialogue can be seen as a bulwark against patriarchal conceit. Sulabha may have lived in the early vedic period, a few centuries before the epic was penned. While patriarchy was at a nascent stage in the early vedic period, it had hardened by the time the Mahabharata was written (between 400 BCE and 400 CE). Sulabha also composed a portion of the Rigveda, Saulabha Shakha, which is now lost; and is listed in the Kaushtaki Brahmina as a revered teacher, to whom salutations must be offered.

Sulabha, whom we neglect at our own peril, can teach us to hone our intelligence and use it for the best of ends. She was an original thinker, articulate, self-possessed and wise to the ways of the world. As scholar Ruth Vanita notes: 'her arguments provide a philosophical justification within Hindusim, for any woman to make unconventional choices. Her arguments... apply to any woman anywhere.'[3]

2 | Lopamudra: Vedic Feminist

Second Millennium BCE, Central and South India

We glimpse a shadowy figure across the sands of time: her name means 'the invisible one'. Piecing together Lopamudra's story, she emerges feisty and multifaceted; the name may also mean 'one absorbed in herself'. Tradition reveres her as teacher of Srividya, worship of the sacred feminine. She was a Rishika and Brahmavadini. One of the few women whose verses are included in the Rigveda, her voice and views—strong, authoritative and distinctive—prevailed over those of her husband, the celebrated sage Agastya. If ever there was a vedic feminist, it was Lopamudra.

Lopamudra is believed to have developed and refined Srividya, which she learnt from Mitreshanatha, and taught Agastya. 'Lopamudra vidya' was codified over the next centuries, and had a faithful following in Kashmir and Kerala, well into sixth century CE, despite the creeping domination of patriarchal brahminism. 'Lopamudra mantra' or Panchadasi is still recited to enhance powers of speech, love and transformation. Lopamudra transmitted Lalita Sahasranama, thousand names of Lalita, to her disciples: Lalita is playful creative energy pervading the cosmos.

Lopamudra was young when she married Agastya. For several years, they did not cohabit. As Lopamudra grew into mature adulthood, she questioned his vow of celibacy. Though Agastya was reluctant to change, he wished to have a son to propitiate his ancestors. They debated the issue of sexuality versus asceticism, an intense exchange, as philosophical as it was practical. Ultimately, Lopamudra was able to convince her middle-aged, celibate husband that in the best kind of life, spiritual and worldly coalesce. Her arguments and methods helped secure the roots of Srividya and Shaktism, which over time crystallized into full-blown doctrines. The sensual is sacred; female and male principles unite and in harmony create the differentiated world: one becomes many.

This complex debate between Lopamudra and Agastya was condensed into a conversation in six verses, which form a sutra of the Rigveda (Rigveda, 1.179). The first two verses were spoken by Lopamudra, the third by Agastya, the fourth by Lopamudra, the fifth by Agastya and the last either by a disciple of theirs, or by Agastya. The sutra dramatically encapsulated the result of a long dialogue between husband and wife—monastic celibacy losing to the doctrine that emphasized integration of sexual and spiritual.

In the first verse, Lopamudra says: 'In our life of many years, through many dawns we have laboured tirelessly day and night. Old age impairs beauty and diminishes bodily strength. Let virile men come near unto their wives.' Her second verse continues, 'For even the ancients, devoted to the pursuit of Truth, in communion with the gods, noble, strong and capable, have not remained brahmacharis forever. Women should come unto their virile men.'

Agastya replies, 'Our meditations have not been futile. If we two now engage, merging as a couple, we will be able to face a hundred challenges and triumph in many conflicts.' Lopamudra says, 'Desire has come upon me for the bull who roars, and is held back, desire engulfing me from this side, that side, all sides.' The poet adds: 'Lopamudra, aroused, draws out her resolute husband, the bull rushes forth, she drains deep and directs his turbulent panting.'

Agastya, having emerged from celibacy, says, 'By this Soma which I have drunk, in my innermost heart I say, whatever offences we have committed, let him forgive us, for a mortal man is full of many desires.' The last verse comments: 'Agastya, digging with spades, wishing for progeny, and strength, nourished both divine and human qualities, and found fulfilment of his real hopes among the gods.'[4]

Thus, their differences were reconciled and companionship ripened into intimacy. Sexuality was negotiated, with Lopamudra initiating and expressing desire frankly and unapologetically; and Agastya responding with passion. Having noted that human beings are full of desire and longing, Agastya thereafter explored kindred points of lovemaking and penance, cherished the celestial and the earthly, and attained immortality through progeny and ascetic practice. So did Lopamudra—who taught Agastya to accept his own desires, and thus revitalized their life. Lopamudra also means 'breaking of the seal'—aptly describing her influence on Agastya's abjuring of celibacy.

Lopamudra urged him, then, to gather wealth to bring up the child they both wished to have. Agastya explored various options and approached Illwala, king of asuras. Appreciating Agastya's supernatural powers, siddhis, Illwala gifted him a golden chariot and gold and silver coins. Agastya returned home after seven years. He asked Lopamudra whether she wanted a thousand sons or just one who could defeat a thousand. Lopamudra replied she would prefer one learned son rather than a thousand evil ones. When Lopamudra delivered a baby, he was born reciting the vedas, for while in the womb, he regularly heard his parents chanting! The child, Dridhasyu, became a celebrated poet.

Lopamudra may have been born to tribal parents in central

India, but was reared by Kshatriyas. According to the Mahabharata and the puranas, Agastya found Lopamudra in the forest, and took the baby to the king and queen of Vidarbha, who adopted her and loved and educated her well. When Agastya returned after several years and demanded her as his bride, the royal parents were reluctant, but Lopamudra agreed: 'He has the wealth of ascetic living. My youth will fade, but his virtue makes him the right person.'

In the Giridhara Ramayana, Agastya wished to marry any daughter of the king of Kannauj. The king married off his daughters elsewhere; and dressed his *son*, Lopamudra, in girl's attire and presented him to Agastya. After the wedding, Lopamudra transformed into a woman: a story ripe with transgender possibilities; on the other hand, Lopamudra, the youngest daughter, may have been brought up as a son. Another meaning of 'Lopamudra' is 'one whose body has long been hidden'.

The Mahabharata describes Agastya and Lopamudra's hermitage at Agastyapuri, in Dandaka forest beside the Godavari. At some point, the couple moved from central to south India. Tamil sources describe their hermitage in Tirunelveli or Thanjavur, where they contributed to the spread of Sanskrit and vedic traditions—irrigation, agriculture, astronomy and medicine. In Skanda Purana, however, Lopamudra was daughter of Kavera, a rishi from Coorg. She agreed to marry Agastya, on condition that he would never leave her. However, he once left her, during a famine. Enraged, Lopamudra became a river—Kaveri—which brought relief and prosperity to the land. The Kodavu people consider Kaveri to be a twin manifestation of Lopamudra.

Agastya has several sutras in the Rigveda which indicate that he helped reconcile conflicts between Aryas and Dasas: 'May each community know refreshment (food) and lively waters.' All this makes us consider Lopamudra and Agastya to be vedic seers, who drew from tribal, Dravidian and Aryan heritage, and advocated plurality and peaceful coexistence. Lopamudra, moreover, asserted the centrality of a primal, vital, creative feminine principal, in human life and the universe.

3 | Chandana: Non-Violent Ways

Sixth–Fifth Century BCE, Bihar

Chandana was the first nun in the Mahavira Jain tradition, a leader and preceptor of the faith. Her story remains very much alive in the Jain imagination. After experiencing immense suffering, she adopted an unconventional way of life, where she found refuge and meaning, opening up a new path for women.

Born a princess, Chandana's father Dadhivahan was Raja of Champa, a republic in present-day Bihar, while Dharani, her mother, was daughter of King Chetak of Vaishali. Her parents named her Vasumati, but due to her gentle and sweet nature, people began calling her Chandanbala, or Chandana. Her father's sister Trishaladevi was Mahavira's mother. Chandana's parents and Mahavira's parents were followers of Parsvanath, the 23rd Jain Tirthankara. She was brought up respecting ethical injunctions of ahimsa, aparigraha and anasakti, that is, non-violence, non-possessiveness and non-attachment.

Chandana's mother's sister Mrigavati was married to Raja Shatnik of Kosambi, who believed in violent conquest and territorial expansion. He challenged Dadhivahan to war. Dadhivahan refused, being a believer in non-violence. His army being tiny compared with Shatnik's, he decided to retreat into the forest. Shatnik sent his men to loot Champa and capture women.

Dharani and Chandana were defenceless. Shatnik's soldiers captured and dragged them to a deserted spot intending to sexually assault them. Dharani committed suicide by pulling back her tongue in such a way as to suffocate herself. The soldiers were horrified. Repentant, they apologized to Chandana and took her to Kosambi.

In Kosambi, a merchant, Dhanavah, bought Chandana, to help his wife Mooladevi with household tasks. Chandana accepted her changed circumstances in philosophical spirit. Helping Mooladevi with housework, Chandana also served Dhanavah, who developed fatherly affection for her. Mooladevi, however, interpreted his affection for the young woman as attraction and became jealous. Once, when he came home from a business trip, Chandana bent down to wash his feet with warm water, her long hair almost touching the ground; he picked it up and put it on her back. This gesture troubled Mooladevi greatly.

When Dhanavah went on another trip, Mooladevi called a barber and got Chandana's head shaved, and hired a locksmith who chained Chandana and locked her in a dark room. Mooladevi wanted her to starve to death. Chandana neither fought back, nor blamed Mooladevi. Instead, she used the confinement as an opportunity to fast and meditate. Chandana reflected on the changes that had beset her—from princess to a starving wretch. She felt amused at the vagaries of fate.

On the fourth day, Dhanavah returned. Shocked to find Chandana chained and starving, he brought her whatever food he could find—a handful of soaked lentils in a winnowing basket—and rushed off to fetch the locksmith. She waited in the dark room, chained, one foot in, one foot out. Before breaking her fast, she wanted to offer food to a Muni.

At that very moment, Mahavira passed outside the house. He had been fasting for five months and 28 days. He refused all food because, unknown to anyone, he had set himself 10 seemingly impossible conditions: he would accept food only if lentils were offered, from a winnow, by a princess, with a shaved head, in chains, one foot in her cell and one out, who had fasted for three days and had tears flowing from her eyes, a chaste woman and would serve him only after all other mendicants had rejected her food offering.

Chandana offered her meagre food to Mahavira. He turned away: most of his conditions were met, but she had no tears in her eyes! When he rejected her offering, tears welled up and flowed down Chandana's cheeks. Mahavira's last stipulation thus fulfilled, he accepted her food offering.

Dhanavah returned. Mooladevi was forgiven. Chandana was freed, and resolved to devote her life to spiritual practice. She became the first Jain nun, ordained by Mahavira.

After Chandana took this step, many other women followed. Chandana led a wandering life, travelling constantly, never spending more than a day in any village, just like Mahavira. Her early inclination towards non-violence, fortitude and compassion became matters of deep conviction. Appreciating her sagacity, Mahavira asked her to head the order of nuns, and she took charge of the ever-growing congregation.

According to the Kalpa Sutra, at the time of Mahavira's attainment of moksha, there were 36,000 Jain nuns and 14,000 monks; 318,000 shravikas (laywomen) and 59,000 shravakas (laymen). With two and a half times as many nuns as monks, and five times more laywomen than laymen in the faith, women had clearly made a place for themselves. They helped develop and spread the faith, and it provided them an alternative space from conventional domesticity, suffering and calamities.

After Mahavira's passing, Chandana continued to build the congregation, and ordain more nuns. She contributed immensely to preserving, enriching and teaching the Jain tenets and way of life. Her interpretations carried forward the original intent, imbued with her sensibilities.

There may have been some precedents within Jainism. Some believe that several millennia before Chandana's time, when Rishabhnath, the 1st Tirthankar, founded the Jain faith, his daughter Brahmi became a nun, along with at least 2,000 other women. During the time of Parsvanath (the 23rd preceptor), some 250 years before Mahavira (the 24th and last preceptor), some 20,000 nuns are said to have attained moksha; as did 1,000 monks.

Despite these astonishing figures, Digambara Jains believe a woman cannot attain moksha until she is reborn a man. It is Shvetambaras who believe women can attain moksha just as a man can. The Shvetambaras believe that Malli, one of the 24 Tirthankaras, was a woman, which the Digambaras deny.

To date we might see Jain nuns, clad in white, barefoot, gentle and austere, carrying with them a wooden bowl for food offerings. They travel, teaching through precept and practise the virtues of simplicity, non-violence and non-attachment, peace and forbearance. Chandana forms a sturdy link in the chain, of a tradition that stretches into the hoary past, and continues to be vibrant today.

4 | Gautami: Beloved Leader

Sixth Century BCE, Nepal and Bihar

Mahapajapati Gautami was the first woman to be ordained within the Buddhist Sangha. Yet, when she first asked to join the order, Buddha would not allow it. She persisted for several years before he opened up the path for her. 'Mahapajapati' means 'leader of a great following'—a prediction made when she was born. And so it came to be: Gautami was a leader among women, and immediately after she joined, so did many others. She practised diligently, became a *theri* (senior nun), taught lay disciples, and ordained and mentored other nuns.

Gautami was born in Devadaha, her father being chief of the Koliyas. Both Gautami and her sister Mahamaya were married to Shuddhodana, chief of the Shakyas. When Mahamaya was pregnant, she travelled from Kapilavastu to Devadaha, but Siddhartha was born en route, in the tree grove of Lumbini. Mahamaya returned to Kapilavastu with her newborn. Gautami was also pregnant, and gave birth to a son, Nanda, a few days younger than Siddhartha. Mahamaya had seemed fine, but died within a week of Siddhartha's birth. Gautami then adopted Siddhartha and brought him up, handing over her own son to a foster mother. Afterwards, Gautami and Shuddhodana had a daughter, Sundarinanda.

Since ancient times, the Koliyas and Shakyas intermarried within themselves. Gautami's brother Supabuddha was married to Shuddhodana's sister, Pamita, and they had a daughter, Yashodhara. Yashodhara and Siddhartha were married, both 16 years old. Several years later, they had a son, Rahula. Soon after Rahula's birth, Siddhartha left the palace. At the time, there was a dispute between the Koliyas and Shakyas, over use of the river Rohini. Some ministers proposed war with the Koliyas, Siddhartha opposed it, but the people's assembly accepted the plan of war. Siddhartha was disturbed by the violence human beings indulge in, and was seeking a way to end it. Seven years after leaving home, he gained enlightenment and founded the Dhamma.

Gautami understood Siddhartha; she herself felt the futility of war. When Buddha visited Kapilavastu, she carefully heard his sermons, and was converted to the philosophy. A few years later, Shuddhodana was ailing, and Buddha came to provide solace. After Shuddhodana died, Gautami asked Buddha to ordain her, and 500 other women. Gautami repeated her request twice, but Buddha refused each time.

Later the same year, Gautami and her band of determined aspirants shaved off their hair, donned ochre robes and walked 250 miles from Kapilavastu to Vaishali, arriving dust-coated, their feet swollen and hurting. Gautami asked Ananda, Buddha's disciple, to speak for them. Ananda reminded Buddha: 'Mahapajapati Gautami was very helpful to the Blessed One—serving as his aunt, foster mother, caregiver and giver of milk, who breastfed the Blessed One after his mother died.' Buddha relented, out of respect and gratitude. Gautami accepted the eight rules he laid down for women (*bhikkhunis*, that is female monks), and was thus ordained.

After Gautami, the other 500 women were ordained. Many

had lost husbands, fathers, brothers or sons in war. They were from royal, merchant, artisan and peasant households; there were also some erstwhile concubines of Siddhartha—including Tissa, Dhira, Vira, Mitta, Bhadra and Upasama. Gautami's daughter Sundarinanda joined, but was conceited about her looks, and half-hearted about the Dhamma. One day, Buddha called for her, created a lovely woman, and showed her this illusory woman passing through youth, midlife, old age, death and decay. Sundarinanda realized the transience of good looks, and the meaning of impermanence, and became a serious disciple.

Gautami progressed rapidly on the path. Buddha appreciated her as one with great experience. Over the years, she tried to change some of the eight rules he had laid down for women. The first rule required all bhikkhunis to pay obeisance to all bhikkhus; Gautami requested Buddha: 'Allow making salutations to take place equally between bhikkhus and bhikkhunis, according to seniority.' Buddha (according to one version) responded by changing the rule thus: a bhikkhuni had to bow only to a monk who was worthy of respect. Part of the reason he made the change was his knowledge that some six monks had bared their thighs in front of nuns. The Buddhist Sangha apparently had its share of sexual tensions and harassment: issues that Gautami would have dealt with. Gradually, Buddha relaxed strict observance of the eight rules. Among other amendments, bhikkhunis were allowed greater autonomy in living and travelling alone (without monks), and in handling ritual observances.

Gautami built up the Bhikkhuni Sangha, ordained a large number of women, and had many disciples, such as Mutta, Mettika, Subha, Therika, Punna, Chitta, Dantika, Gutta and Bhadda Kapalini. Mutta, from a working-class household of Kosala, was mentored by Gautami. Mutta practised, gained insight and exulted:

So free am I, so gloriously free,
Free from three petty things—
From mortar, from pestle and from my hunchback
lord...
Freed from rebirth and death I am
And all that has held me down
Is hurled away...

Gautami ordained and mentored Mettika, who hailed from a wealthy family of Rajagriha; ageing, she went alone to the forest and composed the following:

Though I am suffering and weak,
My youthful spring gone, yet have I come,
Leaning upon my staff, climbed aloft
The mountain peak.
My cloak thrown off,
My little bowl overturned: I sit here
Upon the rock. O'er my spirit sweeps
The breath of Liberty![5]

The Theri Apadana says Gautami died at the age of 120. When he heard she was ill, Buddha came to her room, breaking the injunction that forbade a monk from visiting the room of a nun. Gautami spoke:

'That aim for which one goes forth,
From home to homelessness,
Has been attained by me;
All my fetters and bonds are destroyed.'

Turning to her son Nanda, and step-grandson Rahula (both of whom were monks), she said:

'I have seen the Blessed One,

> This is my last body...
> Maya gave birth to Gautama
> For the sake of us all.
> She has driven back the pain
> Of the sick and the dying.'[6]

Younger nuns wept, but she taught them that separation is inevitable; and going into deep meditation, passed away. Several of the 500 bhikkhunis ordained with her passed away, the same day. In the Kanya Mai temple at her birthplace, Devadaha, as well as in Burmese, Cambodian, Laotian and Thai congregations, the day is celebrated every year, in memory of Gautami, who laid the foundation of the first Bhikkhuni Sangha.

5 | Patachara: Renowned Teacher

Sixth–Fifth Century BCE, Uttar Pradesh

Patachara was a most unconventional woman, who struck out against strictures of class, caste and social morality. She followed her heart; but enormous tragedies engulfed her. After much hardship, she gained peace of mind and developed into a fine teacher. Buddha assigned her the foremost place among those well-versed in the Vinaya (rules of conduct). Patachara's name occurs in the *Therigatha* more frequently than any other bhikkhuni's. She evolved a distinctive style of teaching, imbued with sensitivity and empathy, and became renowned as a teacher. People revered her and flocked to her sermons; this woman, who once had walked the roads, mad with despair and grief.

Patachara's story began with her birth in a merchant household, in Shravasti. When she grew up, she had an affair with a servant working in her home. Her parents arranged her marriage with a young man of their rank. But she told her lover, 'After tomorrow there will be a hundred door-keepers to keep you from seeing me. If you have the spirit, take me with you and depart this very moment!' He brought an elephant and they rode off to his village, and set up home.

Within the year she was pregnant, and wished to go to her parents' home for childbirth. Her husband procrastinated, and she set out alone one day. When he discovered she'd left, he felt guilty, so he pursued and overtook her on her way home. Her labour pains began, and she gave birth on the roadside. She decided to return to their own home, since the reason for going to her parents had passed.

When she became pregnant again, the situation repeated itself, except that when her labour began, they were in the midst of a rainstorm. Her husband went to gather grass to make a shelter, but was bitten by a venomous snake. Patachara gave birth in the lashing rain, and spent the night protecting both children with her body. When day broke, she discovered her husband, dead. Overwhelmed with grief, she resumed her journey, carrying the newborn, leading the elder child by hand. A flooded stream lay across their path; she told the elder to wait while she took her newborn infant across. Leaving him on a pile of leaves, she returned for the first. Looking back, she saw a hawk swoop down upon the baby, so she screamed to scare it away. The elder boy thought she was calling out to him, so he stepped into the river and sadly drowned. The hawk meanwhile carried away the infant.

In despair, weeping and lamenting, Patachara continued walking. Reaching Shravasti, she could not find her old home. People told her that the house had collapsed in the rainstorm, killing all inside, and pointed out a huge pyre, where her mother, father and brother were cremated. She saw smoke still rising, curling upwards. Patachara was inconsolable. She went around in circles, wailing, out of her mind. Rags barely covered her body. Crowds of people followed her, jeering, while others drove her off with sticks. They began calling her Patachara, which means 'she who wanders unclad'; the word also means 'she who wanders wisely'.

One day, she came upon Buddha, giving a sermon at Jetavana. He addressed her directly: 'Sister, return to your right mind!' She felt his loving kindness, and saying, 'Help me', related her terrible story. Somebody threw her a garment, which she wore. Buddha told her she had cried more tears for the dead than fill an ocean. But no kin can help her; upon realizing this, the wise swiftly walk on the road to liberation. Patachara asked to be ordained.

She practised diligently, but could find no peace. One day while bathing, she saw water run down the slope, absorbed by sand, some quickly, some taking longer. She saw that the same happens with humans, some living short, some long, lives. That night when she put off the lamp in her room, she experienced a breakthrough:

> I held back my mind,
> As one would a thoroughbred horse,
> … I used a needle to pull out the lamp's wick,
> As the lamp went out, my mind was free.[7]

One day when Patachara was out walking, a poor Brahmin beggarwoman called Chanda approached her, and told her that her entire family had died of cholera seven years ago; she asked for advice. Patachara could empathize deeply with her despair and help her find new purpose in life. Chanda later wrote:

> Sympathetic to me, Patachara made me go forth,
> She gave me advice and pointed me toward the highest
> goal.
> I listened to her words and put into action her advice.
> That excellent woman's advice was not empty.

Similarly, Uttara, from a merchant family of Shravasti, met Patachara when young, and later paid tribute to her:

> I met a nun I thought I could trust,
> She taught me the Dharma,
> The elements of body and mind,
> The nature of perception, earth, water, fire and wind…

A poem records Patachara teaching a group of 500 nuns, all of whom had lost children to death. She was able to dispel their grief by placing their sufferings in perspective. She helped them heal, even as she had, through the light of reflection and understanding. She spoke comforting, strengthening words:

> You keep crying out, 'My son!'—to that being
> Who was coming or going somewhere else
> …He came from somewhere or other, he stayed a bit…
> He went the way he came, what is there to grieve about?

Each of the nuns repeated Patachara's words and noted,

> She pulled out the arrow that was hard for me to see,
> The one that I nourished in my heart…
> The grief that had overwhelmed me…
> Today…I am without hunger, completely free…

Bowing, they paid their respect to their revered teacher, Patachara, saying:

> 'We have taken your advice, and will live honouring you.'[8]

6 | Amrapali: Wise Ganika

Sixth-Fifth Century BCE, Bihar

Amrapali was a beautiful and talented performing artiste in the republic of Vaishali. The state appointed her 'ganika', a prestigious position that many women vied for. 'Ganika' comes from 'gana', or republic; she was the female counterpart of the 'nagarika' or male citizen—a public personage, rather than private wife. Amrapali was held in high esteem and considered the pride of the city. Later in life, she became a bhikkhuni and realized the impermanence of wealth and beauty. She composed verses which indicate her sensitive, probing mind; she closely observed and documented the changes in her own body:

> Black as night, like the down of the honeybee,
> Curled and flowing was my raven hair—black silk.
> Now, with age, it resembles strands of hemp.
>
> And my eyes, like royal jewels, shone
> Sparkling and resplendent, long, wide and black.
> Now with age, faded, dim, they shine no more...
>
> My earlobes were a thing of beauty, like bracelets
> Fashioned and finished by a master craftsman.
> But now, with age, they hang and droop...
>
> Earlier my teeth dazzled with their whiteness,
> Shining like the colour of the plantain bud.

Now with age, they are chipped, broken and black...

I remember my throat was like a conch-shell,
Well-polished by the sea, delicate and graceful.
Now, with age, my neck is bowed and bent...

Once my breasts were round and full,
They rose into the air, side by side.
Now with age, they sag like empty water-bags...

Oh, the beauty of my body, in the past,
Like a sheet of gold, polished to perfection.
Now, with age, fine wrinkles cover it...

Like the elephant's curving trunk, firm and smooth,
Were my two thighs. That was in my youth, I know.
Now with age, they resemble shafts of bamboo...

Such was this complex form, I called it mine.
Withered now and old, abode of aches and pains,
It is the house of age. See the plaster fall.
What Buddha has said is true—I have no doubt.[9]

Amrapali went through many changes in her life. A gardener in Ambara, a village near Vaishali, had discovered her in infancy, lying under a mango tree; he and his wife took her in and brought her up. When quite young, she was selected ganika, and carefully groomed for the role, through education in 64 arts, including singing, dancing, painting, etiquette, acting, staging plays, reciting poetry, composing, gardening, weaving garlands, preparing drinks, gambling, the art of conversation and the art of love.

As ganika, Amrapali mixed freely with men, and conversed knowledgeably on matters of state and society. A connoisseur of the arts as well as performer, she held soirees where city notables gathered in the evening. Wealthy patrons came for the pleasure of her company, and the opportunity to relax and speak uninhibitedly. A ganika helped keep the youth together through social intercourse, so they could unite against state enemies. The state sometimes asked her to negotiate, or draw out critical information, functioning as a diplomat or spy. Ganikas were close to centres of power, and wielded considerable influence.

Ganikas were the highest tier of 'public women'. According to the law, anybody who abused a ganika was punished. Vaishali, a prosperous city set amid the fertile Gangetic plains, attracted traders, bankers, artisans, performers and vesyas (sex workers). It boasted a democratic ethos, sound governance and guilds for most professions, including, perhaps, for female performers and vesyas. Part of Amrapali's tasks was to supervise the trade.

The position of ganika demanded hard work and dedication. Amrapali earned well, bought choice properties, lived in splendour in a grand mansion with extensive gardens, and ran a large establishment with maidservants, messengers, cooks, bearers, attendants and caretakers. Phenomenally successful, she was desired by many. She was not allowed to marry, but could accept the suit of a wealthy patron. A celebrated ganika like Amrapali would usually select one such person, and take him as her lover. She would neither be owned by him, nor be responsible for carrying on his lineage.

Bimbisara, king of Magadha, had heard much of the beautiful and talented Amrapali. Several fictional accounts hold that when they met, both fell in love with each another. He already had several wives and many children, some older than Amrapali, but the affair with Amrapali had a different intensity; perhaps he was attracted to her sexually as well as intellectually. Amrapali had a son by Bimbisara, named Vimala Kodanna. She brought him up, and he chose to become a Buddhist monk.

Bimbisara, meanwhile, was killed by Ajatashatru, his son and heir. Ajatashatru invaded Vaishali, leading to a 16-year war. It is said that he too was smitten by Amrapali, but she had little to do with this bloodthirsty son of Bimbisara. She observed the treachery of the human heart, the violence of patricide and war, the madness of human ambition, and wished to have none of it.

Buddha, at the age of 80, came to Vaishali and camped in her mango groves. Amrapali listened carefully as he spoke of impermanence. Afterwards, she went up, bowed low and requested him to take a meal at her house. He accepted the invitation. Ruling Licchavi nobles invited Buddha for a meal but he declined, having already promised Amrapali. Eating in a ganika's home, he broke age-old convention and prejudice. Amrapali and her maids served the meal in the courtyard and, thereafter, she donated her jewellery as well as mango groves to the Sangha, and became a disciple.

The mango groves, Ambavana, became the venue for several sermons, including the Amrapalika Sutra, which teaches how to cultivate mindfulness through contemplation of body, feeling and mind, leading to insight and knowledge. Buddha rested for some months at Ambavana, before passing away.

One day, Vimala Kodanna came to Vaishali; Amrapali heard his teachings. She too left home, and ordained as a bhikkhuni. She realized the futility of physical beauty. Finding her own body transformed by time, she wished to transmit to others the insights she now had, the need to turn away from superficial to deeper things. Thus, she composed the fine verses, known as the songs of impermanence.

The wise ganika would be amused to know that there are plans today to install a statue of Amrapali in Ambara—a beauteous, young Amrapali!

7 | Punna:
Slave to Nun

Sixth–Fifth Century BCE, North India

Punna was a slave in the house of Anathapindika, a wealthy merchant in Shravasti, known to be a great devotee of Buddha. Born in this house, she was not free to leave it.

Several times Punna heard Buddha's teachings. She listened carefully, absorbed his message and philosophy, and became a lay follower. Soon she became adept at understanding and recounting the teachings in her own words and interpretations. Members of the household were not aware of this, and continued to treat her as an instrument of labour, as was the lot of servants.

Her many tasks kept her busy from morning to night. If she did not meet the employers' expectations, she was abused and beaten. Fetching water from the river one day, she saw a Brahmin washing himself in the cold water. She said to him, later recounted in verse:

> I carried water,
> Even when it was cold
> I still went down into the water,
> Afraid of the sticks of my mistresses,
> Afraid of their words and their anger.
> But what are you afraid of, Brahmin?

The Brahmin told her that he was bathing in the river because it would wash off his sins, to which Punna responded with impeccable logic and dry humour:

> Who told you,
> Like a know-nothing speaking to a know-nothing,
> That one is freed of the fruits of an evil act
> By washing off in water?
> Is it that frogs and turtles
> Will all go to heaven,
> And so will water monitors and crocodiles,
> And anything that lives in water,
> As will killers of sheep and killers of pigs,
> Fishermen and animal trappers,
> Thieves and executioners,
> Everyone who habitually does evil?
> They are freed from the fruits of their evil acts
> If these rivers can just carry away the evil already done?
> But these rivers might carry away all the good done too,
> You'll be beside yourself about that,
> Aren't you afraid of that, Brahmin,
> Each time you go into the water?

Her witty, ironical remarks cut through a mass of mumbo jumbo, and the Brahmin's mind was cleared of superstition. Punna displayed remarkable grasp and analytical skill, when she enquired whether all water animals would go to heaven and so would criminals, just by a wash in the river. And if a river can carry away evil, she reasoned, surely it can carry off good too. The Brahmin understood he had been on a wrong path, and she guided him further:

> If you fear suffering, if you dislike suffering,
> Don't do action that is evil, whether openly or in secret.
> If you do action that is evil,

Or you already did it,
You won't be freed of the suffering that comes to you,
Even if you jump up and run away…
Develop your moral virtues, that will be for your
benefit.[10]

When Anathapindika learnt how Punna had given teachings and
got a Brahmin to give up empty rituals, and convert to a life of
moral virtue, he was deeply impressed. Realizing that she should
not be trapped in household chores, he set her free. Punna went
forth and joined the bhikkhunis, becoming one among them.
Being already advanced in her thinking and merit, she soon
became a senior nun. It was a good life, freely chosen—from slave
to nun.

8 | Visakha: Philanthropist-Benefactor

Visakha was Buddha's chief female lay disciple, patron and benefactor. She saw to the welfare and maintenance of the Sangha by careful donation of immense wealth. Committed to the faith, she revered Buddha, but also relished being a homemaker, and wearing fine clothes and jewellery. Scholar Nancy Falk states that 'the grand heroine of Buddhist storytelling is... Vishakha, a daughter and wife who belonged to the early community and who never took the nuns' vows.'[11] Her philanthropy exactly matched that of Anathapindika, the chief lay disciple among men. Visakha served as one of Buddha's primary aides in dealing with the public—he often turned to her when something needed to be arranged with the community.

Visakha used her riches to good purpose. Her father Dhananjaya was a wealthy merchant; her mother Sumana brought her up affectionately. She was seven years old when Buddha visited her hometown, Bhaddiya. She listened to his sermon, and it appealed greatly to her, as well as to her maidservants. At the age of 16, she married Punnavaddhana, son of Migara, a financier. Her father gifted her untold gold, jewellery, silks, food stuff and cattle as dowry. At Shravasti, people showered gifts on her, which she generously redistributed. Her father-in-law wanted her to follow their faith, and threatened to send her away. Hearing this, she herself ordered preparations to be made for her return to her parents. Migara apologized, and allowed her to invite Buddha to their house. Hearing Buddha's sermon, he was converted. Migara was enormously grateful towards Visakha and declared he would treat her as his mother—so she came to be called Migara-mata.

Visakha gave birth to 10 sons and 10 daughters, each of whom had similar number of children, and so on down to the fourth generation. She was reputed to have the strength of five elephants, and work tirelessly. Daily she fed large numbers of monks at her house, visited Buddha in the afternoon for sermons whenever he was in Shravasti, and then went round the monastery inquiring into the needs of monks and nuns. Buddha called her an ideal benefactor, with both a love of giving and abundant wealth to give. He contrasted this with people who have wealth but don't give, like garland makers who have flowers but lack skill to make good garlands.

Visakha asked Buddha for eight boons: as long as she lived, she be allowed to give rain clothes to monks and nuns; food for those coming into Shravasti; food for those going out; food for the sick; food for those who nurse the sick; medicine for the sick; a constant supply of rice gruel; and bathing robes for nuns. These eight boons indicated how keenly she observed the needs of the nuns and monks. Buddha asked how these boons would provide inner benefits to her; she replied: 'If bhikkhus say so-and-so has died, I shall ask: "Did that bhikkhu or bhikkuni ever come to Shravasti?" If they say yes, I shall conclude that surely a rains cloth was used by that bhikkhu or bhikkuni, or food when coming into Shravasti, or food before leaving, or food for the sick, or food for a sick nurse, or medicine for the sick, or morning rice gruel. I shall be glad. When my mind is happy, my body will be tranquil. When my body is tranquil, my mind will become concentrated. That will develop spiritual faculties and powers in me. This, Lord, is the benefit I foresee for myself in asking the eight boons.' Buddha appreciated her answer, and granted her the eight boons.

Visakha often wore fine clothes, jewellery and perfume even to monasteries, although later she voluntarily gave these up. One day, she lost some extremely expensive jewellery while visiting the Sangha. When the monks sent it to her house, she wished to gift it to them, but they said they had no use for riches. She then decided to use an amount equalling the value of the ornament, to build a new monastery. The monk Maha Moggallana stayed on in Shravasti and helped construct the Pubbarama, or Migaramatupasada Monastery. When the monastery was completed, Visakha walked round it in delight, singing with joy, accompanied by children, grandchildren and great-grandchildren. Pubbarama was one of the most important monasteries built in Buddha's time, where he spent six rainy seasons.

Visakha was well respected in the Sangha. She was authorized to arbitrate issues and disputes that arose among the nuns; and between nuns and monks. A number of nuns were housed in Pubbarama, and Visakha was in charge of managing the nuns' section.

Buddha imparted a number of teachings to Visakha. One evening, she was horrified to find some nuns drunk, dancing and singing crazy songs; they asked her to join the party and raise a toast to Buddha. Puzzled by the custom of drinking alcohol, which makes one lose one's senses, she sought Buddha's counsel. He explained the origin of alcohol, from fermented fruit and water, which someone first found naturally in the crevice of a tree, and consuming which people felt a false feeling of well-being.

One hot afternoon, Visakha was angry with tax collectors who were arbitrarily overcharging duty on her goods, making her costs escalate. Buddha calmed her mind, singing:

'Painful is all subjection,
Blissful is complete control.
People are troubled by common concerns,
Hard to escape are the bonds.'

Another time, Visakha was broken-hearted due to her granddaughter Sudatta's sudden death. Buddha asked her whether she would like to have as many children as there were people in Shravasti, to which she joyfully agreed. He asked her how many people in Shravasti die every day. She answered, 'Shravasti is never free from people dying.' Buddha said: 'Visakha, those who have a hundred dear ones have a hundred sufferings... Those who have one dear one have one suffering. For those with no dear ones, there are no sufferings. They alone are without sorrow, without suffering, without desperation.' These teachings comforted her.

Visakha lived a long and healthy life, and it is said that even in old age, she looked youthful.

9 | Sumangalamata: Set Free

Sixth-Fifth Century BCE, North India

Sumangalamata came from a working-class background; her husband was a weaver of sunshades and mats. Living in the city of Shravasti, often there wasn't enough to feed everyone, and after feeding her husband and children, she went to bed hungry. Husband and wife were ill-matched. Torn by conflicting emotions, Sumangalamata often felt angry and miserable, even as she brought up the children and looked after the household. Would it not be wonderful, she sometimes thought, to move away from this hell, this morass of endless needs, and find tranquility?

Her children grew up. The firstborn, a son called Sumangala, left home to join the Buddhists. He had always been close to his mother, and empathetic to her suffering. Seeing how his life changed, Sumangalamata realized that she too could transform her life. She left home and joined the bhikkhunis. She found here a wider world, where she could savour life in a way she had never thought possible.

One day, while reflecting on her previous life, she was much affected, her insight quickened, and she sang of freedom:

'A woman well set free! How free I am,
How wonderfully free, from kitchen drudgery,
Stained and squalid,

Free from the harsh grip of hunger,
And empty cooking pots...
Free too of that unscrupulous man,
The weaver of sunshades.
Calm now and serene I am,
All lust and hatred purged,
I dwell at ease beneath the shade
Of spreading boughs,
And contemplate my happiness.'[12]

Sumangalamata's song has a startling resonance with contemporary issues—domestic work, poverty, relationship agonies, domestic violence and the difficulties of leaving a bad marriage; also, the search for happiness, and the possibility of transforming life. Her words express a tremendous sense of release, peace and contentment.

10 | Bhadda Kundalakesi: Good Fortune

Sixth–Fifth Century BCE, Bihar and Uttar Pradesh

Kundalakesi was born in a wealthy family of Rajgir, her father a financier. When she grew up, she was secluded within the house, as was customary for girls from wealthy families. She had a razor-sharp mind, but no occasion to apply it. As she grew older, she needed a purpose in life, but was never allowed to venture out alone or meet interesting people. One version of her life story says her parents locked her in a room at the top of their seven-storey mansion to keep her secure. She was called Kundalakesi, 'curlylocks', because of her unruly, curly hair; the name also means good fortune. But she was pining away with a nameless disease. She had a turbulent youth, but her intense quest for meaning yielded fruit, and late in life she exclaimed with quiet satisfaction:

> 'The name I was called means good fortune,
> It now becomes me.'

Returning to the days of her youth, we find Kundalakesi in her parents' home, looking out of a grilled window. Suddenly she saw a thief, Sattuka, chained and being led to execution. She took a fancy to Sattuka and in a trice, discovered a purpose in life: she would rescue and marry this man. She told her father she wished to marry this man; insisted it was her destiny. Her father was perplexed. He had never quite understood this moody, brilliant child of his, but was fond of her, and indulgent in his own way. The wily banker used his influence to bribe the guards, and secured Sattuka's release. He had him bathed, dressed in fine clothes, and presented to Kundalakesi. Sattuka and Kundalakesi were duly married.

She was happy with her husband, who seemed devoted to her. He was from a good family, his father a minister in a royal court. Everybody was relieved, and rejoiced. However, it was a fool's paradise that Kundalakesi was dwelling in, for, at heart, the man was not reformed.

Sattuka told her that when the guards were taking him up a cliff for execution, he had appealed for pardon, and promised to make an offering to the deity, should he be released. He asked her to accompany him, to make the offering. Highly excited, she agreed. Dressed in finery, at his bidding, she put on all her ornaments—necklaces, rings, bracelets, earrings, toe rings. They set off by carriage towards the cliff. Leaving behind carriage and attendants, the two climbed up towards the summit.

At the summit, Sattuka asked her to take off all her jewels, wrap them in her outer robe, and hand these to him. Harshly he rebuked her, 'You think I am in love with you, you fool! I want your wealth. I have no use for you, so today is your last day on earth!' In a flash, Kundalakesi saw him for what he was: cruel and unrepentant. She felt terrified, but using her wits, said: 'This is the last I will see of you! All I want is a last embrace, and then take the jewels, and kill me!' He granted her this wish, and they embraced. Kundalakesi leaned over, her weight on him, making him lose balance, and at that moment, she gave him a hard push, so that he fell backwards over the cliff.

The moment of crisis was also, for her, a moment of awakening. She saw how deluded she had been, and decided to change entirely the course of her life. In any case, she knew there would be no place for her at home or in society, for she had murdered her husband.

Kundalakesi went to a Jain monastery and was ordained as a nun. She chose the severest forms of asceticism: her hair was torn out, and she wore just one shapeless cloth. With other nuns, she took to a life of constant travel, often coated with dust, begging for alms. She kept speaking to people on questions of ethics, life and death. She acquired a reputation as a debater, who won every argument with her sharp reasoning. Arriving at a village, she would stick a twig in the sand; if anybody knocked it down, it was signal for a debate. She sought somebody wiser than her, from whom she could learn.

One day, she reached Shravasti and, as was her wont, stuck a branch into the sand. Sariputta, a disciple of Buddha's, came that way, and asked children to knock the stick down. A crowd gathered, as the two began their debate. Kundalakesi lost; Sariputta won the debate. The same day she went from the shelter where she was staying to the Gijjhakuta mountains, where Buddha was camping. She bowed low, and he said to her, 'Come, Bhadda' (Bhadda means elderly, venerable). That was her ordination. Joining the Buddhist Sangha, Bhadda Kundalakesi continued a travelling life, debating less and teaching more. Buddha declared Bhadda Kundalakesi the nun foremost in quickness of understanding.

Towards the end of her life, she recalled her life in verse, the years as an itinerant Jain nun:

Once I wandered with hair cut off,
Covered with dirt, wearing only one cloth,
I thought there was a fault where there was none,
And I saw no fault where there were.

And then, as a Buddhist:

> Chinna, Anga, Magadha, Vajji, Kasi, and Kosala
> For 50 years I enjoyed the alms of these places,
> Never incurring a debt…
> This Bhadda, who is quite free from all ties.[13]

11 | Uppalavanna: Fearless One

Sixth–Fifth Century BCE

Uppalavanna was the daughter of a wealthy merchant of Shravasti. She was beautiful, like the dark blue uppala lily, after which she was named.

When she came of age, kings and noblemen sent proposals for marriage. There was such a competition for her hand that her father feared there would be conflict between the powerful suitors. Moreover, none of them seemed trustworthy. Uppalavanna was quite disengaged from all the fuss around her. Seeing how it was, her father one day suggested she leave all this, and go forth into monastic life.

This was just what Uppalavanna wanted. Gladly and readily, she left behind the crowd of unsuitable men, and stepped into a different life altogether. She joined the bhikkhuni sangh.

She underwent training as a novitiate. As part of her training, she chose to reside in a forest hut for solitary meditation. An erstwhile suitor, her cousin Nanda, pursued her into the forest, entered her hut when she was outside and hid under her bed. When she came to sleep, he jumped out, attacked and raped her. Uppalavanna was devastated.

After this incident, Buddhist nuns were forbidden to travel alone or live as solitary hermits. Over the centuries, Buddhist women questioned this injunction, and it was reversed by several monastic orders.

Uppalavanna remained within the community of nuns. The trauma she experienced drove her to face her own vulnerability, and she developed extraordinary inner strength. Over time, she healed. She gave a sermon which has come down to us, known as 'Uppalavanna Sutta', which unfolds in the form of a conversation with Mara, personification of evil.

Mara, desiring to arouse fear, trepidation and terror in Uppalavanna, approaches and addresses her:

> 'Having gone to a flowering sal tree,
> You stand at its foot all alone, bhikkhuni.
> There is none whose beauty rivals yours:
> Foolish girl, aren't you afraid of rogues?'
> Uppalavanna confidently asserts:
> 'Though a hundred thousand rogues,
> Just like you might come here
> I stir not a hair, I feel no terror,
> Even alone, Mara, I don't fear you.
> I can make myself disappear,
> Or I can enter inside your belly.
> I can stand between your eyebrows
> Yet you won't catch a glimpse of me.
> I am the master of my own mind,
> The bases of power are well developed;
> I am freed from every kind of bondage,
> Therefore I don't fear you, friend.'[14]

Mara, defeated, departs. Uppalavanna says,

> 'The aim for which one goes forth from the home to the
> homeless state,
> That aim has been attained by me—all bonds are
> destroyed.

My defilements are burnt out; all future births completely
destroyed.
Having severed my bonds like a she-elephant, I live
without taints.'

Uppalavanna was singled out by Buddha as an example
for fellow bhikkhunis to look up to, one of his two foremost
female disciples (along with Khema); and a leader. She excelled
in psychic power. Once, Uppalavanna gave 500 bhikkhunis a
teaching on the inevitable loss of all that is beloved and pleasing.
Her story spread far and wide, and appears in popular renditions
in Mongolia, Tibet, Japan and Korea.

12 | Kosala, Chellna, Khema: Magadha Queens

Sixth-Fifth Century BCE, East India

Kosala Devi was Queen of Magadha (558–491 BCE), married to Bimbisara. Her father, Mahakosala, was king of Kosala. At her marriage, Kosala Devi moved from Shravasti, capital of Kosala, to Rajgir, the Magadhan capital. Kosala Devi was Bimbisara's principal queen, his first wife. Their marriage ended the long-standing hostility between Magadha and Kosala.

Chellna was Bimbisara's second wife. She was a Lichhavi princess, daughter of King Chetak of Vaishali. Chetak was brother of Mahavira's mother, Queen Trishala; Chellna was thus first cousin to Mahavira, the Jain preceptor. Bimbisara, a patron to Buddha, was also a patron of the Jains.

Buddhist tradition records Ajatashatru as Kosala Devi's son, but according to Jain tradition, he was Chellna's son. Other children of Bimbisara included Halla and Vahalla, born of Chellna; Vimala Kodanna, born of Amrapali; Abhaya, born of Padmavati; Kala, Shilavat, Jayasena and a daughter Chundi, from other wives.

According to the Buddhist Attakatha, during her pregnancy, Kosala Devi craved to drink blood from her husband Bimbisara's arm; the king obliged her. When the child, Ajatashatru, was a few months old, he had a painful boil on his finger due to which he cried pitiably. Bimbisara sucked the pus out of the little finger, relieving the pain. When Ajatashatru grew up, he became extremely ambitious. His friend Devadutta advised him to kill the king. Bimbisara, meanwhile, wished to retire and stepped down voluntarily. Yet, Ajatashatru threw his father into prison at Rajgir, and planned to starve him to death. Kosala was allowed to meet him, and daily took small food packets into the cell, hidden beneath her hair and in her golden slippers; when she was caught, Ajatashatru prohibited her visits, and had Bimbisara physically tortured.

Meanwhile, Ajatashatru had a son, whom he loved greatly; Kosala reminded him how much Bimbisara had loved him when he was small. Suddenly, Ajatashatru was filled with remorse, and ordered that his father be released. When Bimbisara saw the servant coming with an axe to cut his chains, he thought the man was sent by Ajatashatru to hack him to death. Bimbisara killed himself, before that eventuality.

After her husband's death, Kosala Devi died of grief. Jain texts relate basically the same story, except for the major difference that Chellna Devi is Ajatashatru's mother, and it is Chellna who carries out the stratagem of providing nourishment to the imprisoned Bimbisara.

Khema was Bimbisara's third wife. She was daughter of the chief of the Madra clan of Punjab. She grew up in luxury, princess of the Madra kingdom, indulged and cared for. 'Khema' means security and is sometimes used as a synonym for enlightenment.

Soon after her arrival at the palace at Magadha, Bimbisara realized that Khema was proud of her good looks. He wished for Khema to meet Buddha, but she refused, thinking Buddha would rebuke her because of her vanity and attachment to sensual pleasures. Bimbisara got poets to recite poetry about the beauty, harmony and peacefulness of the monastery where Buddha was staying, and because Khema loved the beauty of nature, she decided to visit the monastery. There, she met Buddha.

Khema was drawn to the teachings, and in time became a bhikkhuni. She composed a dialogue with Mara, who tries to attract her with promises of sexual pleasure; Khema responds thus:

> This foul body, sick, so easily broken, vexes and shames me,
> My craving for sensual pleasures has been rooted out.
> The pleasures of sex are like swords and stakes,
> The body, senses and the mind
> Are the chopping board on which they are cut...
> What you take as pleasures are not for me,
> The mass of mental darkness is split open.
> Know this, evil one, you are defeated, you are finished.[15]

Khema became one of the two foremost female disciples of Buddha (the other was Uppalavanna). In the Khema Sutra, she preached to King Prasenjit, answering his queries with analytical knowledge and clear exposition. He was was amazed at her uncommon wisdom, and acknowledged her superiority to him. Khema's exchange with a powerful king indicates how well respected she was. She also taught many others, such as her friend Vijaya, guiding her to become a bhikkhuni.

13 | Mallika, Visavakhattiya, Vajira, Sumana: Kosala Royalty

Sixth–Fifth Century BCE, North India

Mallika was the daughter of a garlandmaker, in the royal palace at Shravasti. Attracted by her sweet nature, King Prasenjit married her. Although his third wife, she became the principal queen, and exerted considerable influence on his attitudes and policies. She was respected for her opinions, compassion and patience. She built a large hall in her private garden Mallikaarama among evergreen trees, for conducting discussions on ethical conduct and spiritual matters. Mallika had a daughter, Vajira. When Vajira grew up, she married Ajatashatru, king of Magadha.

One evening while Mallika was in the palace balcony looking across the river, Prasenjit asked her whether there was anyone in the whole world she loved more than herself. He expected Mallika to say she loved him more than her very life; but she replied calmly, that she knew of no one dearer to herself than herself. Prasenjit felt let down. Mallika questioned Prasenjit whether he loved anyone more than himself. He haltingly conceded that self-love was uppermost in every creature.

One night, Prasenjit had a succession of 16 perturbing dreams. When he woke up from these nightmares, great fear seized him. Next morning, Brahmins advised him to sacrifice animals, but Mallika was horrified. She exclaimed: 'Where did you ever hear of saving the life of one by the death of another?' Finally, the king discarded all plans for animal sacrifice.

Apart from Mallika, Prasenjit had various wives including Visavakhattiya, Ubbiri and the sisters Soma and Shakula. Mallika lived without envy or jealousy, in peace and harmony. It appears Mallika died rather suddenly, leaving Prasenjit grief-stricken and inconsolable.

Visavakhattiya was the daughter of Nagamunda, a Naga slave woman, and a Shakya prince, Mahanama. When Mahanama arranged the match between Visavakhattiya and Prasenjit, he concealed the fact of her mother being a slave. Prasenjit married her under the impression that she was of royal parentage.

Visavakhattiya and Prasenjit had a son, Vidudabha. But then, somehow, Prasenjit got to know about Visavakhattiya's mother. When he realized the Shakyas had tricked him by marrying Vasavakhattiya to him without revealing that her mother was a slave woman, he demoted both mother and son in the palace hierarchy to the status of slaves.

Visavakhattiya was miserable at her changed circumstances, and Vidudabha was resentful. When he grew up, Vidudabha revolted against Prasenjit as revenge. Prasenjit quelled the rebellion, but a little later, when he was away from Kosala, Vidudabha staged a coup. Prasenjit went to Magadha to seek help from his son-in-law Ajatashatru (who was married to Prasenjit's daughter Vajira) to regain the throne. But that night, Prasenjit fell ill and died, and Ajatashatru performed his funeral rites.

Vidudabha now reigned as king of Kosala, and Visavakhattiya regained high status. Vidudabha also attacked the Shakyas of Kapilavastu as revenge, although it was his mother's natal place. The war he waged left behind a trail of destruction; innumerable women were widowed and children orphaned.

Vajira, or Vajirakumari, was princess of Kosala, daughter of Prasenjit and his principal queen, Mallika. When Vajira was born, Prasenjit was disappointed that the child was a girl. Around the same time, his other wife Visavakhattiya gave birth to Vidudabha. Buddha assured Prasenjit that he was fortunate to have a daughter, and told him that women were sometimes wiser than men. This in fact rings true for both Mallika and her daughter, Vajira.

Vajira grew up in the palace at Kosala, under the loving care of her parents. Meanwhile, Ajatashatru, the young king of Magadha, waged war against Kosala. He did so although Kosala was his mother's natal place and Prasenjit his maternal uncle. He confiscated the revenue from Kashi village, which had belonged to his mother Kosala Devi. In the battle between Prasenjit and Ajatashatru, Prasenjit emerged victorious, but he spared Ajatashatru's life, since Ajatashatru was his nephew. A peace treaty was negotiated, under which Prasenjit gave Vajira in marriage to Ajatashatru.

Vajira was 17 years old at the time. Prasenjit gave the disputed Kashi village to Vajira as part of her dowry. Vajira was Ajatashatru's chief queen. Under Ajatashatru, Magadha became the most powerful kingdom in north India. Vajira was queen of Magadha from 492 to 462 BCE. According to Jain tradition, Ajatashatru had eight wives, including Padmavati, Dharini and Subhadra.

Vajira and Ajatashatru had a son, Udayabhadra. Vajira brought him up within the palace with notions of goodness and fair play that she had learnt from her mother, Mallika. However, Ajatashatru was ambitious and expansionist, and trained his son in warfare. She could not protect Udayabhadra from this powerful paternal influence.

When Udayabhadra grew up, he assassinated his father,

Ajatashatru. Just as his father had, he took over the kingdom, well before the appropriate time. For five generations, in fact, the dynasty witnessed patricide, the reigning king killed by an ambitious son. Women's efforts to the contrary, failed.

Sumana was the daughter of Mahakosala, king of Kosala. She grew up in the palace at Shravasti. Sumana witnessed intrigue and war, saw members of her family fight and kill, all for the sake of power and pelf. She experienced the moderating influence of Jain and Buddhist faiths, and absorbed the wisdom of non-violence.

When quite young, Sumana met Buddha with her brother, Prasenjit. She immediately wanted to leave palace life, and enter the Buddhist order. But she felt responsible for the care of their grandmother. Due to this, she delayed her departure from the palace, and devoted herself to looking after the elder lady, who survived to the age of 120. Prasenjit too was fond of his grandmother, and filled with grief when she died. Sumana, having spent a few decades caring for their grandmother, knew that death was inevitable. She herself was ageing.

Sumana was finally able to renounce the royal life and go forth to become a nun. She gifted their grandmother's possessions, including much treasure in carpets and shawls, to the Buddhist order. She passed away within a few years of joining the Buddhisht Sangha.

Buddha, discerning the maturity of her knowledge, said:

'Happily rest, venerable elder! Rest, wrapped in robe you yourself have made.
Stilled are the passions that raged within, cool are you now, knowing Nibbana's peace.'

14 | Sanghamitra: Overseas Mission

281–202 BCE, Madhya Pradesh, Bihar and Sri Lanka

Sanghamitra, nearly two millennia ago, travelled to Sri Lanka, where she set up the order of bhikkhunis, and is held in deep reverence to this day. In Sri Lanka, people celebrate the day of the December full moon as 'Sanghamitra Day.'

Sanghamitra was the eldest daughter of Devi (Vidisha-Mahadevi) and Ashoka, the Mauryan emperor. Devi was Ashoka's first wife, and was born and brought up a Buddhist. Devi's father Dhaniram was a merchant in Vidisha. Ashoka, as a young man, was governor of Ujjain, and fell in love with Devi while posted there. They had two children—Mahendra, in 285 BCE and Sanghamitra, in 282 BCE. When Sanghamitra was born, Ashoka was 23 years old. She knew her grandfather, Bindusara, was emperor, but in faraway Pataliputra. Ashoka was posted in central India for over a decade. Then around 273 BCE, Bindusara fell ill and died; Ashoka returned to Pataliputra, battled with and defeated several rivals, and around 268 BCE, was consecrated. All this time, Sanghamitra and Mahendra lived on in Vidisha with their mother.

Devi lived her whole life in Vidisha, while Ashoka moved permanently back to Pataliputra. The *Mahavamsa* states that

Devi chose to remain behind, rather than go live as queen in Pataliputra. The same year, Sanghamitra, aged 14, was married to Agnibrahmi, Ashoka's sister's son. Sanghamitra and Agnibrahmi lived in Pataliputra, and had a son, Sumana. At the age of 18, Sanghamitra took ordination into Theravada Buddhism. Her brother Mahendra also received ordination at the same time. Ashoka's efforts to mould Mahendra to become heir to his throne were of no avail. Soon, Sanghamitra matured into an Arhat Theri (senior-most among nuns). Later, Agnibrahmi and Sumana also became Arhats.

Ashoka, meanwhile, married Asandhimitra, his chief queen, with whom he had no children; and Karuvaki, with whom he had a son, Tivala. In 263 BCE, Ashoka invaded Kalinga. The carnage, in which over a lakh died, horrified him, and Ashoka turned, finally, to non-violence. Devi, steadfast on the path since long, was a strong influence on Ashoka, showing him the possibility of a peaceful and generous life. Sanghamitra and Mahendra too chose their mother's faith over their father's empire.

A few years later, Ashoka sent Buddhist missionaries to Sri Lanka, led by Mahendra. Before setting out, Mahendra visited his mother at Sanchi, near Vidisha, where he lodged in a sumptuous vihara that she had built. Devi, intent on creating something beneficial, had planned and initiated construction of the grand complex of monuments at Sanchi—the Sanchi Stupa—which Ashoka later actively supported. It seems that Devi shared a bond with Ashoka, and remained a guiding force throughout his life.

Mahendra travelled to Sri Lanka and successfully ordained monks, including King Tissa. Tissa's sister-in-law Queen Anula and thousands of women converted too; but only a Theri could ordain them. Tissa sent emissaries to Ashoka with a letter inviting the 'profoundly learned' Sanghamitra to Sri Lanka. Mahendra too wrote to his father with the same request.

Ashoka was greatly troubled at the prospect of sending his daughter away, but Sanghamitra appealed to him: 'Great King! The females to be ordained in Lanka are many; on that account it is essential that I should go.' Finally, Ashoka agreed. Her son Sumana was already in Sri Lanka with Mahendra. An important part of Sanghamitra's preparation for her mission was a trip to Bodh Gaya, where a branch of the Bodhi tree, under which Buddha had attained enlightenment, was ceremonially cut for her to carry to Sri Lanka.

Sanghamitra was 32 years old when she undertook the momentous journey in 250 BCE. From Pataliputra, she travelled to Tamalitti in Bengal, where a royal ship awaited. The Bodhi sapling, in a golden vase, was placed safely in the ship. Ten bhikkhunis travelled with Sanghamitra—Uttara, Hema, Pasadpala, Aggimitta, Dasika, Pheggu, Pabbata, Matta, Malla and Dhammadasiya. The entourage included several men of royal lineage from Magadha and scholars, traders, herdsmen, craftspersons, weavers, potters and indigenous people.

Sanghamitra's ship landed at Jambukola in north Sri Lanka, where King Tissa received her with veneration and escorted her to the capital, Anuradhapura. En route, they halted at Tivakka village. In Anuradhapura, the Bodhi sapling was planted in the Mahameghavana Grove by the king, in the presence of Sanghamitra and Mahendra.

Sanghamitra ordained thousands of women from diverse backgrounds, and established the Bhikkhuni Sangha, which flourished. On one occasion, 96,000 bhikkhunis are said to have gathered in Jambudipa; though this might be an exaggeration, the order was clearly thriving. Sanghamitra pursued efforts to enhance the status of woman in Sri Lanka. In Anuradhapur, she initially lived in Upasika Vihara, with the bhikkhunis who had accompanied her. Later, Hathalakha Vihara was constructed for her, along with separate dwelling places for other bhikkhunis, so that they could reside in quietude. Her brother Mahendra lived in Mihintale near Anuradhapur, residing in a cave, Mahinda Guhawa.

Sanghamitra never returned to the land of her birth. She passed away aged nearly 80, a couple of years after her brother's death. King Uttiya performed Sanghamitra's last rites. She had selected the spot for her cremation—in front of the Bodhi sapling, already a stately Bodhi tree with fruit, seeds and aerial roots. Uttiya got a Stupa built over Sanghamitra's ashes. For a week, ceremonies were held in her honour throughout Sri Lanka.

The Bhikkhuni Sangha established by Sanghamitra flourished and spread to China, Myanmar, Thailand and other parts of Southeast Asia. At a monastery in Nakhon Pathom, Thailand, a statue of Sanghamitra is the main deity, her image flanked by 13 bhikkhunis. In Sri Lanka, bhikkhunis performed welfare activities, integrated within society, living within countless monasteries. By the late tenth century CE, however, they had lost much of their original spiritual autonomy and status. During the eleventh century CE, Buddhism virtually disappeared from Sri Lanka, precipitated by the Chola invasion. In the eighteenth century, the Bhikkhuni Sangha was re-established; later, the Unduvapa Poya festival was revived— popularly called 'Sanghamitra Day'—to commemorate her arrival from India. Ten nuns initiate the celebration, and day-long prayers are offered. It has been proposed that the day be celebrated as Women's Day in Sri Lanka, as a tribute to Sanghamitra's unique life and extraordinary contributions.

15 | Leima Laisna: Just Rule

First Century CE, Manipur

Leima Laisna is often called the first queen of Manipur. She and Nongda Lairen Pakhangba established the Ningthouja dynasty in 33 CE. This was the ruling dynasty right up to 1891—nearly two millennia—making it the longest ruling dynasty anywhere in the world! One of the most significant contributions of Leima Laisna was 'Pacha Loishang', an all-women court which dealt with a wide variety of cases. She personally presided over the court, with sensitivity for the welfare of the people.

Manipur was once 'Sana Leibak' or gold country, land of blessed existence. The kingdom set up by Leima Laisna and Nongda Lairen Pakhangba was prosperous and well governed. Their coronation was held one Monday at Kangla, in present-day Imphal, while royal bards sang the *ougree*, a song in praise of the gods, wishing prosperity for the kingdom.

Leima Laisna and Nongda Lairen Pakhangba were Meitieis, the majority ethnic group of Manipur. Leima Laisna was born in the Poireiton lineage. She and her brother, Chingkhong Poireiton, travelled from a subterranean region in the east to Imphal valley, with many others of the Poirei tribe. Leima Leisna brought 200 varieties of vegetables and fruit with her—a hundred meant to be cooked, a hundred to be eaten raw. Chingkhong Poireiton brought fire, and this first fire still burns at Andro village of Imphal valley. Meitei literally means 'fire-bringer', and to date, most Meitei families keep the fire burning in the *phunga* or fireplace in their homes.

Leima Laisna was respected as a Maibi, or priestess. According to some accounts, she had two husbands—Nongda Lairen Pakhangba and his brother. Nongda Lairen Pakhangba married thrice, his other wives being Laikhurembi and Lainaotabi.

Nongda Lairen's mother, Leinung Chakkha Yabirok, had three husbands. Nongda Lairen had no clear knowledge of his father; according to some accounts, Kangba, or Tupu Likleng, was his father. He assumed the title Pakhangba to link his name with the mythical ruler god, Pakhangba, which literally means, 'one who knows his father'. The genesis myth in Manipur tells of Sidabi, the female godhead and Sidaba, the male, who had two sons, Pakhangba and Sanamahi. Sidabi favoured the younger son Pakhangba, while Sidaba favoured the older son, Sanamahi. Sanamahi is enshrined today in every family home, as ruler of the inner world, while Pakhangba is worshipped as ruler of the external world. Leima Laisna and Nongda Lairen adopted the Pakhangba symbol, a dragon-headed serpent.

Leima Laisna and Nongda Lairen moved their kingdom towards low-lying areas in Imphal valley, after water started draining slowly at Chingnunghut in southwest Manipur. They found a suitable dry spot, set up their capital there and named their palace Kangla (which means dry land).

They consolidated their kingdom, setting up several administrative departments, including the Pacha Loishang. There was a Department of Justice, which was run by women, and handled cases particularly relevant to women, including family conflicts, violence, theft and territorial conflicts. This arrangement for dispensing justice was unique in its concern with women's issues and rights. Leima Laisna was largely responsible for establishing the Pacha Loishang, and ensuring its smooth functioning.

During their reign, several people migrated towards Imphal valley. Integrating them within this fertile valley was a challenging task. Nongda Lairen and Leima Laisna handled the situation carefully, allowing diverse migrant groups to settle at different places.

The reign of Leima Laisna and Nongda Lairen marked the beginning of Meitei state formation. They laid the foundations for a dynamic society and distinctive culture, which flowered during subsequent centuries. The socio-economic structure transformed from tribalism towards feudalism, within a strong, stable monarchy. The *Cheitharol Kumbaba* (royal chronicles of Manipur) records Nongda Lairen Pakhangba's reign as lasting for 120 years: 33–154 CE.

Pakhangba was succeeded by his son, Khuiyoi Tompok, who continued the legacy of peace and stability. Known as the inventor of the drum (*pung*), technical innovations in metallurgy took place during his reign. Subsequently, a number of kings and queens ruled from the royal palace in Kangla, Imphal. Meitei monarchy consolidated its position vis-à-vis other ethnic groups who resided in the hill regions, through force and ritual. Conflicts occurred, as well as peaceful coexistence. Manipur developed a sophisticated pluralistic culture, with intricate literature, dance and drama, and excellence in sports.

In 1891, the British defeated Manipuri forces and captured Kangla, which is central to people's memory of a time when Manipur flourished as an independent kingdom. But Kangla remained closed to the public even after 1947, an extremely sore point with the citizens. Paramilitary forces were headquartered within the Kangla complex. Powerful people's movements, including indefinite fast by young Irom Sharmila, and the nude protest by elderly Meira Paibis (women activists, literally meaning 'women carrying burning torches') outside Kangla gate in 2004, finally induced the government to restore Kangla to the people of Manipur (in 2005).

Manipuri women's radical demand for justice hails back to a tradition inaugurated by Leima Laisna. Women of Manipur have consistently led struggles for justice. The two Nupi Lans (women's wars)—in 1904 and in 1939—resisted colonial exploitation, in particular, British demand for forced labour, and artificially created famine due to export of rice. Since the 1970s, Meira Paibis have been a strong force for justice, fighting alcoholism and drug abuse as well as atrocities by the armed forces. Irom Sharmila, who fasted for 16 years demanding justice, was supported by bands of women on unbroken relay fast, continued for several years.

Leima Laisna's daughters carry on her superb legacy: justice by women, for women, for all.

16 | Naganika: Wheels of Fortune

First Century BCE, West, Central and South India

Naganika was queen of the Satavahana dynasty, a powerful kingdom that lasted over 400 years (approximately 200 BCE–220 CE). We know Naganika through the inscriptions she got engraved, found in rock-cut caves at Naneghat in the Western Ghats (in present-day Maharashtra), as well as coins she issued. The coins bear her name, 'Naganikaya', calligraphed in Prakrit, the language of the common people. These are rare finds indeed, evidence of the authority Naganika commanded. Coins travelled far and wide; and here they were, heralding to the world the pre-eminence of their queen.

The Naganika inscriptions tell us a great deal about her life and times. She was widowed; the inscriptions include a eulogy to Satkarni I, her husband who died an untimely death. Naganika herself came from the Amgiya family that ruled over parts of Maharashtra; while Satkarni I was son of Simuka, founder of the Satavahana dynasty. Satkarni I had extended the Satavahana kingdom through conquests and the inscriptions refer to him as Dakshina-Pathapati—'Lord of the Southern Regions'.

Naganika held sway over this vast empire, reigning with sagacity for several years until her son Vedishri came of age. She ruled one of the biggest kingdoms in ancient India, often allying with her father Maharathi (great warrior) Tranakayira Kalalaya. She was probably the first woman in India's recorded history to take over the reins of a large kingdom. Under her, the Satavahanas flourished: their power and prosperity was further enhanced.

The inscriptions that Naganika commissioned were public documents, historical accounts widely accessible not only in language and style, but also in terms of their location. Naneghat was on a much frequented trade route between Kalyan and Junnar. During Satavahana rule, trade with Rome flourished through ports like Sopara and Bharuch. Inland trade picked up as the state, under Naganika, improved roads and modes of transport. The sheer volume of coins testifies to the importance of trade and the wealth being generated.

Though Naganika was ruler after Satkarni I's death, an inscription tells us she 'lived like an ascetic'. Inscriptions at the Satavahana family shrine, or Devakula, situated in a cave at Naneghat pass, mention a long list of sacrifices and donations by various persons, including Naganika. An inscription states that a queen who was daughter, wife and mother, well acquainted with ceremonies and vows, performed 20 vedic sacrifices including Ashvamedha Yagna. Some of the sacrifices she offered were proscribed to females, so either Naganika took liberty with the rules, or there was some leniency for royal women. Inscriptions describe details of the sacrifices and donations; in some, she herself paid the sacrificial fees. The same cave has life-size sculptures of a few members of the Satavahana dynasty: King Simuka Satavahana, Queen Naganika, Prince Bhayala, Maharathi Tranakayira and Prince Haku-Sri—their features destroyed by the ravages of time. She was the only woman among this illustrious set, just as she was the only woman we know of among the Satavahanas who offered vedic sacrifices, and the only one depicted on coins.

The Naganika coins are of alloyed copper, round or square in shape, and bear the name 'Naganikaya' in a rectangular cartouche, and around it, the legend bearing her husband's name in a clockwise fashion. The coins also bear the figure of a horse along the left margin of the cartouche—which is uniquely significant in light of the Naneghat inscriptions, which have informed us that a queen performed the Ashwamedha Yagna.

A later queen of the Satavahanas, Gautami Balashri followed Naganika's example by commissioning inscriptions, which provide us with historical insights. She commissioned these at the Pandavleni caves in Nashik, after the death of her son, Gautamiputra Satkarni (first century CE). Gautami Balashri called her son a 'king of kings', and noted that he revived Satavahana power by defeating the Shakas, Pahlavas and Yavanas. Evidence indicates that Gautami Balashri ran the administration during the last years of Gautamiputra's reign, partly because he was ill, or preoccupied with military operations.

Names of several Satavahana kings, after Naganika's rule, were derived from their mothers' names, denoting the high status that 'queen mothers' commanded. Gautami, Vasishti, Madhari and Hariti were the mothers, respectively, of Gautamiputra Satakarni, Vasishtiputra Pulomavi, Madhariputra Sakasena and Haritiputra Satkarni. These were women with strong personalities, and held in high esteem. Naganika was historically the first powerful Satvahana queen: evidently she was an exemplar and a trendsetter.

17 | Auvaiyar:
Sangama Singer

Second-Third Century CE, Tamil Nadu

Auvaiyar was a poet of the Sangama Era (approximately 300 BCE to 300 CE). Some 59 poems in the Sangama corpus are by Auvaiyar, making her the most prolific among the 28 women poets, and more prolific than most of the male poets as well. Her poems are in various Sangama literature anthologies—*Puranuru, Kuruntokai, Narrinai Akananuru*—and the poems are rich in imagery and drama:

> The red blazing sun creeps in the sky,
> Raging as a fire in the forest,
> And the silk-cotton tree is leafless
> Yet in flower without a bud,
> Like a long array of red lamps
> In the month of Kartikai
> Lit happily by bustling women…
> If only he'd spend the time with me,
> It'd go fast
> If only he'd walk swiftly with me
> In the dunes
> Overhung with flowering boughs,
> All fragrant…[16]

Auvaiyar's poetry dealt with a range of themes, from *akam* (inner, romantic), to *puram* (wars, politics). In the aesthetic scheme of the time, akam implied love poems; puram extolled brave warriors. Mothers sang of rearing sons for war, as in the following:

> There, in the very middle of battle-camps that heaved
> like the seas...
> Cleaving through an oncoming wave of foes, forcing a
> clearing,
> He had fallen in that space between armies,
> His body hacked to pieces:
> When she saw him there, in all his greatness,
> Mother's milk flowed again
> In the withered breasts of this mother
> For her warrior son
> Who had no thought of retreat.

Auvaiyar was brought up in a Palar family of traditional bards. She picked up lyrics and tunes easily, and began travelling across the Tamil country with her (adoptive) father, and other singers and dancers; her mother travelled less, due to childcare and housework. According to legend, Auvaiyar and her six siblings were abandoned by their (biological) parents Pakavan, a Brahmin, and Ati, a Dalit, on Pakavan's insistence. Ati wept as she abandoned her firstborn, Auvaiyar: 'Oh who will take care of my little one?' The baby confidently reassured her; and did, in fact, find a loving home with the Palars. Her siblings too were well cared for; Mariyamman was adopted by a washerman's family and later composed poems on ethics; Atiyaman became a chieftain; Uruvai, adopted by toddy dealers, became a dancer and poet; Kapilar was adopted by a Brahmin family; Valli by basketmakers; and Tiruvalluvar was reared by a Dalit family.

Growing up with bands of itinerant Palar singers and Viraliyar dancers, Auvaiyar consciously opted for a single life. People believe she appealed to Murugan (Lord Ganesh), to help her avoid marriage, and he helped out by transforming her into an elderly woman. Delighted, she escaped the limitations marriage imposed on women, and was able to immerse herself in creative expression. Sacrificing youth, she gained autonomy, and became the wandering teacher she so wanted to be. She was free to sing, compose and travel through the world.

The Sangama Era was marked by urban prosperity in south India, and flourishing trade with Southeast Asia, Sri Lanka, China and the Roman kingdom. In the second century CE, the Chera dynasty ruled far south, Pandyas in central Tamil Nadu, the Cholas farther north. The fertile river valleys had a thriving pastoral and agricultural economy.

The culture of the age took poetry very seriously. Chieftains and kings extended patronage to poets, whose eulogies helped them legitimize and consolidate political power. The relationship was reciprocal: poets received gifts in cash and kind. Auvaiyar travelled, like others of her ilk, on foot, bullock cart, caravan, sometimes chariot. There were wells, tanks and rest houses along the roads. Sangama texts vividly describe markets of Puhar and Madurai, selling flowers, garlands, aromatic powders, betel leaf, shell bangles, cloth, garments, wine and bronze statues. Itinerant traders carried paddy, salt and pepper to the interiors, and brought goods to the ports.

Auvaiyar sang her verses, among the ordinary people as well as in chieftains' mansions and palaces. She shared gruel with poor farmers and composed songs for their enjoyment and edification. Kings and chieftains valued her sagacity and invited her to stay on in their courts, but she preferred to be always on the move. She spoke with royalty on equal terms, correcting them when they were wrong. According to her, there were two castes—generous people belonged to the high, while the miserly belonged to the low.

Auvaiyar wrote many poems in praise of Atiyaman Neduman Anji and his family. Anji was her chief patron: he trusted and respected Auvaiyar for her wisdom and judgment. Once, anxious about the aggressive attitude of a neigbouring chieftain, the Tondaiman of Kanchi, he appointed her ambassador to help avert war. Auvaiyar proved herself a shrewd diplomat. When the Tondaiman took her to his well-stocked armoury, she responded with a poem praising the shining weapons of war; but then remarked that her own king's weapons were broken, having pierced their enemies, and now lay in blacksmiths' sheds. She thus indicated that Anji's weapons were frequently used, to annihilate enemies. Tondaiman was impressed by her words, and war and bloodshed were averted.

In several poems, Auvaiyar praised Anji's generosity—his gifts of clothes, good food and toddy. The greatest gift he gave her was the rare *nelli* (gooseberry) fruit, plucked from a mountaintop, which conferred immortality. Rather than keep the fruit for himself, he gave it to Auvaiyar, valuing her life and art.

Anji set up alliances with Chola and Pandyan kings, but ultimately was defeated by the Chera king, Perunjera Irumporai, whose kingdom extended from the eastern to western oceans. Anji died fighting during an expedition in Pali, north Malabar. Anji's death was a big blow for Auvaiyar. She wrote:

> If he found a little liquor, He would give it to us.
> If he had more, he would drink happily, while we sang.
> Where is he now?
> If he had even a little rice, He shared it, in many plates.
> Where is he now?
> … He gave us, of the flesh on the bones.
> Where is he now?

Wherever spear and arrow flew, He was there.
Where is he now?
… The spear that pierced his chest, pierced at once
The eating bowls of great and famous minstrels…
It went right through the subtle tongues of poets…
No more, no singers any more, nor anyone to give
anything to singers…
As in the cold waters, jalap flowers blossom, large, full of
honey,
But die untouched, unworn,
There are many now living, and dying…

Auvaiyar lived a long and productive life, breathing her last in
Muppandal, a village in Kanyakumari district. Occupying a
special place in popular imagination, she has morphed into the
archetypal wise elder-woman—(the literal meaning of 'Auvaiyar').
Avvai Vizha festival is held every year in Thulasiyapattinam
village, Nagapattinam, to celebrate her life and literature.

18 | Prabhavatigupta: Across Empires

Fourth Century, North, Central and West India

Prabhavatigupta was the daughter of Chandragupta II of the powerful Gupta dynasty (375–414). Her mother, Kuberanaga, was of Naga lineage. An Allahabad Pillar inscription mentions the marriage of Chandragupta II with Naga princess Kuberanaga. Born of mixed parentage, Prabhavatigupta later combined, during her own reign, two leading empires of the age—the Guptas and the Vakatakas.

Prabhavatigupta was married to Rudrasena II, ruler of the powerful Vakataka dynasty of western India. Their marriage sealed a political alliance between the Gupta and Vakataka dynasties. Prabhavatigupta moved from Pataliputra, her natal place, to the royal palace in Nandivardhana, the Vakataka capital near Ramtek hill, some 30 kilometres from Nagpur. The Vakatakas ruled also from Mansar in Nagpur district, and Paunar, in Wardha.

Before Prabhavati's time, bloody conflict had raged between the Guptas and Vakatakas. There is some evidence that Rudrasena I, who ruled from Nandivardhana (reign 330–355), was killed in battle by Samudragupta. It was Rudrasena I's son, Prithivishena I, who arranged the match between his son Rudrasena II and Samudragupta's granddaughter, Prabhavati. Thus, she occupied a critical and specific historical location, personifying the bridge between two empires which, between them, covered much of the subcontinent.

Prabhavati and Rudrasena II had three sons—Divakarasena, Damodarasena and Pravarasena. She lost her husband within a few years of marriage. All three boys were still infants when their father passed away. Rudrasena II died young, having ruled for barely five years (380–385).

Prabhavati put her personal grief aside and took over the reins of the Vakataka empire. She was regent for the next 20 years. She understood statecraft well, having observed how her father had conducted matters, and then her husband. Prabhavatigupta had a lively mind and was ambitious as well. During her rule, she combined the interests of both Gupta and Vakataka dynasties. Closely allying herself to the Guptas, her natal people, she gave equal weightage to the Vakatakas, the dynasty to which she belonged by marriage. In fact, under her, the two kingdoms virtually functioned as one, sometimes called the Gupta-Vakataka empire.

Prabhavati issued copperplate inscriptions, in which details of the Vakataka and Gupta empires were routinely mentioned. She issued coins, another important source for the history of the time. She often sought the advice of her father Chandragupta II, especially in the early years of her reign. Running the affairs of the Vakataka state was no easy matter, and she faced many challenges with calm good sense. She also extended support to her father's campaign against the Shakas of the Western Shatrapas. Her grandfather, Samudragupta, had come in contact with the Western Shatrapas a few decades earlier, but it was only at the end of the fourth century that the Gupta empire was able to defeat them and annexe Malwa and Gujarat. Prabhavati's strategic support was crucial to the success of this venture.

Chandragupta II's chief queen was Dhruvasvamini. Vishakhadatta's play *Natya Darpana* had a sequence wherein

Chandragupta II's elder brother Ramagupta agreed to surrender Dhruvasvamini to Shaka ruler Rudrasimha III, when defeated in war; Chandragupta II, however, refused to surrender her, and instead went himself disguised as Queen Dhruvasvamini, and killed Rudrasimha III. While this is a fictional narrative, clearly there was long-standing enmity between the Guptas and Shakas; and women were, as usual, part of the booty of war. Interestingly, Chandragupta II, Prabhavatigupta's father, is portrayed as taking enormous risks in order to defend women (or at least one woman).

Close cooperation between daughter and father continued throughout Prabhavatigupta's reign. Prabhavatigupta's elder son, Divakarasena, died in the year 400. She continued at the helm of affairs in the Vakataka empire until the younger son, Damodarasena, came of age in 405 CE. Meanwhile in the Gupta realm, Chandragupta II ruled until his death in 414 CE; succeeded by his son Kumaragupta (his son with Dhruvasvamini).

The Vakatakas were patrons of the arts, architecture and literature. The Vakataka Fort at Nandivardhana was a grand structure, and its ruins are still a sight to behold. The rock-cut Buddhist viharas and chaityas of the Ajanta Caves at Aurangabad— today a UNESCO World Heritage Site—were built under the patronage of Vakataka emperor, Harishena (reign 475–500), a descendant of Queen Prabhavatigupta.

19 | Karaikkal Ammaiyar: Keeping Rhythm

Fifth–Sixth Century, Tamil Nadu and Puducherry

Her poetry is set in the cremation grounds. Hair matted, body shrivelled, eyes gleaming, Karaikkal Ammaiyar sings and plays cymbals, keeping rhythm as Shiva dances, while corpses burn and turn to ash:

In this miserable burning ground
young ghouls scavenge the desolate theatre,
finding nothing to eat, disappointed,
settle for sleep

At twilight
flawlessly, in time to the rhythm
of heavenly drums
effortlessly bearing fire in his palm
the beautiful one dances. (*Decade-2*, v. 7)[17]

Karaikkal Ammaiyar's 143 verses are compiled into four collections, an integral part of the Tamil Shaivite canon: *Arputat Tiruvantati (Sacred Linked Verses of Wonder)*, with 101 verses; *Tiruvirattai Manimalai (Sacred Garland of Double Gems)*, with 20 stanzas; and two hymns on Tiruvalankattu (*Decade-1* and *Decade-2*), each an 11-verse poem set to music. Her hymns on Tiruvalankattu are a passionate account of Shiva's cosmic dance, even as scavengers howl and ghoulish devotees *(pey)* hover around.

Her verses seem to transform terror into beauty.

Karaikkal Ammaiyar composed in the people's Tamil. In portraying Shiva as the protector of humankind, she addressed an emerging Shaivite community with the vision of bhakti—personal devotion—as a means of salvation. She sings of Shiva who burnt the demons of the triple cities by a single flaming arrow; and swallowed poison during the churning of oceans:

> In times of yore
> the lord who bears the cobra
> drank poison from the awesome ocean
> churned by the celestials,
> his throat darkened
> like a shadow across the silvery moon
> that crowns his red, snake-holding matted locks.
> (*Wonder*, v. 55)

The poet identified herself in the signature verses of *Wonder* as 'Karaikkal pey'—the ghoul from Karaikkal. Rejecting social orthodoxies, rules and obligations, she sublimated worldly desires to become Shiva's attendant, and engage in a life of spontaneous worship:

> I aspired to only one thing
> settled on it and left the rest
>
> I kept in my heart only that lord
> whose crest bears the Ganga
> whose matted locks
> are adorned with sun and moon
> whose palm holds the flames—
> I have become his servant. (*Wonder*, v. 11)

Karaikkal Ammaiyar's poetry reveals her questioning mind and philosophical search. Having rejected the paradigm of domestic order and wifely virtues, and become an ascetic, she reflected deeply on humanity and divinity. In the opening verse of *Wonder*, she asked:

> Birth in this body
> enabled me to express
> overflowing love
> Through speech,
> and I reached your sacred henna-red feet.
>
> And now I ask,
> o, lord of the gods
> whose neck shimmers black,
> when will the afflictions
> that birth in this world enables, ever end? (*Wonder*, v. 1)

Her poetry reveals familiarity with Sangam literature, Sanskrit mythology, Tamil epics and Shaiva Tantric practices. Perhaps she performed Tantric practices at night in the cremation ground; intimacy with death allowed her to live intensely, with singular focus. Overcoming the fear of death, she created a space in the heart for meditation. Fire may terrify us, or illuminate, depending on our consciousness. Karaikkal Ammaiyar's devotion lets her live in bliss, even amid decay and destruction. Shiva's dance burns away illusions:

> If you consider the One whose complexion
> Is like the red rays of the setting sun,
> And smoldering fire,
> And whose matted hair hangs down,
> You would say that to those who have surrendered to him,
> He shines like a golden flame;
> But to those who move away without taking refuge in Him,
> He has the nature of leaping fire. (*Wonder*, v. 82)

Karaikkal Ammaiyar was historically the first of 63 Tamil Shaivite saints: Nayanars. She played a key role in initiating the Shaivite bhakti movement (sixth–twelfth century). Her hymns were sung in many Shiva temples. Sundarar in the ninth century, and Nambi Andar Nambi in the twelfth, refer to her in their writings, as pey or demon devotee; and as a maternal figure for Shiva.

Chembiyan Madevi, tenth-century Chola queen, introduced Karaikkal Ammaiyar's iconic figure into many temples: emaciated, with matted locks, sitting at Shiva's feet, rapt in his cosmic dance, marking rhythm with cymbals. This icon is found in Thanjavur and Cholapuram, and Shaivite temples across Southeast Asia. One of the earliest of these sculpted images can be seen in Cambodia's Banteay Srei (Citadel of Women).

In the twelfth century, Cekkilar penned Karaikkal Ammaiyar's biography, as part of a compilation of the lives of the 63 Nayanar saints. Today, her life story as narrated by Cekkilar is widely known, and enormously influential in the popular imagination of her. His narrative has her born into a wealthy merchant family in the port town of Karaikkal (in present-day Puducherry), and named Punithavati. When she came of age, she was married to Paramatattan, a merchant. One day, a Shaivite mendicant came to their door. Punithavati fed him curd rice and a mango. At lunchtime, Paramatattan ate one mango, and asked for the second. Punithavati appealed to Lord Shiva, and a fresh mango appeared in her hands. Paramatattan challenged her to produce another mango, so Punithavati prayed, and a mango flew into her hands. Unnerved by her miraculous powers, Paramatattan abandoned Punithavati and settled elsewhere. When Punithavati's relatives discovered his whereabouts, they took her there. But Paramatattan, his second wife and child, prostrated at Punithavati's feet. He explained that he regarded her not as wife, but as a goddess.

Punithavati appealed to Shiva to release her from her youthful body. Her body transformed into the body of a pey—a 'body of bones... a female wraith of shriveled breasts, swollen veins, protruding eye-balls...'[18] Freed of worldly attachments, she walked to Mount Kailash, making the last part of the journey on her hands so as not to defile the sacred mountain. Shiva and Parvati rose to welcome her, addressing her as 'Amma'; from this comes the name by which she is known, 'Revered Mother from Karaikkal'. She asked to sit at his feet, singing while he danced. Shiva directed her to Alankatu, the forest of banyan trees. Travelling again on her hands, she settled in the wild jungles of Alankatu, where Shiva performed his 'tandava dance' in the midst of cremation pyres. She witnessed the beauty of his dance, and spent the rest of her life composing and singing, in praise and worship.

20 | Khona: People's Scientist

Fifth–Twelfth Century, Bengal, Odisha, Tripura and Assam

'*Ghorilebari, Sajaile tari*'—'if you have surrounded the house with plants, you have arranged the world.' The pithy adage, composed by Khona centuries ago, is cited to date in the Chittagong region. Khona's sayings are popular in Bengal, Bangladesh, Tripura, Odisha, Assam and Nepal. She forecast weather, gave advice on crops, plants and trees, and how homes should be planned so as to maximize benefits of sun, wind, water bodies and livestock, and ensure human health and well-being. Being well-versed in astronomy, she linked the influence of celestial bodies with practical knowledge, relevant to daily life. She pursued Charvaka philosophy, which denounced religious orthodoxy and promoted logic and enquiry.

Quite the ecologist, Khona supported sustainability: 'In the same field, mustard and mung bean can be grown. The farmer is delighted since two crops grow on the same field.' It is not as if Khona invented these methods: rather, she observed farmers' practices, experimented herself, and deduced what was of value and worth. She was intimate with the land and acquainted with the ordinary ways of life.

Combining astronomy, agro science and botany, she observed: 'If it rains in the month of Chaitra, it is good for crops. If the month of Kartik is not windy and has mild rain, that year will yield double the usual quantity of crop.' Advice she gave has seeped into folk consciousness, guiding farmers: 'Cow dung and rotting vegetation have unpleasant odour and are deadly if consumed, but on the other hand, are extremely good for trees, as manure.'

Khona examined minute details of plants and trees, their effect on environment and people, and recommended some as beneficial: '*Neem Nishindajotha, manush ki more totha* [Where there are neem and nishinda (a mint-like herb), people do not die].' Today, neem is known across the world for its powerful medicinal properties!

Her advice was detailed and practical: 'The process to grow shali (a type of rice): these crops should be arranged in parallel rows in the field and the crops should be tied together in small groups. If this is followed, there will be good harvest and the farmer will be happy with Khona's advice.'

She emphasized hard work: 'The farmer who works with his attendants in the field gets maximum profit from the harvest. The farmer who stands under an umbrella and supervises, gets half the profit. The farmer who sits at home and expects his work to be done by others gets nothing, and never has rice in his home to eat.'

Khona's advice combined landscape design and architecture with ethno-botanical observation of plants and trees, and public health. One of her couplets goes: 'Duck in east, bamboo in west, banana in north, empty in the south. Build your home on a high and spacious platform.' On the east side of the dwellings was to be the pond; bamboo trees on the west to protect from sun and keep the house cool; banana trees in the north would allow wind and diffuse sunlight; the entrance to the house would be to the south.

Rural people practising eco-friendly agriculture and architecture have honoured Khona's legacy over the ages. Her principles influenced even the design of the grand parliament building in Dhaka—whether or not architect Louis Kahn had studied Khona's maxims, his design incorporated several principles first formulated by her—including the imperative of using indigenous, readily available local material.

Khona's social commentary was sharp: '*Bramun, bosak, bash— tine bastunash* (Brahmins, tamarind and bamboo trees [planted too close to the house]—all three wreak destruction).' She spoke of the value of amicability, which allows people to live together happily despite hardship: 'If good hearts prevail, nine people can live on one couch.'

Khona's words occupy a special place in the hearts of people. They trust her robust common sense, as reflected in the well-known adage she coined: 'A little bit of salt, a little bit of bitter, and always stop before you are too full!' Mothers in Bengal often teach their children basics of good eating habits, nutrition and health through such sayings.

We are not sure of Khona's life story, or when she lived. *Khonar Bachan* (Khona's words) have come down to us through centuries of oral history, as they have guided countless common people in their daily lives. During recent decades, *Khonar Bachan*—a compilation of her sayings—has been oft-published; and two television serials made on her life (*Khona* on Zee Bangla, 2009; *Khanar Bachan*, Colors Bangla, 2019). A research scholar has written a thesis on Khona's contributions to 'vernacular architecture[19], and a contemporary poet writes:

In Bengal in the Middle ages
Lived a woman Khona, I sing her life
The first Bengali woman poet
Her tongue they severed with a knife...[20]

It is said that Khona's astrological predictions were more accurate than those made by her well-known father-in-law, Varahamihira, one of the nine gems in Vikramaditya's court. Some say that Vikramaditya had declared her a tenth gem; others say that Varahamihira got Khona's tongue sliced off, and she bled to death. She was punished because the established astrologers were furious, since she was smarter than them. There is no evidence for any of this, only widely divergent stories.

We have no way of confirming whether she grew up princess of Sri Lanka (as some sources declare), or was the daughter of an Acharya in Chandraketugarh, Bengal. We cannot ascertain whether she indeed married astrologer Varahamihira's son Prithuyasas (also an astrologer), or the why and wherefore of the dilapidated brick structure that bears her name at Berachampa (near Chandraketugarh): was it a temple or an observatory?

Her name means 'a moment'. She came and went, like a brilliant flash of lightning illuminating earth and sky, leaving behind an astonishing legacy of timeless wisdom.

21 | Andal: Forever Young

Ninth Century, South India

More than a thousand years after she lived, Andal's songs are still sung at festivals and wedding rituals. Many revere her as a saint. How did a woman so young—16 years old when she passed away—attain such exalted status? It is a story that feels like a dream.

Periyalvar, a temple attendant, found her as an infant, lying calmly under a tulsi plant, in the Srivilliputhur temple garden. His wife and he joyfully adopted the baby girl, naming her Kodai, 'given by the gods'. She grew up absorbing simple rhythms of life, exposed to literature, music and poetry in beautiful surroundings. Periyalvar, a devotee of Vishnu, composed cradle hymns for infant Krishna. Every day he wove a garland for the temple deity. Quietly, Kodai often wore the garland, savouring its fragrant flowers; later Periyalvar would duly dedicate it to Vishnu. But one day, Periyalvar found her wearing the garland, and admonished her, for he felt the garland had been desecrated. That night, Periyalvar dreamt of Vishnu, asking him to daily offer garlands that had first been worn by Kodai. Periyalvar interpreted the dream to mean that Kodai was very special—an incarnation of Lakshmi. Gradually, as her childhood name dropped away, she became known as Andal—'she who rules'.

As Andal grew into teenage years, she became an ardent devotee, in love with Vishnu! She was 13 or 14 when she composed *Tiruppavai*, a composition of 30 verses. In it she depicted rural life and emotions, young women singing in the cool month of Marghazhi, heralding Pongal, the harvest festival. Gopis, the cowherd girls, in love with Krishna, bathe in the river, anoint themselves with turmeric paste and pray for a fruitful life. Spirited, energetic Andal, a gopi herself, calls out to the lazy ones to join in worship and earn eternal happiness.

When Andal was 15 or 16, she composed *Nacchiyar Tirumozhi*. Here, she sang passionately of her longing for union with her lord, in 14 long poems. Of these, the sixth—the wedding hymn 'Vaaranam Aayiram'—got incorporated into the standard Tamil Vaishnava wedding rituals. Ironically enough, while girls around her dreamt of marriage, Andal firmly refused to marry. In the bloom of youth, she directed her passion towards Vishnu, in the form of Sri Ranganatha. She composed intense, sensuous poetry, with fine imagery and delicate emotion:

> The velvety red
> of the ladybirds
> whose flutter fills the air
> in the dark grove of Maliruncolai
> brings to mind
> the glowing red
> of kumkum powder
> on my dark lord's forehead.
> Once he churned the ocean
> for the nectar of the gods
> using Mandara mountain
> as a churning rod.
> I flounder in the net
> of that lord
> of the handsome shoulders.
> Can I escape alive?[21]

Andal expressed an abundance of desire; the erotic tone led orthodox scholars to keep *Nacchiyar Tirumozhi* from wide circulation. She declares her passion for the 'lord dark as a rain cloud', with 'coral lips', broad shoulders and lotus eyes. Body and spirit throb as one; her human love is coterminous with divine. For Andal, merging with Krishna is linked to survival:

> Tell him I will survive
> Only if he will stay with me
> For one day
>
> Enter me
> So as to wipe away
> The saffron paste
> Adorning my breasts.[22]

Andal pines for the absent one, enlisting birds and monsoon clouds as her messengers. In the *Nacchiyar Tirumozhi,* she appeals, commands, enrages, despairs, then grows calm: 'At least let him look me in the face, utter the truth and give me leave to leave', and then:

> Arrayed in playfulness, his dark
> Cloud essence rains down bliss
> Amidst our unrecognized thirst.[23]

After completing *Nacchiyar Tirumozhi*, one night, Andal dreamt of Vishnu, inviting her to his shrine at Srirangam. She dressed in bridal finery and flower garlands, and went to the rendezvous. People believe she reached the sanctum sanctorum, and merged with the deity. Andal, the human girl-woman, disappeared.

Andal the poet lives on. She was a young woman—today we would call her adolescent—with agency, following her heart. Audacious, she composed poetry from the depth of her being— and it was no half-baked drivel. We know her today, through her powerful literary works. *Tiruppavai* has been translated into several languages and the verses are recited by countless young Tamil women during Marghazhi. And 'Vaaranam Aayiram' is routinely part of the rites and rituals repeated in countless weddings.

Andal is the lone woman among 12 Alvar saints—all of whom composed hymns, in language accessible to the common person. Alvars were bhakti poets who attracted followers from diverse social strata, particularly marginalized castes and communities. One of the Alvars, Thirumazhisai, was brought up by a tribal couple, and always said he was Avarna—not of the four varnas.

Andal is frequently positioned next to Vishnu, as goddess Bhudevi (Lakshmi). She is celebrated at many festivals dedicated to her. Aadi Pooram festival marks the adoption of Andal by Periyalvar; on this day, the deities Andal and Ranganatha are taken out in procession in decorated palanquins.

Within the Vishnu temple at Srivilliputhur, her hometown, Andal's bronze icon is enshrined. Every year her garland, of tulsi, sevanthi and sampangi flowers, is taken to Tirupathi Venkateswara temple (Andhra Pradesh) on a particular day. And Tirupathi Venkateswara's garland is sent at the same time to Srivilliputhur, where it is worn by Andal.

Classical dancers choreograph and dance to her songs. And poets, who read Andal's complex imagery, are full of wonder, at the pure heart and consummate skill of one so young. A visitor to the Srivilliputhur temple found a feisty 73-year-old, resplendent in Kancheevaram silk, reciting verses in deep resonant tones; later she confided that she considered her widowhood to be a boon: 'Before I was cooking, cooking, cooking. Now I can talk, talk, talk, sing, sing, sing... Marriage is like slavery... but now I am free... Now, I take orders only from her.'[24] She pointed to Andal, standing serene, timeless and free within the shrine.

22 | Didda: Mountain Queen

924?*–1003, Kashmir

Didda ruled in Kashmir for 50 years: nearly half of it as absolute sovereign. She earned the rare distinction of bringing stability into the fractious kingdom. Didda's father-in-law, Parvagupta, was a clerk until, in 949, he killed King Sangramdeva and grabbed the throne, only to die within a year. His son Kshemagupta took over, and proved as incapable as his young wife, Didda, was capable. Kshemagupta married Didda immediately after assuming power, slyly calculating that her royal lineage would provide legitimacy to his rule.

Didda's father was Simharaja, king of Lohara, and her maternal grandfather was Bhima Shah, powerful ruler of Kabul and Gandhara. Didda was in her mid-20s when she married, later than the usual age of marriage—quite likely because she suffered from a disability. Historian Kalhana described[25] her as 'Charanhina' or lacking one foot—but she went everywhere, often carried around by Valga, a woman appointed for the purpose. Didda already had a mind of her own, and understood well the business of statecraft. While Kshemagupta spent his time drinking, gambling and hunting, Didda took over the reins of government in Srinagar. Coins minted in those years carried their joint names—'Di-Kshema'.

---

*All dates with '?' are meant to denote the historical ambiguity of the said dates.

Didda's influence created enemies for her, such as Phalguna, the prime minister, whose daughter Chandralekha was also married to Kshemagupta. Didda gave birth to a son, Abhimanyu. Her grandfather, Bhima Shahi, paid a visit, meeting his little great-grandson and building a temple, Bhimakeshava. However, in 958, Kshemagupta contracted a violent fever during a jackal hunt, and died.

Courtiers gathered for the funeral, and pressured Didda to commit sati along with Kshemagupta's other queens, including Chandralekha. Didda refused, arguing she must live to protect her son. Little Abhimanyu was crowned and Didda began ruling as regent. Didda and her son were surrounded by threats to their life. Kshemagupta's sister's sons, Mahiman and Patala, surrounded them at Padmasvamin temple with the intention of killing them off, but Didda managed to turn the tables and assassinate them, and bribe and placate their allies. Through military prowess and clever stratagem, she suppressed a revolt by the Damaras, feudatory landlords of Poonch and Rajouri, who were uniting against her.

Abhimanyu, on reaching adulthood, took over from his mother. However, he died shortly thereafter (972), leaving behind three small sons. Didda resumed rule as regent. Abhimanyu's eldest son, Nandigupta, was declared king, but died in 973; his younger brother Tribhuvangupta was crowned and Didda continued as regent. Two years later, Tribhuvangupta died, and Didda crowned her youngest grandson, Bhimagupta. In 981 CE, Bhimagupta too passed away. It is often assumed that Didda got her grandsons killed, for the sake of power, though there is no evidence for this view. In any case, a ruler of her calibre should not have been required to step down, handing over the kingdom to an inexperienced youngster. Didda was a seasoned statesperson, much respected by the people.[26]

Didda was monarch in her own right for 22 years (981–1004 CE). She quashed rebellions that arose periodically, using a combination of appeasement and ferocious reprisal. Kalhana remarked:

> The Lame Queen, whom no one had thought capable of stepping over a cow's footprint, got over a host of enemies just as Hanuman got over the ocean... Treacherous ministers who for 60 years had robbed 16 kings, from King Gopala to Abhimanyu, of their dignity, lives and riches, were quickly exterminated by the energy of Queen Didda.[27]

It is entirely possible that the deaths of her son and grandsons were caused by illness or accidents; Didda would have been devastated by feelings of sorrow and loss. She constructed Abhimanyusvam temple and Abhimanyupura town (Bimyan), to honour the memory of her son. In memory of Valga, her loyal maidservant, Didda built Valgamath. She built over 64 temples, rest houses, monasteries and towns—including Diddapura town and Diddamath (now Diddmar area of Srinagar); and issued white metal and copper coins carrying the legend 'Sri Didda', along with Goddess Arodoxsho, goddess of abundance.

Her prime minister and army commander, Tunga, served Didda well. He was of humble origin: a herdsman from Poonch, she had promoted him out of turn. Extremely capable, he held these posts for nearly four decades—throughout Didda's regime, and thereafter too. Much younger than her, he was rumoured to be her lover; this was pure speculation rather than proven fact. More power to her, however, in case there was any truth in the rumour!

When Didda was in her late 70s, she decided to choose an heir. She called together several boys from her natal family, placed a heap of fruit between them, and asked them to pick up the maximum number. The youngsters grabbed and fought, except for Samgramaraja, who merely incited others to fight, and calmly gathered the booty, ending up with the maximum number. Didda adopted Sangramaraja—son of her brother Udairaj, king of Lohara—and declared him her heir. She made Samgramaraja and Tunga take an oath that they would work together.

By grooming Samgramaraja for the responsibility, Didda ensured smooth transition of power—very rare in those days. Samgramaraja lived up to the trust reposed in him, and was able to maintain a stable kingdom, partly because of the strong army and administration he inherited from Didda. When Mahmud of Ghazni attacked Kashmir in 1015 and 1023, Samgramaraja was virtually the only king in India to beat him back. The Lohara dynasty remained in the seat of power in Kashmir for over three centuries.

23 | Akkamahadevi: Naked Truth

Twelfth Century, Karnataka

Akkamahadevi's nonconformist ways caused consternation in conservative society. A rebel and early bhakti poet, she wrote:

> I'm not one to be afraid,
> Whatever you do
> I exist, chewing dry leaves,
> My life resting on a knife edge...[28]

Born in village Udutadi, near Shimoga (Karnataka), she was initiated into Virashaivism as a young girl. According to popular legend, Kaushika, a local chieftain, wished to marry her. Although she was not keen to do so, the marriage took place, partly through coercion. He tried to subjugate Akkamahadevi, and she suffered greatly. Finally, she threatened to leave if he continued to force himself upon her. When he still insisted on violating her, she left home and family, in a radical move—radical in any age or time.

Her *vachanas* (spoken free-verse poems) portray her unpleasant experience of intimacy: her lover turned her body into an object of desire. She seeks the divine lover, who respects her Self, and rejects the human lover, who detracts and denies her selfhood. Akkamahadevi rejected existing marital relationships, in favour of perfect union with a perfect being. Her poems are intensely passionate, yearning for 'Chennamallikarjuna (Lord White as Jasmine)', who is exactly as she wants him to be:

> I love the Handsome One:
> he has no death,
> decay, nor form,
> no place or aspect,
> no end nor birthmarks.
> I love him, O mother. Listen.
> I love the Beautiful One
> with no bond nor fear,
> no clan no land,
> no landmarks
> for his beauty.
> So my lord, white as jasmine, is my husband.
> Take these husbands who die,
> decay, and feed them
> to your kitchen fires![29]

In another vachana, she tells us with simple emotion how she severed links with her mother and her birthplace, and set out on a solitary journey. Alone, she wandered far, cowed down neither by threats nor attacks, deprivation nor starvation; over vast tracts, in what is today Karnataka and Andhra, in search of meaning and fulfilment.

Akkamahadevi gave up clothing: she walked naked. It is believed that long tresses covered her body. She was scornful of those who misunderstood and questioned her renunciation of clothes. Already, she had been violated in her own home; so what more was there to fear? She asserted her right to be exactly as she was, out in the world; refused to shrink into a corner, become invisible, limit herself or compromise with her freedom.

You can confiscate
money in hand;
can you confiscate
the body's glory?
Or peel away every strip you wear,
but can you peel
the Nothing, the Nakedness
that covers and veils?
To the shameless girl
wearing the White Jasmine Lord's
light of morning,
you fool,
where's the need for cover and jewel?[30]

To men who dared to try and harass her, Akkamahadevi spoke with calm reason, putting them in their place. She pointed out the fallacy in their perceptions—they were attracted by her body; but she had no sexual interest in them:

Brother, you've come
drawn by the beauty
of these billowing breasts,
this brimming youth.
I'm no woman, brother, no whore.
...All men other than Chennamallikarjuna
Are faces to be shunned, see, brother.[31]

Seeking philosophical discussion and human kinship, Akkamahadevi made her way to Kalyana, the Virashaive stronghold, where Basavanna and Allamaprabhu resided. Allamaprabhu put her through a test—he initiated a debate which Akkamahadevi engaged with. She later documented the extensive dialogue, conveying philosophical complexity in fine verse. Allamaprabhu was unable to defeat her; her claim to spiritual equality was accepted. She joined the community, a highly respected member, and took part in many gatherings of the learned. An accomplished thinker, quite at home with sophisticated logic, she became a senior teacher of the faith.

Akkamahadevi resided in the hermitage at Kalyana, its first female *sarana* (renunciant). She influenced 50 successive women yogi saranas, some of whom composed vachanas: Neelambika, Lakkamma, Satyakakka, Muktayakka, Gogavve and Rekkamma. The women saranas initiated reforms, including discarding of customs on the 'five pollutions', which restricted women's activities during menstruation, childbirth and widowhood. Wanting women to enjoy freedom and mobility, they initiated new rites to celebrate womanhood.

Akkamahadevi's poetry challenged caste and gender, and asserted women's right to autonomy and active desire. Virashaivas opposed Brahminism and Jainism, which had ossified into the religion of powerful business families and ruling dynasties. In speaking of direct relationship with the divine, Akkamahadevi resisted established hierarchies at multiple levels. Her vision united corporeal and spiritual in intimate union, redolent of the everyday world and yet deeply transformative. Her poems speak of forbidden love, fulfilled love and the longing of separated lovers. She claimed agency and sexuality in her own radical way, on her own terms, absolutely subversive of social moralities. She wrote, of herself:

> She has lain down
> with the Lord, white as jasmine
> and lost caste.[32]

Akkamahadevi recorded her spiritual-intellectual journey in simple, lively language, to startling effect. Her metaphysics was centred on human existential crisis, and the possibility of developing wider consciousness. Legend states that she meditated in a cave near Srishaila, experiencing successive states of consciousness, until she achieved ecstatic union, her body disappearing into Chennamallikarjuna. She was just in her early 20s.

Mahadeviakka, like Andal, Auvaiyar and Karaikkal Ammaiyar, rejected patriarchal marriage, but they adopted somewhat different approach and strategies. Auvaiyar and Karaikkal Ammaiyar in a sense denied their sexuality by circumventing youth; and transformed sexual energy into a powerful force which won them independence, acceptance, even awe. Andal and Mahadeviakka, on the other hand, developed an emobodied, sensual mysticism. Andal's passionate songs were absorbed into the Tamil canon, contained within the framework of a bride's longing, and impending marriage. Mahadeviakka poses perhaps the most radical challenge to patriarchal society; her critique is direct, expressed clearly, and evades easy framing or containment.[33] Three hundred and fifty vachanas of Akkamahadevi have come down to us, and constitute scripture for the Virashaiva sect. Nearly a millennium after she lived and died, her poetry is widely read, recited and sung. These are testimonies of human aspiration, demanding an impossible perfection—and bending reality to make the impossible possible.

24 | Razia: Sultan of Hindustan

1205–40, Delhi

hen Razia came to power, at age 31, she proclaimed herself 'Sultan'—supreme, second to none; emphatically *not* 'Sultana', the term generally used for a Sultan's wife. Razia was sovereign ruler of vast territory, stretching from Lahore to Bengal, Punjab hills to Gwalior. She was devoted to her job. A historian describes her as: 'wise, just, generous, patron of the learned, dispenser of justice, protector of her people, leader of her armies, endowed with all the admirable attributes and qualifications necessary for a ruler.'[34] He adds, sadly: 'What advantage were all these attributes to her, when she was born a woman?' Within four years her reign was cut short by an elite coterie, her life brutally truncated.

Razia's mother Qutub Begum was daughter of Qutubuddin Aibak, founder of the Slave (Mamluk) Dynasty; her father, Iltutmish, was the third Sultan of the dynasty. Both Aibak and Iltutmish began their career as slaves, but worked their way up to high positions and became free men. Aibak was appointed governor of Lahore by Mohammad Ghori, and after Ghori's death in 1206, established the Slave Dynasty. Iltutmish was Aibak's son-in-law and governor of Budaun, where Razia was born.

When Razia was five years old, her grandfather, Aibak, died suddenly. His son Aram Shah took over as Sultan, but within a year, Iltutmish marched against Aram Shah and defeated him at Bagh-i-Jud near Delhi. Razia's life changed: her father was now Sultan; her maternal grandmother Shamshad Begum was Valide Sultan (queen mother). Now living in Delhi, Razia studied, played sports and learnt warfare, just like her brother Nasiruddin. Her half-brothers Ruknuddin and Bahram were born to a slave woman, Shah Turkan; she also had a sister, Shazia, and younger brother Qutubuddin.

Iltutmish expanded the Sultanate, introduced administrative and military reforms, completed the Qutub Minar, and built madrasas, dargahs and the first mosque in India—Quwwat-al-Islam. Suddenly in 1229, Iltutmish's heir Nasiruddin, died; Iltutmish constructed a mausoleum, Sultangarhi, in commemoration.

Iltutmish appointed Razia his regent when he went to war in Gwalior; returning after a year, he discovered that she had handled the job exceedingly well. His experience of slavery gave Iltutmish a healthy disdain for social hierarchies, and a respect for competence and hard work: he saw in Razia 'the signs of power and bravery'. According to some accounts, he publicly declared that she would be his successor.

When Iltutmish died in 1236, courtiers sidelined Razia, and raised Ruknuddin to the throne. Ruknuddin and his mother Shah Turkan killed Razia's younger brother Qutubuddin, and plotted to kill Razia. Razia then made a rousing public speech: 'My brother killed his brother and now wants to kill me. Do remember my father, his good deeds and benevolence to all.' Recalling her father's desire that she succeed him, Razia appealed for support and promised a just regime. She won over the army, courtiers and citizens; they stormed the palace. Ruknuddin and Shah Turkan were imprisoned, and eventually killed.

Razia was crowned in November 1236—Jalalat-al-din Razia Sultan. She established her authority, and Friday namaz was read in her name, confirming her status as temporal and spiritual head. Being a Turk and a Sunni, she owed allegiance to the Abbasid Caliphate, who recognized her as 'Malika' of Delhi.

Razia was energetic and hard-working. She built roads linking villages and cities, with small forts along the way. Protecting the culture of Hindus and Muslims alike, she established schools and libraries stocking works of philosophy, literature, science, law and spirituality. She presided over the administration, introduced reforms in the army and conquered new territories. Initially, her throne was separated from courtiers and the public by a screen, but soon she began appearing unscreened and unveiled. She rode out on horse or elephant. Amir Khusro wrote: 'She tore away the veil, the lioness showed so much force that brave men bent low before her.'[35] Early in her reign, she minted coins bearing the legend 'pillar of women, queen of the times, Sultan Razia, daughter of Shamsuddin Altumish the Great Sultan'. By 1238, she had enough confidence to mint coins exclusively in her name, 'Al-Sultan al-Muazzam Razziyat al-Din (Razia the Great Sultan)'.

Turkic nobles were upset by Razia's independent thinking. To loosen their grip in court, Razia appointed trustworthy slaves and others to high positions. Altunia, a senior slave, became governor of Tabarhind; Aytegin became amir-hajib (lord of the court) and Malik Yakut, an Abyssinian, became amir-i-akhur (master of the stables). Those resentful of her power slandered her by linking her name with Altunia, and then with Malik Yakut.

Incited by unscrupulous courtiers, who tempted him with visions of becoming Sultan, Alltunia rose against Razia Sultan; he captured and imprisoned her in Qila Mubarak, Tabarhind. A few days later, courtiers crowned Razia's half-brother Bahram. Altunia realized he had been tricked into conspiring against Razia. At this point, Razia and Altunia married—a pragmatic decision, because by combining forces, they could try to reclaim her lost kingdom.

Their ragtag army advanced towards Delhi, but Bahram, with the levers of power at his command, easily defeated them. On 14 October 1240, Razia was killed.

Some say she fought valiantly until struck by an arrow; Ibn Battuta, writing some hundred years after the event, provided a different version. Her army vanquished, Razia fled into the countryside; she found a peasant tilling the soil and, exhausted, asked him for some food,

> He gave her a piece of bread which she ate and fell asleep;
> and she was dressed like a man. But, while she was asleep,
> the peasant's eye fell upon a gown... studded with jewels...
> He realized that she was a woman. So he killed her,
> plundered her and drove away her horse, and then buried
> her in his field.'[36]

He was caught when trying to sell the valuables. A shrine was built there and Razia's tomb, by the banks of the Yamuna, at Kaithal, became a place of pilgrimage.

In Old Delhi, at Bulbul-i-khana lies a dilapidated tomb marked 'Razia, Sultan of Delhi.' Probably, her remains were later reinterred there. A twin tomb may be her sister Shazia's, who, some say, stayed with Razia till the end. Though details of Razia's life and death remain elusive, her name is known to all, her memory inscribed in the collective consciousness. Although queen for less than four years, Razia's rule stands out for its vigour and relative strength: both brothers who ruled before and immediately after her, had much shorter reigns; nor have they left any mark in popular memory.

25 | Rudrama:
Rudradeva Maharaja
1220?-1289, Telengana and Andhra Pradesh

R udrama, of the Kakatiya dynasty in south India, was formally known as Rudradeva Maharaja. She was at the pinnacle of a powerful dynasty, sovereign as kings generally were, but seldom queens. In fact, in her one person Rudrama combined king and queen: similar in this to Razia Sultan, who preceded her by just a few decades.

Born around 1220 to King Ganapatidev and Queen Somalidevi, she was named Rudrambadevi at birth; at the time of her coronation in 1259, she was renamed Rudradeva Maharaja. Rudrama had a younger half-sister, Ganapamba, born to Bayyambika. Both Rudrama and Ganapamba were carefully brought up and well educated, in Warangal, capital of the Kakatiyas.

Around 1240, Rudrama married Chalukya Veerabhadra of Nidadavolu; the couple lived in Warangal. They adopted two girls—Mummadamba and Ruyyama. Mummadamba married Mahadeva II of the Chalukyas—Veerabhadra's younger brother; and Ruyyama married Induluri Annayadeva of the Kolanu dynasty. When a son was born to Mummadamba, Rudrama adopted him—the little boy, Prataparudra, grew up in the palace, calling his grandmother, Rudrama, 'Mother'.

In 1259, Ganapati, who had been king since 1199, abdicated

in favour of his daughter, Rudrama. He assisted her for a couple of years, and then retired completely. He passed away in 1269. Rudrama handled incessant attacks on the kingdom—by the Pandyas, the Eastern Ganga dynasty and the Yadava of Devagiri. When the Yadavas laid siege on Warangal, she routed them after 15 days of fighting, pursued them into their territory, and released their soldiers only after payment of a huge ransom; she distributed this money among her soldiers. Sources suggest that Veerabhadra accompanied Rudrama in some battles; but he too died in 1269, the same year as Ganapati.

Kotagiri copperplates of 1273 record: 'to Ganapati was born a daughter Rudramamba, or Rudrambika, the sole champion of the world and spotless like the crescent moon... She was firmly holding the earth with her fierce and flashing prowess which terrified the enemies with fear of death.' Another inscription states that after Ganapati's death, his daughter Rudramadevi protected the earth as well as he had.

Rudrama launched a policy by which people from ordinary backgrounds could be appointed to high posts in the army and administration, earlier reserved for the elite. She initiated welfare programmes, built hospitals and introduced the tank system of irrigation to bring vast tracts under cultivation. She completed the Warangal Fort to protect the city from further sieges.

Rudrama faced rebellious feudatories as well as external aggressors. Ambadeva, of a powerful Kayastha lineage, attacked her kingdom from 1273 onward. Though she lost some territories in southwestern Andhra and Guntur, she was able to ward off his attacks and retain control over most of her kingdom. Around 1280, she handed over some of her duties to her grandson, Prataparudra, whom she had trained well in statecraft and war; he had a bent for literature as well.

Ambadeva launched a massive attack on Warangal in 1289.

Rudrama, around 70 years old, led her forces into battle. Her army lost, and Rudrama died on the battlefield. At Pochalamma temple of Bollikunta village in Warangal, two recently discovered magnificent granite sculptures depict Rudrama's crucial last battle. D. Kanna Babu, of the Archaelogical Survey of India, explains that the statues clearly portray 'Rudrama Devi's commanding and imperial personality with characteristic gesticulations of a ferocious warrior... She was a brave general, administrator, strategist, trendsetter and philanthropist.'[37] While one statue shows her on horseback, wielding a sword, the royal umbrella overhead, the other has her slumped on the horse, tired and sorrowful, with a buffalo, vehicle of Yama, nearby, suggesting her final journey from this world.

Rudrama is remembered in Telangana as a determined and just ruler, and brave warrior. Popular tradition holds that she lived to 80 years, and died around 1296. Interestingly, Marco Polo visited India sometime between 1289 and 1293, and wrote:

> [T]he kingdom of Mutfili was formerly under the rule of a King, and since his death, some forty years past, it has been under his Queen, a lady of much discretion, who for the great love she bore him never would marry another husband. And I can assure you that during all that space of forty years she had administered her realm as well as ever her husband did, or better; and as she was a lover of justice, of equity, and of peace, she was more beloved by those of her kingdom than ever was Lady or Lord of theirs before... It is in this kingdom that diamonds are got...[38]

Historians have generally identified Rudrama as the queen Marco Polo mentioned; and it is true that diamonds, including the world-famous Kohinoor, were mined within Kakatiya territory. An alternative theory is that the queen Marco Polo described was in fact Rudrama's sister, Ganapamba: she had married Betadeva, Kota chief of Dharanikota; and ruled for well over 40 years after Beta's death (around 1251). Motupalli (possibly Marco Polo's 'Mutfili') was an important port town in Ganapamba's kingdom. She too was reputed to be a wise and enlightened ruler, though the territory over which she ruled was much smaller than the Kakatiya kingdom. A third possibility is that Marco Polo unwittingly mixed up the attributes of the two sisters, Rudrama and Ganapamba, and wrote up a joint description. There were anyway startling parallels in their trajectories—brought up together, widowed early, each became a sovereign ruler in her own right, with a reputation for wise governance.

Rudrama's grandson Prataparudra succeeded her on the Kakatiya throne. He inherited a thriving kingdom which he governed well. He was also a noted littérateur in Telugu and Kannada. However, Prataparudra was forced to become a tributary of Alauddin Khilji, of the Delhi Sultanate. In 1323, Alauddin Khilji had him arrested and ordered that he be brought to Delhi; en route, Prataparudra committed suicide, near the Narmada River in central India. Thus ended the Kakatiya dynasty—which Rudrama had defended lifelong.

26 | Unniyarcha: Martial Artiste

Thirteenth Century, Kerala

The tale of Unniyarcha is preserved in popular ballads of North Malabar.[39] She was an expert martial artiste, a Dalit and a 'MeToo' veteran: she used her skills to fight ruffians who were harassing women. She brought an end to violence against women in her area, and ushered in communal harmony between different communities. In a famous episode, she defeated a large gang of ruffians who had tried to abduct her, and compelled them to give up their nefarious activities.

Unniyarcha was born in the house of Puthooram, renowned for the ancient martial art, Kalaripayattu. Unniyarcha's father, Kannappa Chekavar, was a Kalari master. Unniyarcha grew up practising Kalaripayattu rigorously from the age of seven, along with her brothers Aromal and Unnikannan, and cousin Chandu.

At the age of 14, Unniyarcha married Kunhiraman, also a martial arts practitioner. One day, Unniyarcha decided to visit an Ayyappan temple a few miles from their village, but her mother-in-law forbade her because she would have to pass Nadapuram village, where gangsters were known to rob and molest. Unniyarcha, not to be deterred, exclaimed:

Born in the famous Puthooram family,
As the fearless daughter of Kannappan,
Born with valour and courage,
I can't stay back like a coward.

Declaring that even if there were thousands of opponents, she would deal with them, Unniyarcha set off, her urumi, a flexible whip-like sword, tied around her waist, and husband, Kunhiraman, in tow. He went reluctantly, apprehensive of the dangers ahead; as they approached Nadapuram, she noticed how fearful he was, and reproached him:

> I, a woman do not tremble,
> Then why do you, a man, tremble?
> Doesn't matter if thousands come to attack,
> I belong to Puthooram.
> Have you ever heard that women of Puthooram
> Sent their men to be killed?

At Nadapuram Bazaar, the ruffians surrounded them, gagged and bound Kunhiraman, and attempted to carry off Unniyarcha. But she brandished her urumi and injured many of the men through a splendid performance of Kalari techniques. When they persisted, she killed a few and threatened to destroy all the rest. Her opponents prostrated at her feet, apologizing and begging her to let them go. Unniyarcha's brother Aromal, a fearsome warrior like herself, arrived on the scene.

Unniyarcha challenged the chief to a duel, but he was reluctant, and continued to appeal for mercy. His wife rushed in with gifts of gold and jewellery for Unniyarcha. In the interests of peace, Unniyarcha finally agreed to pardon the gangsters, on condition that they would never again harass any woman of the area. The chief promised that henceforth he and his men would never trouble women. Unniyarcha released them, and went ahead triumphantly to the Ayappan temple, Kunhiraman at her side. When she returned home, Unniyarcha handed over the booty to her mother-in-law and proudly announced that she had brought Kunhiraman back unharmed!

The ruffians were Jonaka Mapillas—seafarers who had settled in coastal Kerala. Some Jonakas carried on honest trades, but others indulged in abducting women, and were involved in the Arab slave trade. Unniyarcha's victory over this dangerous gang gave courage and much relief to local people, and helped fuel an uprising against the slave trade. Simultaneously, more of the Jonakas settled into a peaceful way of life, seeking to coexist with mutual friendship.

Unniyarcha was also called Puthooram Putri; the Puthooram clanspeople were Ezhavas, a Dalit caste. The ballad of Unniyarcha tells us she had one son, Aromalunni. At the age of 21, she was widowed. She brought up her son, even while fighting—and winning—some 64 duels, ankams. She remained closely bonded with her brothers Aromal and Unnikannan, both renowned Kalariyapattu practitioners. Her cousin Chandu, however, bore them a grudge because in his youth he had wanted to marry Unniyarcha, but she had refused, and her brothers had supported her decision. To take revenge, Chandu treacherously killed Aromal. Unniyarcha, in grief and fury, determined to wreak revenge on Chandu. She trained her son Aromalunni and nephew (Aromal's son) Kannappanunni, in Kalariyapattu, and once they grew up, sent them to behead Chandu. As they went, she gave a stern warning:

> If you die fighting,
> I will receive your body in silken clothes and give you a
> proper funeral.
> But if you receive an arrow from a hidden foe,
> I will wrap you in green leaves and perform no
> ceremonies!

The young men brought back Chandu's severed head; thus fulfiling her vow. Later on, though, Aromalunni wished to marry

Chandu's daughter, and Unniyarcha agreed, albeit reluctantly. After her daughter-in-law settled in, Unniyarcha announced her plan to go to Omalur temple for seven days of fasting and prayer.

Aromalunni offered to go with her but she refused, saying: 'Your mother never needed anyone's support, even in her youth.' She advised him to come to the temple on the seventh day. When her son and daughter-in-law reached the temple, Unniyarcha had already passed away; her body lay by the river which flowed next to the temple. She chose to die the way she had lived—strong, dignified and self-reliant.

27 | Janabai: Dalit Radical

1298–1350, Maharashtra

Janabai worked her entire life as a servant, bonded to a particular household. Within this oppressive situation, she became, startlingly enough, a poet. Though Janabai could never emerge from menial service, she infused it with dignity and power, creatively subverting the social order. Some 300 of her *abhangs* (devotional poetry set to music) are sung even today by devotees, as they walk the road to Pandharpur. Janabai's songs remain popular; her work challenges the prejudices of caste and gender. In a profound critique of conventional morality and society, she wrote:

> Let me not be sad because I am born a woman.
> In this world, many saints suffer the same way.[40]

At the age of seven, Janabai's mother died, and her father sent her to live and work with the Shetty family, in Narsi village near Hingoli. Her status was of a dasi, duty-bound to execute an endless series of tasks. Yet, an element of playfulness entered into what were otherwise utterly lonely tasks. Vithoba performed with Janabai tasks society considered low and dirty, such as cleaning floors and carrying garbage.

> Jani sweeps the floor,
> The lord collects the dirt,

Carries it upon his head,
And casts it away.
Won over by devotion,
The lord does lowly chores!
Says Jani to Vithoba,
How shall I pay your debt?

The family was Varkari, like herself, a sect that preached egalitarianism, and Sant Namdev was a member of the household. Yet, Janabai had to work long hours with little respite, and was subjected to restrictions on her movements, even in the realm of worship. Janabai survived her harsh circumstances by developing an unusual intensity of devotion. She experienced Lord Vithoba—chief deity of the Varkaris—as a beloved companion. The support she drew from her friend Vithoba lightened her tasks. He was always there for her; often they were co-workers, labouring in tandem; he even became a woman sometimes, working with her, grinding, pounding, collecting cow dung.

Solicitous and loving, he performs acts of personal caring for Janabai, as a mother, sister or woman friend might—bathing her, washing her soiled clothes, helping her carry water. A direct, one-to-one relationship with the deity was characteristic of the bhakti movement, but Janabai took it to new heights and surprising directions. There was an exceptional intimacy, as Vithoba not only helped her perform mundane and repetitive tasks of grinding and pounding rice and millets, and gathering dung for fuel, but also looked after her, rubbing her back, oiling and combing her hair:

Mother is dead, father is dead
now, Vitthal, take care of me
O Hari, my head is itching
I am your child

And have no one of my own.
Vitthal says to Rukmini,
'There's no one to care for my Jani.'
Taking oil and comb in his hands
He combs and braids my hair,
Finishing the braid he knots it.
I say, now please rub my back.
Jani says, 'O Gopala,
Help celebrate the festival
Of the powerless'.[41]

Janabai felt elated to have this loving, caring presence in her life, a deity-friend accessible to the powerless. She expressed solidarity and spoke for other working women too. The wandering singer she encountered was, like herself, a poet who sang her own songs. In imagination, Janabai transformed into this independent figure that nobody dared control. Such women were shamed and stigmatized for walking free and performing in public. Transgressing further, Janabai imagines setting up business not only as a public singer, but also a slut:

Cast off all shame,
And sell yourself
In the marketplace;
Then alone can you hope
To reach the Lord.
Cymbals in hand,
A veena upon my shoulder, I go about;
Who dares to stop me?
The pallav of my sari
Falls away (A scandal!);
Yet will I enter
The crowded marketplace

Without a thought.
Jani says, 'My Lord,
I have become a slut
To reach Your home.'[42]

In a radical inversion, by dint of the persecution she suffered, the disreputable labouring woman laid claim to the shelter her friend Vithoba offered. She truly deserved it, rather than respectable people leading comfortable lives. Janabai raged against the duplicity prevalent even in Namdev's household, the saint who preached spiritual equality:

Your wife and mother stay at your feet
And sons are placed proudly in front,
This woman is kept on the doorstep
No room for the lowly inside.[43]

Only Vithoba was genuinely concerned about her, whereas for others, she was merely of functional value. An apocryphal story relates that one day, Krishna was invited for a feast at Namdev's house, but sensing Janabai's depression, he lost his appetite. She cleared away the soiled plates. Later, Krishna went to her hut and finished eating the leftover food from his plate, helped Janabai grind grain and, tired, fell asleep. He left hastily for temple service next morning, leaving behind his jewels and blankets. When these were found in her house, she was accused of having stolen them and sentenced to death. Krishna interceded and saved her.

Janabai's poems peeled away layers of hypocrisy that tenaciously clung to the upper castes, and claimed rights to worldly and spiritual goods, for the labouring Dalit. She realized that the elite were dependent on the services of the poor; in similar vein, the Lord was nothing without the love and service of His devotees. She inverted the spiritual hierarchy, taking charge.

This Shudra woman, whose entire life was completely hemmed in, took control of the divine:

> I eat god
> I drink god
> I sleep
> On god
> I buy god
> I count god
> I deal with god
> God is here
> God is there
> Void is not
> Devoid of god
> Jani says:
> 'God is within
> God is without
> And moreover
> There is god to spare.'

Janabai is today revered as a saint. Her poetry has been integrated deep into the Varkari corpus. She developed a creative response to injustice and inequality, and her imaginative and ironic inversions, embodying social critique, continue to inspire. Ordinary people draw solace from her words, songs of resistance par excellence.

28 | Lalla: Perfect Hermitess

1320–1392, Kashmir

Lalla has been called 'the perfect hermitess'.[44] She was a learned woman who left home and hearth, to wander and seek wisdom. Her words and ideas have seeped into and become an integral part of Kashmir's culture. Hindus and Muslims alike claim her; even though she rejected orthodox religiosity. She wrote:

> Your idol's stone, your temple's stone,
> All's stone tied from top to toe
> Dense Brahmin, what do you worship?
> Bind breath to mind instead.[45]

Iconoclastic, she spoke up for the sanctity of authentic experience. Variously called Lalla, Lalla Arifa, Lalleshwari and Lal Ded, she voiced her direct personal realizations through verses called *Vakhs*, meaning 'voice' or 'sentence'. Lalla's Vakhs are the oldest known specimens of literature in the Kashmiri language. Their imagery was familiar, the meaning direct and sharp; her Vakhs appeal to scholars as well as peasants, and form part of common parlance in Kashmir.

Lalla was born in Pandrethan village near Srinagar, to an ordinary Pandit family. She liked to learn from their family priest Sidhha Srikanth; a scholar and yogic practitioner, he must have found her unusually alert and engaged. At the age of 12, she was married in Pampore, to a man who turned out to be as crude as she was subtle and sensitive. Her mother-in-law starved Lalla, habitually placing a large stone in her food bowl, covered with a thin layer of food. Nobody knew about Lalla's hardships, as she went about quietly performing her domestic tasks.

One festival day, when she was 24, Lalla took her pitcher to the Jhelum to fill water. Several women had gathered for the same chore, and one of them teased her, 'You will have tasty dishes to eat today!' Lalla, heavy of heart, replied: 'Whether they eat lamb or sheep, Lalla will get her stone as usual.' When this remark reached her father-in-law, the truth tumbled out, leading to an uproar. The upshot was that Lalla left that house, never to return.

She did not seek refuge with her parents. From that day on she fended for herself, preferring solitude to cruel social intercourse. Wandering alone through forests and hills, she ate odds and ends, slept in mountain caves or pilgrim shelters, and discarded clothing altogether. In her 'fine madness', she became utterly devoid of self-consciousness:

> The guru gave me but one word of wisdom
> From the outside bade me turn within
> That word for me, Lal, is the surest prophecy
> And that is why I dance in naked abandon.

Subjected to insults and harassment, she did feel vulnerable:

> When will the shackles of shame be broken?
> When to jibes and taunts indifferent I'll be?
> When will the robes of pride burn away?
> Only when the mind horse tamed will be.

As she roamed about, she observed much, and remarked on the vagaries of human nature:

> A learned one I saw die of hunger
> Like a leaf falling away in winter wind
> A fool I saw beating his cook
> And I wait for the lure of life to fall off.

Lalla sought a deeper connection with her own self, and practised taming her mind. As insight matured and understanding developed, she grew self-possessed.

Her verses were a mix of common sense and mystical depth. She experienced the ups and downs of life, and revealed gems of truth, teachings for anyone who would listen:

> A moment ago, I saw a river in spate
> There is no bridge or ferry now
> A moment ago I saw a bush in bloom
> There is no thorn or flower now.

Lalla broke away from dogma and empty ritual, and gave sage advice, with confidence and rare authority:

> Fool, there's no merit in fasts and rites
> No merit in serving your body food
> No merit, fool, in comforting yourself
> Look inward—this is good advice.

Lalla's transformation was complete; but the journey had been hard:

> I, Lal, set out, hoping to bloom like a cotton flower
> But was beaten and trampled by ginner and carder
> Shredded and spun into so fine a yarn
> And hung and hit by the weaver on his loom
> Thrashed and kneaded on the washerman's stone
> Pasted and plastered with soap and clayey earth
> Till the tailor's skilful scissors worked on my limbs
> And I found my place in the highest abode.

Mystics, fakirs, sadhus and philosophers gravitated towards Lalla's extraordinary wisdom. Kashmir was an arena of fertile philosophical debate at the time. Different creeds were learning to coexist, in an atmosphere of intellectual freedom. Lalla contributed to building a syncretic philosophy, in which elements of Buddhism, Sufism and Shaivism fused, lending a distinctive flavour. Lalla synthesized diverse elements, showing that the essence of spirituality was the same whether in Shaivism or Sufism. People from all walks of life and diverse backgrounds respected and learnt from her.

She rejected all authority except one's own practice and insight. The quintessential solitary pilgrim, her commitment was to the self: Lalla, the lotus blooming among reeds in stagnant waters:

> The vast plan of the Void I crossed alone
> I, Lal, left reason and memory behind
> Communing with myself, I found myself
> Among what reeds my lotus bloomed.

And finally, Lalla could say:

> Wear the robes of wisdom,
> brand Lalla's words on your heart,
> lose yourself in the soul's light,
> you too shall be free.[46]

In Kashmir, Lalla's memory is woven into the collective psyche, her impact undiminished.

She is like a patron saint, and at the same time, a wise grandmother. Compassionate, she shows a path out of suffering and assures us that the truth is within our grasp.

29 | Rami:
Heart Washed Clean

Fifteenth Century, Bengal

We know Rami through her poetry: it reveals she was a Dalit, a washerwoman; and that she fell in love, with tragic outcome. The events of her life, linked to the life of poet Chandidas, gave rise to folklore, songs and plays; but it was the sheaf of Rami's own poems, discovered some three centuries after her death, that provided a window into her persona, emotions and experiences. Rami's songs are the earliest songs extant, by a Bengali woman.

Here is her narrative poem, akin to a ballad, recounting traumatic events, with pain, love and understanding:

Where have you gone, my Chandidas, my friend,
Birds thirst without water, despair without rain.
What have you done, O heartless lord of Gaur?
Not knowing what it means to love, you slay my
cherished one.
Lord of my heart, my Chandidas, why did you break
The vows you made and sing in court?
Now evil men and beast come swarming round; heavens
turn to hell
Betrayed by you, I stand in shame; you've crushed my
honour in your hands.

Once, heedless, untouched by Vasuli's threat, you told the
court with pride
You'd leave a brahmin home, you said, to love a washer
girl.
Now, lashed to an elephant's back, you reach me with
your eyes.
Why should the jealous king heed a washerwoman's cries?
Soul of my soul, how cruelly on your fainting limbs the
heavy whip strikes and falls,
Cleave through my heart, and let me die with Chandidas,
my love.

And then the queen fell on her knees, 'Please stop, my
lord,' she cried.
'His singing pierced me to the heart. No more of this, I
plead.
Why must you thus destroy limbs made for love alone?
Free him, I beg of you, my lord, don't make love your
toy.
O godless king, how could you know what love can
mean?'
So spoke the queen, and then, her heart still fixed on
Chandidas, she died.
Rami trembled, hearing her, and hastened to the place,
She threw herself at those queenly feet and wept the
tears of death.[47]

Other poems, along with this one, help us reconstruct her
story. Rami was born in a family of destitute washerfolks. She
wandered hither and thither until she found work washing clean
the Bashuli Devi temple, in village Nanur, Bankura. She was
devoted to her work, and to the goddess Bashuli Devi. The entire

village respected her, for she kept their temple spic and span; and composed and sang verses to the deity.

Chandidas dwelt in the same temple; a warm friendship sprang up between the two poets. Their relationship deepened into intimacy—an intense, passionate involvement, encompassing friendship, companionship and fellow-feeling. This love transgressed social taboos in more ways than one, for not only was it inter-caste (Chandidas being Brahmin) but also egalitarian in terms of gender. In one of Chandidas's poems, he expressed the desire to touch Rami's feet—a radical inversion of the social order. His poems expressed his love as a tender devotee towards the devi; her poems expressed the intensity of her passion in frank and uncompromising terms.

Their love did not go unnoticed. People strongly disapproved of the inter-caste relationship, and took drastic action. Rami got summarily dismissed from her job at the temple; Chandidas was boycotted by his community and sent away from the village in disgrace.

Abused, reviled and stigmatized, Rami railed against the injustice, and decided to leave the village too:

What can I say, friend:
I don't have enough words!
Even as I weep when I tell you this story
My accursed face breaks into laughter!
Can you imagine the cheek of the sinister men?
They have stopped worshipping the devi
And have started tarnishing my reputation.

Let the thunderbolt crash on the heads of those
Who from their housetops shout abuses at good people
I won't stay any longer in this land of injustice,
I'll go to a place where there are no hellhounds.

Rami still held Chandidas in her heart; but further tragedy lay in store. The Nawab of Gaur invited Chandidas to sing at his palace, and though Chandidas had earlier vowed not to do so, he now agreed. The Begum was deeply moved by his singing, and infatuated with Chandidas. The Nawab saw this, and in jealousy and rage, ordered his men to torture the singer to death.

Rami stood among the throng of people who had come to hear Chandidas sing. She noticed the silent exchange between the Begum and Chandidas, and felt it as a betrayal. She saw Chandidas was attracted to the queen, and intense emotion churned within her. Then she heard the Nawab mete out punishment; her beloved Chandidas was tied to an elephant, and whipped mercilessly. Throughout his extended torture, Chandidas's gaze was fixed on Rami, in mute apology, intense love and devotion. Rami wailed and begged that he be let off—but the Nawab was deaf to her appeal. He was deaf to his wife's urgent words too—she asked him to release the man who had so moved her by his singing. The torture carried on, Chandidas was lashed unceasingly until he bled to death. As his life ebbed away in this macabre setting, the queen, beside herself with guilt and grief, fell into a heap, dead. Rami saw the queen collapse, rushed to her side and fell at her feet, weeping inconsolably.

Rami's world collapsed; later she poured out her agony in verse. Possibly, she became a wandering minstrel, at some point finding shelter and employment elsewhere. The poems she composed testify to her courage. She loved against the grain, though often hurt, and respected everyone's emotions, even when they came in conflict with her own. She saw events objectively, and related them in fine poetry; her heart washed clean, even as she had once washed the temple of the goddess Bashuli Devi.

30 | Kanhopatra: Subversive Poet-Saint

Fifteenth Century, Maharashtra

Kanhopatra's story is a searing cry of pain—brutal and disturbing. Though she made every effort to protect herself from assault and exploitation, ruthless patriarchy and imperial power prevailed. She took refuge in the Varkari sect, in a courageous bid to change the circumstances of her life. She found here a moment of rest, wherein she composed the *ovi* and abhangs for which she is well known. But the end, when it came, was swift and violent.

Her mother, Shyama, was a dancer and devadasi, or ganika. She earned quite well and brought up Kanhopatra in comfort, as well as with affection. They lived in Mangalvedha, a town near Pandharpur. Shyama trained her to dance and sing from early childhood, and she showed uncommon talent. On her own, she also picked up Chokhamela's and Soyarabai's songs, Varkari saints who had lived in Mangalvedha a few decades earlier. She found these songs very appealing.

As Kanhopatra blossomed into youth, her beauty attracted men from far and wide. Shyama set her sights high, thinking her daughter could well become a ganika at the court of the Bahmanis, in Bidar. However, Kanhopatra dreamt of freedom, a simple and peaceful life, rather than pursuing her mother's profession. Born in a courtesan lineage, marriage was virtually taboo, in any case. But Kanhopatra might have been compelled to perform for some patrons, her income required to maintain their lifestyle.

One of Kanhopatra's maids, Hausa, was a Varkari. Kanhopatra observed how the faith provided succour to the elderly woman. Sometimes Hausa sang the abhangs of other women-saints, such as Soyarabai. Kanhopatra learnt these songs from her, and they would sing together.

Meanwhile, another insuperable problem arose. The town headman, Sadashiva Malgujar, used to be Shyama's customer years ago, and now wanted Kanhopatra to entertain him. Shyama was completely nonplussed—because Sadashiva Malgujar was probably Shyama's father. Shyama used to have multiple clients at the time, and was therefore not certain of the child's paternity.

In any case, Kanhopatra was extremely reluctant to go with anybody. Shyama tried to politely refuse Sadashiva, but he persisted, and grew aggressive. She informed him that Kanhopatra was probably his own daughter, but he refused to give credence to this, thinking it was a ploy to put him off. He intensified his harassment of the mother-daughter duo. Feeling insulted, getting Kanhopatra became an obsession with him. Eventually, Shyama possibly felt she had no option but to send Kanhopatra to him.

Feeling utterly vulnerable and distressed, Kanhopatra sought a way out. Pandharpur was just about 20 miles away from Mangalvedha, and often pilgrims passed by Kanhopatra's house. One day, a pilgrim, noticing her curiosity, told her that Vithoba would accept her as a devotee—he was generous, wise, beautiful and perfect. She decided to leave home, and go to Pandharpur. She spoke to her mother about Pandharpur, but her mother was preoccupied.

Having taken a firm resolve, Kanhopatra went to Pandharpur, Hausa accompanying her. Seeing the image of Vithoba at the temple, she spontaneously composed an abhanga—expressing how blessed she felt. She found Vithoba beautiful, and began living close by in a hut, Hausa with her, singing every day at the temple, and cleaning it twice a day. People thought of her as a pious destitute girl, and loved her mellifluous voice. Kanhopatra led a simple life and composed and sang ovi and abhangs day in, day out. Many songs chronicled her experiences, and implored Vithoba to save her from further ignominy. She addressed Him as an intimate, sometimes a mother ('Vithabai', 'Krishnai' or 'Kanhai'—the 'ai' suffix meaning 'mother'):

> O Krishna
> Mother
> Heart of my heart
> O dark One
> With beautiful eyes
> Have mercy on me
> My birth is low
> My reputation
> Black as night
> O dark One
> With beautiful eyes, please
> Have mercy on me.
> The Vedas proclaim you
> Champion of the low
> Savior of the downtrodden,
> Like me.
> Kanhopatra surrenders
> Again and again
> O dark One,
> Have mercy on me.[48]

Her songs betrayed her awareness of continuing vulnerability, threats and dangers that she may not have fully escaped. This refuge at Pandharpur was perhaps the only space available in her time and place, to try to forge a different kind of life. Kanhopatra's creativity flowered in this environment: she was respected and felt her own self-respect rise. At the same time, she wrote of having experienced humiliation, ostracism and violation. Emphasizing how it felt to be the object of lustful men, she used a terribly powerful metaphor—her body as food devoured by wild animals—and appealed for protection:

> …When I say I am yours alone,
> Who is to blame but yourself
> If I am taken by another.
> When a jackal takes the share of the lion,
> It is the great, who is put to shame.
> Kanhopatra says, I offer my body at your feet,
> Protect it, at least for your reputation.[49]

The jackals were for real: Sadashiva hatched a barbaric plan. Aware that the Bahmani king kept countless courtesans and was always on the lookout for more, he went and informed the king about the beautiful and talented Kanhopatra. The king sent for her, but of course Kanhopatra refused. He ordered his men to capture her.

The king's soldiers laid siege on the Vithoba temple, and threatened to destroy it unless Kanhopatra accompanied them. Kanhopatra requested a last meeting with Vithoba, and went into the central shrine. There, she died. Devotees believe she merged with the deity. It's possible she committed suicide, or the soldiers killed her in a scuffle when she refused to go with them. Some believe that after she died, river Chandrabhaga flooded its banks, inundated the temple and drowned all the soldiers.

Kanhopatra died within Vithoba's temple. A tree grew from that spot, and is worshipped by countless pilgrims in her memory. She is respected today as a saint-poet, although when alive she was treated as prey to be hunted, ripped apart and consumed.

31 | Molla: Epic Achievement

Early Sixteenth Century, Andhra Pradesh

Molla composed a new version of the Ramayana—in five days flat! The story goes that the poet Tenali Rama, court poet during Krishnadevaraya's reign, challenged a senior poet from Molla's town, Gopavaram, to compose a new Ramayana within five days. Failure meant dishonour for the entire town. Molla took up the challenge, although everybody scoffed at her. People thought it was impossible—for anyone, especially for a woman, and that too Dalit! But Molla went to the village temple, and sitting there, immersed herself in poetic labour. She completed the work within the stipulated days—an astonishing feat. Not only did she restore the honour of her village, she secured a place for herself in history.

Molla, or Mollamamba, was from the potter caste. Her father, a potter by profession, was a poet too, and Molla grew up learning classical literature and Sanskrit poetics. Her Ramayana was superbly crafted, although she described herself as untrained in the rules of grammar, simply a poet, and not a scholar:

I am no scholar,
Distinguishing loan-words from indigenous,
I know no rules of combination
No large vocabulary
I am no expert

In composition and illocution
Semantics and style,
Nor do I know polemics, case relations,
Roots of verbs and figures of speech,
Meter and prosody
Untrained though,
In composing poems and epics
Mastering lexicons and rules,
I do write poems,
By the grace of the Lord
Sri Kantha Mallesa.[50]

Molla credits her abilities to divine grace; and also, the upbringing she received at the hands of her father, Atukuri Keshav Setti. Molla and her father were Virashaivas, a sect which espoused radical social reform—removing discrimination between the sexes and castes, and rejecting human and animal sacrifice. Her mother died when she was a child and her father brought her up. In the introduction to her epic work, she paid him tribute:

My father Keshav
Was pious, friendly, devoted to his guru,
And God, in all his manifestations,
Fixed and mobile,
Shiva's devotee, he was a guru in his own right.
I am God's gift to him, they call me Molla.

She, a girl child, was valued as a gift from God, rather than a curse, and thus she blossomed, self-esteem intact. There was a rare bond of mutual love and respect between father and daughter. Both Molla and Keshav were ostracized and persecuted for their beliefs.

The *Molla Ramayana* is the first known literary work in the Telugu language. At a time when the business of reading and writing was the sole preserve of Brahmins, a Dalit woman writing such an epic was unimaginable. Several scholars later betrayed their own prejudices by theorizing that Molla must have been a brahmin, or else a brahmin foundling brought up by Keshav!

Oral tradition is clear that Molla was a rebel—bold and unconventional. She remained single through life, as testified by the fact that she kept her maiden name, 'Atukuri'. She was familiar with conventions of the royal court, so it seems her life was not confined to the village. There may be some truth in the story that she was a concubine of Krishnadevaraya: though there is no evidence of this.

Molla wrote in the people's language, and helped develop contemporary Telugu. Writing in Telugu, rather than Sanskrit, was a conscious and subversive decision. Arguing that the best poetry communicates directly, and appeals immediately to the senses, she scorned dull, pretentious, obscure and jargonized writing styles:

> As honey sweetens
> The mouth readily
> A poem should make sense
> Right away.
> Obscure sounds and meaning
> Are no better than
> The dumb conversing with the deaf.

The longest chapter in *Molla Ramayana* is 'Yuddhakanda'—the chapter on war. For the most part, Molla's writing was lyrical, with marvellous depictions of nature, as in the following:

> The sun moved in the sky
> From the East to the other end
> Fatigued, perspiring, it plunged
> Into the ocean for a bath.

Molla Ramayana was never admitted into the royal court, because it was, after all, 'Shudra kavya'—poetic work by a Shudra, and that too a woman! It was praised by court critics for its sophistication, style and content, yet the same critics decided it should be banned from being presented in the court.

In the long run, though, Molla won—her impeccably crafted epic is today considered one of the classical Ramayanas in Telugu, and is widely available in many editions. Although silenced in her time due to her caste and gender, her work is popular with laypeople and very well regarded by scholars.

32 | Meera:
No Strings Tied
1498–1556, Rajasthan, UP and Gujarat

Across India, everybody has heard of Meerabai, and heard her bhajans—which are sung in Marwari and Braj-Bhasha, her languages, and also in Gujarati, Telugu, Bengali, Hindi, Marathi and more. Her popularity readily moves across boundaries of language, caste, class, religion and culture not only within India but also beyond. Her life story is invoked by poets and philosophers, psychologists and ecologists, and a multitude of others seeking authenticity, wholeness and healing.[51] Who was this woman, with such power to endure through time and space?

A princess from the powerful Rathore clan, she was married into the proud Sisodia clan, where she refused to conform. Meera was tortured for her transgressions until, in one decisive move, she left the magnificent palace in the fort of Chittor and took to the roads, a pilgrim forever.

When Meera was a few years old, she asked her mother who her groom would be; her mother pointed to a beautiful statue of Krishna. Her mother died while Meera was small, and her father being busy with wars, she was sent to live with her maternal grandfather Dudaji, in Merta; she took the Krishna statue with her. When she married, it accompanied her to her sasural. Her in-laws told her to worship their family deity, but she declined. This was sacrilege; she further broke iron rules of propriety, defying seclusion to meet and converse with wise men. Attempts were made on her life for the threat she posed to the patriarchal family order; but she survived unharmed:

Rana sent a snake coiled in a basket,
Meera kept it by, went to bathe,
Fresh and clean, she took a look, and finding
A sacred garland, wore it round her neck.
Rana sent a cup of poison,
She turned it into nectar
Drinking, Meera laughed—
It was the water of immortality.
Rana sent a bed of nails
For Meera to sleep on
That evening when she went to bed,
She found a sheet of flowers.
Meera's Giridhar always helps
Protect her from danger,
She wanders blissful,
Devoted to her mountain-lifting lord

The 'Rana' Meera is refering to was most likely her brother-in-law Vikramaditya, who became king after her father-in-law and husband passed away. Her husband was perhaps relatively easy-going, but died within a few years of marriage.

Not yet 30, Meera stepped out, something unheard of for a Rajput queen. Emerging from a palace which felt like a prison, she became the woman with long, unbound tresses, under nobody's control, who danced on the streets for joy. The classical image of Meera has her playing the ektara—blissful, revelling in her freedom. Leaving behind families of origin and marriage, luxuries and precious jewellery, she went forth sans attachments—no strings tied:

I will stay no more within your walls, Ranaji,
Dear to me is the company of the wise,
I have cast off veils of honour and shame,
Left behind Merta home of my childhood,
Left the house I was wedded in,
Both homes cracked like a mirror.
The lord lets me glimpse the heart of love
I dance with abandon, joyful,
To my own beat!
Take your ornaments and adornments—
I flung away necklace, bracelets and rings.
I have seen my perfect groom,
My heart knows no other,
I want no more of fort and palace,
Saris of sheer silk,
Meera walks in a trance,
Crazy, with dancing steps,
Her hair loose, all flowing!

She took to a life of freedom, following her heart, rejecting the dictates of family and community. The quintessential rebel, she gave up shallow pleasures, and adopted instead a peaceful, deep and joyful way of life.

She made her way to Vrindavan. Once there, she asked to meet the learned Jiva Goswami, but he refused, having vowed to see no woman. Meera sent back word: 'I thought in Vrindavan there was but one male, the rest all female', for all Vaishnavite devotees were like gopis, each equally beloved of Lord Krishna. Jiva Goswami realized the wisdom in her words, and met Meera with great respect.

She settled down in Vrindavan, at home in Krishna's hometown, part of a community of worshippers:

Dear friend, Brindavan feels wonderful to me,
Each home offers sacred tulsi leaves,
The Jamuna waters flow pure,
We feast on fresh milk and curd.

In my heart You sit, leaf-crowned,
I walk from grove to grove, listening
To the sound of Your flute,
Living without singing bhajan,
Is like tasting food without salt.

It is not as if Meera's journey was easy. Her practice was exacting.
She pined for a perfect world, and perfect worship, but knew that
this was dependent wholly on the intensity and honesty of her
aspiration:

Is this any way to pray?
Bathed and fresh, tilak on forehead,
But a mind full of mud?
Bound by desire, as if by a thread,
The butcher of wrath in the heart,
How will I meet the cow-herder lord?
When my senses, like a greedy cat,
Beg for food, I feed them,
Worship my own small self,
How can the water of prayer
Form a pool upon this rock of pride?
You cannot deceive One who knows your inmost heart
You count with lips the sacred beads,
Not a trace of the lord in your heart
Come cleave to Hari, remover of falsehood,
Give up wanting the world,
Meera serves her mountain-lifting lord,
Gently turns away from craving, detaches from want.

After spending many years in Vrindavan, Meera walked again—hundreds of kilometres, this time to Dwarka, where Krishna spent his last years. She made the Ranchhor temple her home, the spot where Krishna had stayed, by the lapping waves of the Arabian Sea.

One day, while Meera was singing with other devotees at the seaside Ranchhor temple, a delegation of Brahmins came to fetch her back to Chittor. Her in-laws wanted to get Meera back in Chittor. Perhaps they held her profligacy responsible for their defeat at the hands of the Mughals, and wished to punish her or compel her to penitence; or maybe—just maybe—they wished to honour her, since she was by then well respected as a wise and holy woman.

Meera had no interest in stepping back into Rajput feudalism, a realm of brutal wars and female servitude. The delegation, however, refused to return without her. Meera stepped into the temple's sanctum sanctorum and prayed to Ranchhor. Devotees believe she became one with her Lord; others imagine her stepping into the sea. Either way, she was free, and united with the Whole.

33 | Durgavati: Gond Rani

1524–1564, Gondwana and Madhya Pradesh

'Gond Rani Durgavati' is remembered as a brave warrior who refused to submit to the Mughals even when all odds were stacked against her; she preferred to die fighting. A Rajput princess who married a Gond prince, her memory is cherished by indigenous people of central India. Her bravery and determination have become the stuff of legends.

Durgavati grew up in the magnificent precincts of Kalinjar Fort, Banda; her father Keerat Rai, also known as Salibahan, was the Chandela ruler of Mahoba, Bundelkhand. Durgavati lost her mother in early childhood; she had a sister, Kamlavati, and a dear friend, Ramcheri. The princesses enjoyed hunting, horse riding and archery, and became adept at using sword, spear and dagger. Chandela power was at low ebb, battered by invasions over the years; Durgavati took interest in matters of the state.

In 1542, Durgavati married Dalpat Shah, son of Raja Sangram Shah of Garha-Mandla, a powerful dynasty in central India. The marriage was a political alliance between the Chandelas and the Raj Gond rulers of Garha-Mandla. Ballads and folklore of Gondwana tell a more colourful tale: Dalpat Shah once visited Kalinjar, set in the Vindhya range, and he and Durgavati fell in love during a hunting expedition. He sent a formal proposal, but her father disapproved; Durgavati stealthily left the palace, and eloped with her prince.

Durgavati moved across cultures, leaving Kalinjar, and settling in the rugged Singorgarh Fort, in Garha-Mandla (modern-day Jabalpur and Mandla), within the Satpura mountains. She toured on elephant back, visiting remote villages, and meeting local chiefs with her husband and entourage, within the forested hilly regions of Gondwana. Sangram Shah was the forty-seventh king of the Garha-Mandla dynasty which stretched back over a thousand years; he expanded dominion across the Vindhyas and Satpura highlands, including 52 forts and thousands of villages. After Sangram Shah passed away in 1543, Dalpat Shah became king. Chauragarh—over 150 miles to the south, became his capital, though Singorgarh was also used.

In 1545, Durgavati gave birth to Vir Narayan. In 1550, Dalpat Shah passed away. Durgavati, grief-stricken, gathered herself together: she had a kingdom to govern, as regent for her son. Dalpat Shah's younger brother, Chandra Shah, was resentful, but senior ministers supported the queen. Ramcheri, Durgavati's childhood friend, lived in the palace and was a great help to her.

Durgavati proved to be an able administrator. She got rest houses constructed for travellers, encouraged crafts and made a beautiful tank, Rani Taal, in Garha. Cultivators grew so much grain that the surplus was exported to Gujarat and the Deccan. Abul Fazl wrote in *Ain-e-Akbari*, 'During Durgavati's reign, Gondwana became so prosperous that the people gave land tax in gold coins and elephants. The Rani had her own elephant house, where 1,400 war elephants were kept.' Durgavati kept her army in fine fettle. When Baz Bahadur of Malwa attacked her kingdom in 1556, she led the forces to battle, and roundly defeated him.

In 1562, Akbar captured Malwa, and set his eyes upon Gondwana. Legend holds that he sent Durgavati a charkha, insinuating that she ought to be spinning, not fighting battles. She sent him a 'peenjan', hand-carder, to indicate, 'If I should spin yarn, then you should card cotton!' When her advisor, Adhar Simha, pointed out that Mughal forces were incomparably stronger in numbers, with modern weaponry, she replied, 'It is better to die fighting, than live with disgrace and dishonour.'

In 1564, Akbar's general, Asaf Khan, stationed 6,000 cavalry, 12,000 infantry and heavy artillery in the hills of Damoh. Durgavati went into battle with 500 cavalry, some infantry and elephants. She strategized by hiding a large contingent of soldiers armed with bows and arrows in the hills near Singrampur. Mughal troops seemed to be winning when, all of a sudden, a torrent of arrows rained upon them, taking them unawares. Asaf Khan lost this battle—a signal victory for her troops.

Asaf Khan's spies learnt about a secret tunnel leading into the Singorgarh Fort. His soldiers stealthily entered through the tunnel, and created mayhem in the fort. Durgavati, Vir Narayan, Ramcheri and a few hundred soldiers escaped.

Durgavati halted at Narrai, where there was a hilly range on one side, and rivers Gaur and Narmada on the other. Preparing to fight a defensive battle, she placed her troops in position in the narrow defile. Asaf Khan's forces duly arrived and Durgavati, mounted on her elephant Sarman, led her men into battle. Vir Narayan got badly injured, and she sent him to a safe spot. The waters of the Narmada began to rise, hemming her troops in. An arrow pierced her near one eye; undeterred, she calmly removed it, though the point remained lodged in her left temple. Sarman got wounded, and bellowed in pain.

Her ministers asked her to escape, but Durgavati continued fighting. An arrow pierced her on the side of the neck. Bleeding profusely, she requested her mahout, whom she had brought up from boyhood, 'Gannu, take my sword and end my life.'

He said 'I cannot, Rani Ma! Forgive me!' Choosing death over captivity, Durgavati plunged the dagger into her breast. Asaf Khan slaughtered her army, and looted the kingdom. He attacked the Chauragarh Fort two months later, killed Vir Narayan and carried away booty including over a thousand elephants. It is said that 300 women committed jauhar at the fort, but by chance two remained alive, were captured and taken to Agra. One was Durgavati's sister Kamlavati; the other, a young woman who had been engaged to Vir Narayan.

The date of Durgavati's martyrdom, 24 June, is celebrated as 'Balidan Diwas' among the Gonds. People enjoy visiting the museum and memorial at Jabalpur that commemorates her life and times. Madhya Pradesh police has a Rani Durgavati Battalion, with a thousand police posts reserved for women, and several all-women police stations. May the memory of brave Rani Durgavati inspire courage, and respect for women within all of society!

34 | Khivi:
Soul Food
1506-1581, Punjab

Khivi institutionalized the tradition of langar: a space of astonishing generosity. Millions of people eat daily in langars at gurudwaras, delicious and nutritious meals, cooked and served by volunteers. Food is offered to anyone who comes by, with no differentiation on the basis of religion or race. Special langars are often set up by members of the Sikh community to feed destitute people, refugees, victims of earthquake, flood or other disasters. Despite the flourishing world of langars, few people have heard of its progenitor, Khivi.

In the early years of the Sikh religion, langar was popularly known as *Mata Khivi Ji da langar*. Guru Nanak and his wife Sulakhni had initiated food offering to devotees. Khivi expanded the system, and systemized Seva (voluntary service). She showed the way, through the great care she took in preparing each meal. Langar flows from the awareness that food is divine, no one owns it, everyone needs it, and everyone's need is equally important.

Khivi was born in 1506 to Karan Devi and Devi Chand Khatri, a well-to-do couple of village Sarigar, near Khadur in present-day Amritsar district. At the age of 13, Khivi married Lahina, and moved to live with him at Khadur. Five years later, they had a son, Dasu, and then daughters Amro (1532) and Anokhi (1535), and son Datu (1537). Around 1530, Khivi heard of Guru Nanak's teaching from an acquaintance, Mai Bhirai, and Lahina heard of the Guru through Bhai Jodha.

Lahina went to Kartarpur to meet Guru Nanak in 1532, and became a disciple. He stayed on to serve the Guru—sweeping, washing clothes and working in the fields. His understanding of the teachings grew, and so did the Guru's affection for him. After a while, Guru Nanak instructed Lahina to return to Khadur to his family, and spread word of the new faith. Guru Nanak visited the family twice. Khivi too embraced the faith wholeheartedly. Women of the village cautioned her that if her husband became a holy man, he would forsake her, but she knew better. Guru Nanak advocated family life, with equality and respect for women.

In 1539, Lahina succeeded Guru Nanak, becoming the second guru of the faith; he was now known as Guru Angad Dev. Disciples poured in from far and near. Khivi took it upon herself to look after them, presiding over the langar, attending to every detail. The best ingredients were used, and everyone was treated with courtesy. She created a loving atmosphere, which also helped establish the fledgling spiritual community on a strong footing. Her spirit of hospitality has been widely emulated over the centuries.

Guru Granth Sahib, the holy book of the Sikhs, explicitly mentions Khivi, noting that this noble woman provided comfort to pilgrims, like a tree with deep leafy shade; she distributed rich fare such as kheer, which tasted like ambrosia. Meals were served with equal respect without distinction of caste, creed or colour. Since Khadur was situated by the Beas River, many travellers ate at the langar, before or after crossing the river, and thus got naturally attracted to the new faith. Langar became a unique and integral part of Sikh culture. While Guru Angad spread Sikhism in congregations (Sangat), Khivi effectively did the same through the community kitchen.

Langars offer food free of charge; expenses are met out of donations by members of the community. Sikhism preaches that everyone should earn their livelihood through their own hard work. Guru Angad Dev earned his living by twisting coarse grass, called *munj,* into rope, used for making cots. And Khivi, stepping out of the limited boundaries of the domestic, used her culinary, organizational and managerial skills to set up and run the langar.

Khivi and Guru Angad led a life of rustic simplicity. They loved children—their own and others'. Daily they set aside time to teach children, watched them at play and delighted in their clever ways. From children's games, the Guru would often draw out practical lessons for the congregation.

Khivi was a kind mother, with great confidence in her children. The elder daughter, Amro, married Jasoo, of Basarke village. Amro sang sweetly, and people would gather to hear her sing the Sikh *shabads* (hymns from the Guru Granth Sahab). Amar Das, a young relative of her husband's, was very moved by her singing, and Amro persuaded him to go seek the blessings of Guru Angad. Amar Das did so, and became a devoted follower of Sikhism; Guru Angad selected him as his successor.

Guru Angad said to Khivi, 'I know you approve of my selection of Amar Das, but what of your sons?' She replied, 'They are proud of being Guru's sons. Be kind to them and show them the right path.' When Guru Angad passed away in 1552, Datu declared himself the heir and gathered a small following. When Datu developed headaches, Khivi persuaded him that the sure way to a cure was to accept the rightful Guru. She explained: 'Your father's decision was based on merit. Your father too became Guru on the basis of merit; this is Sikh tradition.' Datu agreed to go with her to Guru Amar Das, who, when he heard Mata Khivi was coming, ran out to meet them halfway. Thanks to Khivi's timely intervention, Sikhism was spared a schism.

Khivi continued supervising the langar for Guru Amar Das. When Guru Amar Das organized the Sikhs into specific districts and jurisdictions called Manjis, he appointed Amro to head a Manji. Amro's responsibilities included spreading the teachings, collecting revenue and caring for the welfare of the people. To date, a pond at Basarke is called Bibi Amro Da Talab.

Khivi lived to the age of 75, some 30 years beyond her husband. She saw five Gurus during her lifetime; Guru Arjun Dev attended her funeral to pay his respects. Mata Khivi's legacy is alive today in the langar served in every gurudwara in the world.

35 | Gulbadan: Insider Historian

1523–1603, Kabul, Agra, Delhi and Lahore

Gulbadan Begum was in her 60s when she wrote *Humayun-nama*, a lively history of the early Mughals. Hers is a multilayered narrative, vibrant with details of travel, daily life, innumerable characters and their eccentricities and activities; it is in fact the inner history of empire. Gulbadan wrote in Persian, interspersed with her mother tongue, Turki. Akbar had asked her to write whatever she remembered of her father, Babur, and brother, Humayun. Gulbadan mused: 'I was eight years old when my exalted father passed away, and therefore may not remember much, yet in obedience to the royal command, I set down whatever there is that I have heard and remember.'

Gulbadan described women's worlds, and complex webs of relationship. She revealed that when 12-year-old Babur's father died, his hardy grandmother Aisan Daulat guided his steps, as well as mother Qutlugh Nigar—through harsh Central Asian terrain, frequently living in penury, until, a decade later (1505), Babur conquered Kabul.

Babur married Maham Begum, with whom he had five children; four died as infants, while Humayun survived. Dildar Begum, a later wife of Babur's, also birthed five children: Gulbarg, Gulchehra, Hindol, Gulbadan and a son who died in infancy.

Maham Begum, the senior queen, adopted Hindol; when Gulbadan turned two, Maham adopted her as well. Gulbadan was always very fond of Maham, Dildar and her other 'mothers'— Gulrukh and Mubarika (other wives of Babur).

The harem, we learn from Gulbadan, was a place of immense camaraderie, shared activities, fun as well as hardship. Its inhabitants included wives of the king, children and a multitude of other female relatives. Gulbadan's aunt Khanzada Begum— Babur's eldest sister—was held in great respect. In 1501, Babur had given Khanzada to Shaybani Khan Uzbek, ruler of Samarkand, in exchange for his own freedom; Shaybani divorced Khanzada after a few years and gave her to Sayyid Hada; Hada was killed in battle against the Shah of Persia, who immediately, and with great respect, sent Khanzada back to Babur. Babur welcomed his sister back with gratitude and full honour. The Mughals appreciated Khanzada's sacrifices; Babur made her Padshah Begum (first lady of the empire). Khanzada married Mahdi Khwaja, a minister in Babur's court, and raised his little sister Sultanam.

Babur established the Mughal empire in Hindustan in 1526—defeating Ibrahim Lodi and taking over Badalgarh (Agra Fort). Babur sent rich gifts for the family in Kabul, including for little Gulbadan. Then Babur fell ill, poisoned by Buwa Begum, Ibrahim Lodi's mother; he sent away the bereaved lady to Kabul, but she committed suicide en route.

In January 1629, six-year-old Gulbadan and Maham Begum set off from Kabul, travelling by horse litter, through over a thousand kilometres of changing terrain, reaching Agra in June. Babur was eagerly awaiting their arrival; they spent pleasant days in Agra, Dhaulpur and Sikri—where 'Baba' (as Gulbadan called him) would sit and write his book (*Baburnama*).

Soon the entire harem arrived, as well as 96 venerable old Timurid ladies who settled in Agra at Babur's insistence; he provided homes to all, and they laid out exquisite gardens along the Yamuna. The very next year, however, tragedy struck: first Humayun fell ill, and Babur prayed that he be taken away instead; Babur indeed passed away. Gulbadan described poignantly the grief that engulfed everyone: 'Black fell that day for children and kinsfolk and all. They bewailed and lamented; voices were uplifted in weeping; there was utter dejection.'[52]

Maham ran the royal household under the new emperor, her son Humayun; she held a grand feast to celebrate his victory at Chunar. But then she contracted a 'disorder of the bowels,' which proved fatal. Maham's death left 10-year-old Gulbadan heartbroken: 'I felt lonely and helpless and in great affliction. Day and night I wept and mourned and grieved.'[53] Humayun visited her often, a kind and gentle brother. Soon, Gulbadan moved in with Dildar, her biological mother.

Gulbadan penned detailed descriptions of a magnificent Mystic Feast organized by Khanzada, with dazzling décor, revelries and legions of guests; and in 1537, a splendid wedding celebration between Hindol and Sultanam. Gifts exchanged included

> nine tipuchaq horses with jewelled and gold-embroidered saddle and bridles; gold and silver vessels and slaves, Turki and Circassian and Abyssinian... and... nine jackets with garniture of jewelled balls, one of ruby, one of cornelian, one of emerald, one of topaz, and one of cat's-eye.[54]

Gulbadan married Khizr Khvajeh Khan, a cousin and Chagatai nobleman, in Humayun's employ. Around the same time, Humayun lost the Battle of Chausa (1539). Gulbadan's half-brother Mirza Kamran took her from Agra to Lahore, though she resisted: 'he took me by main force, with a hundred weepings and complaints and laments, away from my mothers, and my own mother and my sisters, and my father's people, and my brothers, and parted us who had all grown up together from infancy.'[55] In hindsight, it was a sensible move, because within days, Humayun was defeated in the Battle of Kannauj (1540), and with that the Mughals lost Hindustan; the entire court and harem fled to Lahore and further.

Gulbadan spent the next 15 years in Kabul with the family, including Khanzada, Dildar, Gulchehra, as well as her own husband and young children. Kamran tried to tempt her husband to plot against Humayun, but Khizr Khan remained loyal to Humayun, much to Gulbadan's relief. Their son Saadat-yar, when he grew up, also joined Humayun's service.

Humayun marched through Sind, where he married 14-year-old Hamida, who initially 'resisted and discussed and disagreed' but, after 40 days of persuasion, agreed to his proposal. Hamida had a rough time travelling, heavily pregnant, through rugged terrain, semi-starved, until they found shelter with a Rajput family in Amarkot. On 15 October 1542, she gave birth to Akbar. Next year, Hamida and Humayun travelled to Persia. Gulbadan met Humayun (in Kabul) after a gap of five years: 'freed of the moil and toil of separation, we were lifted up by our happiness… There were many festive gatherings, and people sat from evening to dawn, and players and singers made continuous music…'[56] Humayun gave land, salaries and pensions to soldiers who were with him in Chausa and Kannauj, and to widows and children of those who had been killed.

Gulbadan wrote accounts of battles, some of which she witnessed. Kamran took up arms against Humayun, and Hindol, fighting for Humayun, was killed in battle. Gulbadan was devastated: 'Would to heaven that merciless sword had touched my heart and eyes, or my son Saadat-yar's, or Khizr Khwaja Khan's! Alas! a hundred regrets! Alas, a thousand times alas!'[57] Khizr Khan took Hindol's body to Jalalabad, and arranged the burial. Humayun's amirs counselled harsh punishment for Kamran, saying: 'This is no brother! This is your Majesty's foe!' Humayun hesitated: 'Though my head inclines to your words, my heart does not.'[58] But finally, he ordered Kamran to be blinded.

Gulbadan's manuscript ends abruptly; the rest is lost. We know that in 1555, Humayun re-established Mughal rule in India; and Akbar succeeded him the next year. In 1557, Gulbadan, Hamida and other members of the harem joined Akbar. For the rest of her life, Gulbadan remained an active and highly respected elder member of Akbar's harem. She moved as his capital moved— Delhi to Agra, Fatehpur Sikri to Lahore and finally, back to Agra.

Timurid women—Gulbadan along with Ruqaiya and Salima (Akbar's wives) and several others—were extremely influential, and integral to the building of the empire. They were independent-minded, hardy women, who knew the peripatetic life of old. Gulbadan savoured the settled, comfortable life with equal elan and took a lively interest in life around her. Hamida was her closest friend. All the Timurid women wore Turkic-style comfortable qabas (long and loose women's garments) and conical hats, and retained their spirit of adventure.

In 1575, Gulbadan, Hamida, Salima, Sultanam and many other Timurid ladies went on hajj! They left Fatehpur Sikri for Surat, where they were grounded for several months, before setting sail for Jeddah (1576). They spent three and a half years in Arabia and made the hajj four times, performing all the rituals, giving alms and lavish gifts. Their return was delayed by a shipwreck in Aden; they reached home in March 1582. Three years later, Akbar shifted the capital to Lahore; Gulbadan wrote the *Humayun-nama* there.

When Jahangir rebelled against Akbar in 1601, Gulbadan, Hamida, Salima and Ruqaiya made a direct intervention. Akbar was on the verge of pronouncing severe punishment; the elderly ladies made a loud and fervent plea for mercy within the court. In deference to his honoured kinswomen, Akbar pardoned his errant son. There were many ways, we could say, in which Gulbadan literally 'wrote' the history of the empire.

Gulbadan died at a ripe old age. Hamida and Ruqaiya were with her unto the end. Hearing Hamida's affectionate words, Gulbadan quoted the verse, 'I die—may you live!' Akbar carried her bier; and later often lamented that he missed his favourite aunt.

Gulbadan's chronicle has generally been marginalized by emperors and historians, in favour of dry official accounts; sadly so. Its full-blooded style brings alive an era, and characters who emerge as composite human beings, not mere figments of royalty.

36 | Bega: Begum Builder

1511–1582?, Central Asia, Agra and Delhi

Bega was 19 when she became empress. Years later, she chose to move away from palace life; and dwell near an incredibly beautiful monument that she had conceived and constructed. A passionate, strong-willed woman who knew love and loss, she created poetry in stone, fusing Persian and Indian styles. Humayun's Tomb was her legacy for posterity— the first magnificent Mughal mausoleum, archetype for the Taj Mahal.

Bega hailed from Badakhshan, Afghanistan, bordering Persia; her father Yadgar Beg Taghai was Maham Begum's brother, Humayun's maternal uncle. When Babur sent 12-year-old Humayun to Badakhshan as his regent, Bega was eight years old. Eight years later, they married. In 1528, they had a son, Al-Aman, who died in infancy. Humayun complained of the remoteness of Badakhshan; Babur wrote back: 'No bondage is like the bondage of kings.' At Babur's behest, Humayun came to Agra, and upon Babur's demise, became emperor.

Bega came to India for the first time in December 1530, reaching four days after Babur's death. Gulbadan (Humayun's sister) tells a tale official historians never would: Maham Begum 'had a great longing to see a son of Humayun. Wherever there was a good-looking and nice girl, she used to bring her into his service. One day, after Babur's death, she brought a maid, saying, "Humayun, Maywa-jan is not bad. Why do you not take her into your service?" So, at her word, Humayun married and took her that very night.'[59]

Three days later, Bega Begum arrived, and soon was pregnant. Maywa-jan too announced her pregnancy. Maham waited with bated breath for a son to be born to either. Bega gave birth to a daughter, Aqiqa Banu. The tenth month passed, and it became clear that Maywa-jan had been fibbing: she hadn't been pregnant at all!

Bega settled into the duties of queen, and brought up little Aqiqa. Humayun languished under the burden of kingship, and frequent battles. Often he visited women relatives, young and old; Gulbadan describes one such occasion when, one night in 1535, night singers entertained and everyone slept in a vast tent. Bega, perhaps missing the time and attention he gave her in Badakhshan, voiced a spirited complaint next morning:

Bega Begum woke us up, and said, 'It is time for prayers.' His majesty ordered water for ablution, so the begum knew he was awake. She began a complaint, and said to him: 'For several days now you have been paying visits in this garden, and not one day have you been to our house. Thorns have not been planted on the way to it. We hope you will deign to visit our quarters also, and to have a party and a sociable gathering there... We too have hearts.' Humayun heard her out, went for his prayers, then gathered all the sisters and begums, and said to Bega, 'Bibi, what ill-treatment at my hands did you complain of this morning? That was not the place to make a complaint.' To everyone, he said, 'You all know that I have been to the quarters of the elder relations. It is a necessity laid on me to make them happy... I am an opium-eater. If there should be delay in my comings and goings, do not be angry with me...' Bega drily commented: 'The excuse looks worse than the fault! ...What remedy have we? You are Emperor.' She wrote a letter and gave it to him, and he made it up with her.[60]

Humayun took the harem along with him wherever possible, even to war. In 1539, he fought the Battle of Chausa in Bengal; the Ganga and Karmnasan rivers flooded the ground where his troops stood, and inundated the harem tents. Several women were lost, captured or killed; Bega was captured by Sher Shah Suri, and seven-year-old Aqiqa disappeared.

We will never know what Bega experienced as a prisoner of war; Abul Fazl claimed she was treated honourably, but strangely, Gulbadan remained silent on the matter. Bega was sent back to Humayun with Sher Shah's general, Khwas Khan, perhaps within the year, though it may have been longer.

Bega suffered abduction and captivity; her little daughter met an unknown fate. Sher Shah further defeated Humayun at Kannauj (1540). The royal family fled to Lahore, then Kabul; Humayun went to Sind, then Persia. We don't know whether Bega accompanied the family; or was still Sher Shah's captive. Gunwar Begum, another of Humayun's wives, gave birth to a daughter, Bakhsi-banu (1541). Humayun married Hamida and had a son, Akbar, who was sent to the family in Kabul for safekeeping. By then Bega was back, living amid the family; Gulbadan writes that Bega was knowledgeable in herbs and medicine, and cured baby Akbar's toothache with a healing paste.

Bega met Humayun after many years when he reached Kabul in 1545. She was his senior-most queen and, despite travails and separations, they shared a bond of affection. Bega felt keenly the sharp edge of suffering; but reconciled to the inevitable, and lived with grace and dignity. She was part of a spirited family, the women sometimes accompanying Humayun to battle; at other times for excursions, such as an extended picnic at Laghman (1549): '... It was a moonlight night. We talked and told stories...' In the morning, Bega and some other begums took so long putting on their 'head-to-foot dresses', that Humayun grew impatient. Humayun enjoyed visiting orange gardens with Bega, Hamida and others.[61]

Bega heard of Humayun's victories in Hindustan in 1555, and was devastated by news of his sudden death in Delhi's Purana Qila. Soon Akbar sent for the royal family, which resettled in Delhi and then in Agra.

But Bega hewed her own path. In 1560–61, she built the Arab Sarai, a caravansarai in Nizamuddin, a resting place for travellers. In 1564, she went on a three-year pilgrimage to Mecca, earning the epithet 'Haji Begum'. She brought back Persian artisans and the architect Mirak Mirza Ghiyas.

Bega commissioned Humayun's tomb at her own cost, employing local masons who worked under Mirak. She chose the site, beside the Yamuna, and supervised the project—its massive domes, intricate inlay work and charbagh with flower beds and fruit trees. Humayun's remains were reinterred in this stately monument, which towered over the city and became its most conspicuous landmark. Next to this mausoleum, Bega established a madrasa for girls.

Akbar entreated Bega to join the royal family in Agra; he was very attached to her. She, however, preferred to live on her own, free of intricate hierarchies. Whenever she visited Agra, she was received with enormous warmth. She passed away, aged around 70, and Akbar escorted her body to Humayun's Tomb, where she was buried.

Jesuit priest Antoine de Monserrate wrote in 1591:

One of his wives had loved Emaumus [Humayun] so faithfully that she had a small house built close by the tomb and watched there till the day of her death. Throughout her widowhood she devoted herself to prayer and to alms-giving. Indeed, she maintained 500 poor people by her alms. Had she only been a Christian, hers would have been the life of a heroine.[62]

Is that Bega, chuckling in her tomb?

37 | Maham Anaga:
Intricate Mother-Work

Sixteenth Century, Central Asia, Agra
and Delhi

Maham Anaga was with Akbar from the minute he was born: the only stable presence in his life for the next 20 years. She supervised his 11 wet nurses when he was an infant, and ensured every aspect of his welfare. As he grew into boyhood, she taught him right from wrong. After he became emperor at 14, Maham was a trusted advisor, and grew increasingly powerful; however, her life came to an abrupt and tragic end.

Hamida gave birth to Akbar in a remote Sindhi outpost. Fourteen months later, when she and Humayun fled to Persia, other family members took the child to Kabul, along with Maham and his other caretakers. Maham, as chief caretaker, continued to play a key role in Akbar's upbringing. Jiji Anaga, the chief wet nurse, had a unique importance too: other wet nurses often complained that the baby wanted only Jiji's milk! Family women also doted on little Akbar—Khanzada, Sultanam, Gulrukh, Dildar, Gulchehra, Gulbadan, Bega Begum and others.

Maham and Jiji were quasi-mothers who guarded the child through difficult times, danger and turmoil. By the time his parents returned from Persia, Akbar was an active three-year-old. Maham Anaga continued to watch over him, and was much respected for her good sense and intense commitment. Akbar had 'great affection for Maham Anaga, on account of her assiduous attention and service'.[63]

Maham Anaga accompanied 13-year-old Akbar when he came with Humayun to India. She shared the triumph of his first victories and the re-establishment of the Mughal empire; and was there when Humayun suddenly died, and Akbar was crowned emperor. Through all this, Hamida and the legion of aunts and stepmothers were far away, in Kabul. When they arrived in India the next year, Akbar sent Maham to receive them, 'who, on account of her abundant sense and loyalty, held a high place in the esteem of the Shahenshah, and who had been in his service from the time of the cradle till his adornment of the throne, and who trod the path of good service with the acme of affection'.

Trustworthy Maham Anaga slid into the role of political advisor for the young emperor. He accorded her a seat on the platform next to his throne. Bairam Khan was Akbar's prime minister, but by 1560, Maham and Hamida Begum persuaded Akbar that Bairam Khan was disloyal; Akbar demoted Bairam Khan. Maham's son-in-law, Shahabuddin Ahmad Khan, took charge of state affairs. Maham became extremely powerful and her family, including husband Nadim Koka and son Adham Khan, aimed for high posts.

As a symbol of her stature and munificence, in 1561, Maham Anaga constructed an expansive mosque-cum-madrasa, Khairul-manzil, adjacent to Purana Qila, Akbar's seat of power in Delhi. Khairul-manzil, meaning 'most auspicious', was Delhi's first monument built by a Mughal woman. It had an imposing red sandstone gateway, prayer hall decorated with enamelled tiles and a double-storey madrasa for girls with an enclosed garden. Maham's name was inscribed on the central arc of the prayer hall.

Maham was exceedingly proud of her son Adham, but aware

that he lacked propriety and realpolitik. Ten years older than Akbar, Adham had helped guide the child in many sporting activities; they used to go hunting together and engage in trials of strength. Adham was married to Javeda Begum in 1552, and had two sons and two daughters. In 1561, Akbar appointed him general and sent him to Malwa, where, in the Battle of Sarangpur, Adham defeated Baz Bahadur. He was tempted to keep for himself the enormous treasures he looted, including several women dancers.

Getting wind of Adham's intentions, Akbar straightaway went to Malwa. Maham too sped there, and persuaded her son to give everything over to the emperor. Adham kept two of the dancers, and Maham tacitly allowed it. But when she heard that Akbar knew of this, Maham got the two girls secretly killed. In deference to Maham, Akbar did not say anything to her or Adham. But five months later, he recalled Adham Khan, in effect stripping him of his position.

Meanwhile, Jiji Anaga's family steadily gained influence. Shamsuddin Atga Khan, Jiji's husband, had saved Humayun's life at the Battle of Chausa, and was held in great respect ever after. In 1561, Akbar appointed him prime minister. Jiji's sons and several extended family members also gained high positions. Competition sprouted between Maham's and Jiji's families, and took gruesome form. Adham walked into court one day, with his attendants, and summarily executed Atga Khan.

Akbar took decisive action. Rushing out from the inner quarters, scimitar in hand, he struck Adham a blow, crying, 'Fool! Why did you kill my Atga?' He got Adham thrown from the terrace, a fall of some eight feet, but Adham survived. Akbar had him thrown again head-first; his skull smashed. Akbar went to Maham Anaga himself, and gently told her: 'Adham has killed Atga.' The mother heard, stunned. He continued: 'We have inflicted retaliation upon him.' She whispered: 'You did well!'

The good woman fell ill with shock and grief. On the fortieth day, she passed away. Adham was flung down from a height of eight feet, but Maham Aanga's fall was from far greater heights. Her exalted position had been won through a lifetime of sincere labour, and was well-deserved. She came crashing down due to a tragic quirk of fate; her prestige and dreams shattered along with her power.

Akbar got built a stately mausoleum in Mehrauli, for Maham Anaga and her son, Adham Khan. For Atga Khan, he made a beautiful mausoleum next to Nizamuddin dargah. As for Jiji Anaga, she lived on; as did her son Aziz Koka, who was a few days younger than Akbar. Akbar always excused his flaws, saying, 'Between Aziz and me there is a river of milk which I cannot cross!' Fortunately for Aziz, he committed no crime as great as Adham's, and thus never fell through the cracks of imperial favour and disfavour.

38 | Abbakka: Abhaya Rani

Sixteenth-Seventeenth Century, Tulunad and Karnataka

Abbakka, queen of Ullal, a port town in Tulunad on India's west coast, confronted ferocious attacks, and repulsed them repeatedly, earning the sobriquet 'Abhaya Rani'— Fearless Queen. Local stories, songs, Yakshagana and Bhuta Kola narrate Abbakka Mahadevi's story, portraying her as strong and beautiful, and recounting her great deeds.

'Abhaya Rani' in fact is a composite of two Abbakkas: Abbakka I (reign 544–82) and Abbakka II (reign 1606–23). Both were Chowta rulers of Ullal, feudatories of Vijayanagar kingdom. Living in the cosmopolitan setting of Ullal, the queens spoke Tulu as well as a smattering of other tongues.

Abbakka I was crowned queen of Ullal by Raja Tirumala Raya III, her mother's brother. After his death, she took charge of the small state (1544). Abbakka was married to Lakshmappa Banga, of the Mangalore ruling family. Chowtas as well as the Banga dynasty were Jains. Under the matrilineal system Aliyasantana, daughters stayed on in the natal home, and husbands could come live with them. Lakshmappa however maintained Mangalore as his base; he took over as the ruler of Mangalore in 1545. Abbakka and Lakshmappa had three children—two daughters and a son. Their daughters grew up in Ullal; the son probably died young.

Lakshmappa himself passed away early, in 1556.

Abbakka was well-versed in business matters, and became known in the Arabian peninsula as 'Pepper Queen'. Ullal was a hub for the flourishing spice trade. The Portuguese, however, with their powerful naval armada, already dominated the Arabian Sea; they demanded tax (known as *kappa*) from Indian seafarers, traders and rulers. Abbakka categorically refused. She continued sending ships laden with pepper, ginger and other commodities to Arabia and Persia.

In 1556, Commander Don Alvaro da Silveira led an attack on Ullal, but was defeated by Abbakka's army. The following year, the Portuguese plundered Mangalore (where Kumaraya, Lakshmappa's nephew, now ruled). A year later, they attacked and ransacked Ullal, before being ejected: they were unable to occupy the city. Abbakka maintained diplomatic relations with Cochin, Calicut and Keladi, and with their support, sent a spice-laden ship to the Arab peninsula. The Portuguese captured the ship mid-sea. In retaliation, Abbakka attacked a Portuguese factory in Mangalore. She rejected a treaty proposed by the Portuguese, but did agree to pay a small tribute.

A decade later, General Joao Peixoto invaded Ullal. Abbakka's army put up strong defence, but the Portuguese captured the city. Abbakka escaped, took refuge in a mosque, and the same night, gathered 200 soldiers and launched a surprise attack. In the ensuing battle, Peixoto was killed, 70 Portuguese soldiers were taken prisoner and the rest forced to retreat. Abbakka also compelled the Portuguese to retreat from the Mangalore Fort. Her daughters fought alongside their mother.

In 1569, the Portuguese regained the Mangalore Fort, and threatened to burn Mangalore if Kumaraya supported Abbakka. Kumaraya began to conspire against her. The Portuguese passed a series of edicts against Abbakka, dubbing her alliance with

Cochin illegal, and trade with Persia an unfriendly act. They demanded rights to set up trading posts at Ullal, as intermediaries for all commercial transactions. Abbakka scornfully dismissed their unjust demands, and continued strengthening diplomatic and defence ties with neighbouring states.

In 1581, Goa's viceroy, Anthony D'Noronha, led battleships with 3,000 soldiers to Ullal, in a predawn attack. Abbakka roused her soldiers: 'Let us fight them on land and sea, on the streets and the beaches.' Battle raged, and in a barrage of gunfire, Abbakka was wounded; her soldiers carried her to a safe spot, concealed from the enemy. She died a few months later.

∽

Abbakka I was succeeded by Thirumala Devi (1584–1606), perhaps one of Abbakka's daughters—we know little about her reign. In 1606, Thirumala Devi was succeeded by Abbakka II— most likely her daughter, or niece. Abbakka II was another 'Abhaya Rani'—as courageous and fearless as her namesake ancestor, Abbakka I. She continued trading with the Middle East, rejecting Portuguese controls.

In 1618, the Portuguese captured a ship of hers returning from Persia, laden with merchandise. Planning to attack Ullal, they brought their naval armada all around the port. Abbakka laid careful plans. Around midnight, her soldiers and fishermen sailed out in country boats, and threw thousands of burning coconut torches and *agnivanas* (fire arrows) at the Portuguese warships. Sails caught fire, the warships sank, men jumped into the sea. Some 200 were killed by Abbakka's soldiers, and the rest forced to retreat.

Portugal, the powerful maritime power of the time, was repeatedly defeated by tiny Ullal! Tales of intrepid Abbakka spread far and wide. Italian traveller Pietro Della Valle, curious about the woman known all over Europe for having made Portugal bite the dust, came to meet her. She was returning from overlooking an irrigation project in Manel village, accompanied by a few soldiers with shields and swords, and an attendant holding a palm-leaf umbrella overhead. Barefoot, clad in plain cotton wraparound, and white cloth draped over head and upper body, she was sturdy and dignified. Pietro's interpreter introduced him and his travels. Abbakka enquired: 'After seeing the Great Turk, Persian Emperor, Mogul Emperor and Venkatappa Nayaka, what is there to see in this wilderness?' He replied, 'I came only to see you, Your Majesty. You are well known in my part of the world!'

Pietro was impressed with what he learnt about Abbakka: 'She was little at home but, rising at break of day, went forthwith to her works and there stayed till dinner… active and vigorous in actions of war and weighty affairs… She was employed a good while in doing justice to her subjects.'[64] She hired people of diverse religions and sects in her army and administration, and was a benevolent ruler.

The Portuguese, however, continued their relentless attacks; and were finally able to capture and imprison Abbakka; we do not know the year. She rebelled in prison, challenging their unjust acts; they killed her, not knowing how else to deal with a queen who refused to submit to their tyranny.

39 | Harkha:
Great Adventurer
1542–1623, Amer and Agra

People admire the elegant mosque of Mariyam Zamani Sahiba in Lahore, little knowing that behind the title stands a Rajput woman, Harkha Bai! Traversing boundaries of culture and faith when she married Akbar, history knows Harkha[65] as 'Mariyam-uz-Zamani' ('Mary of the World'). Yet she gave up neither faith nor clothes nor food habits, continuing as a Hindu, within the Mughal harem. In her late years, she turned successful trader and ship-owner. An observer wrote: 'The Great Mogul's mother was a great adventurer, who caused the Great Mogul to drive the Portingals out...'[66]—we shall see how and why.

Harkha Bai's father, Bharmal Kachhwaha, Raja of Amer, had sought Akbar's protection to retain his tiny kingdom. To solidify the alliance, he offered his eldest daughter in marriage. She became the first Rajputani to marry into the Mughals: it was a minimalist wedding, at Sambhar, where Akbar camped en route from Khwaja Moinuddin Chishti's dargah at Ajmer. Harkha and Akbar were both 20 years old. Her brother Bhagwant Das and nephew Man Singh accompanied the couple, and joined Akbar's service. Over time, Harkha and her relatives played significant roles in the consolidation of Mughal rule in India.

Harkha was not expected to relinquish her own customs. Her mother-in-law Hamida Banu remembered being sheltered by a

Rajput family in Sind, where she had given birth to Akbar. Harkha brought Hindu deities and rituals with her, and maidservants; swirling ghagras, colourful odhnis and chunky jewellery; and injunctions against beef, garlic, and perhaps meat altogether. Akbar began to sit in at havans and celebrate Diwali, renounced beef, fasted on certain days, and later got the Ramayana and the Mahabharata translated into Persian, and illustrated. He conjured up Din-i-Ilahi, accommodating plurality of faiths as doctrine and administrative policy.

Akbar appealed to Sufi saint Salim Chishti for a son. Akbar already had wives, and several children, but all died in infancy. Salim Chishti blessed him and forecast three sons. When Harkha was heavily pregnant, Akbar moved her to Chishti's humble home in Sikri. In August 1569, Harkha gave birth to Jahangir; Chishti's daughters and daughters-in-law were Jahangir's wet nurses. A miniature painting shows Harkha reclining, wearing a fine gold-embroidered odhni and head ornament, Hamida next to her on a chair, wearing conical hat and qaba, flanked by many relatives and attendants, some in Turkic gear, some Rajasthani, and one of them is holding a newborn.

Akbar built Fatehpur Sikri adjacent to Salim Chishti's dwelling, and shifted the Mughal capital there. For the first time, Mughal women were kept in separate, enclosed space: perhaps Rajput customs influenced him in this too. Harkha bonded with the Timurid women. Hamida, Gulbadan, Sultanam and even Harkha's co-wives Ruqaya and Salima, all doted on her son Jahangir. Akbar had two more sons from serving women, and married several more wives, including Rajput princesses of Bikaner, Jaisalmer and Dungarpur; but none gained Harkha's status.

Harkha's nephew Man Singh became a successful general, helping expand Mughal territories. He rebuilt the Amer Fort.

Harkha visited Amer often, remaining close to her natal family. In 1585, her niece, Manbhawati Bai (Man Singh's younger sister), married Jahangir; bride and groom were both 15 years old. The wedding, with mixed Muslim and Hindu ceremonies, was in Amer. Harkha welcomed Man Bai into the harem; two years later, Man Bai gave birth to a son, Khusrau, who grew into a genial, popular young man.

None of Akbar's sons met the high expectations he had from them. Murad and Daniyal died of ailments caused by alcohol and opium addiction. One faction in court favoured Khusrau as next emperor, rather than the feckless Jahangir; Man Singh was part of this faction. Timurid elder women, however, favoured Jahangir, and represented frequently in his favour. Before passing away, Akbar appointed Jahangir his heir. The worst victim of these court intrigues, involving her husband Jahangir and her son Khusrau, was Man Bai. She lost her mental balance, and in May 1605, consumed poison, ending her life. Khusrau made a bid for the throne, but was defeated by Jahangir, imprisoned and half-blinded.

Harkha negotiated her way within the maze of familial loyalties, kinship ties so intimate and insistent, yet discordant, contentious and fractured. Balanced and mature, she steered her course wisely. Becoming queen mother at the age of 65, she used the position to advantage. Widowed and powerful, she carved out an independent, active life.

Harkha was accorded a high rank, and generous allowance. Courtiers, merchants and ambassadors gifted valuables, knowing she had influence with Jahangir. Harkha invested her money and participated in trade, employing agents and financial advisors. She owned a large vessel, *Rahimi*, 'the great pilgrimage ship'—with room for 1,500 passengers. It transported indigo, cotton, silks, leather, metal, carpets, spices, opium and jewels from Surat; and returned with gold, silver, ivory, pearls, perfumes, wines, brocade, cutlery and glassware. She built a garden and baoli at Bayana, to ensure water for the cultivation of indigo, which she bought and exported, making excellent profits.

From the Timurid kinswomen who had gone on hajj (in the 1560s), she heard how the Portuguese controlled maritime routes, and harassed pilgrims and traders. In 1613, the Portuguese captured her ship, filled with goods and 700 pilgrims, took it to Goa and refused to return it. Mughal emperors generally ignored the Portuguese menace, but a direct assault on the queen mother was unforgiveable. Jahangir immediately stopped all traffic at Surat; seized the Portuguese town of Daman; shut down all Jesuit churches and withdrew allowances to priests. This was the beginning of the end of Portuguese presence in India; Jahangir did everything possible to freeze them out. Thus, Harkha, who herself never set eyes on the Indian Ocean, played a key role in ridding it of Portuguese piracy.

Jahangir constructed a mosque in Lahore in honour of his mother, with large prayer halls, beautiful floral frescoes and geometric designs. An inscription over the northern gateway notes: 'The founder of the edifice, the site of salvation, is Begum Mariyam Zamani.' She lived a full life; and after her death in 1623, Jahangir built for her a beautiful mausoleum, next to his father Akbar's tomb in Sikandra. It is known as 'Mariyam's Tomb', or the mausoleum of Mariyam-uz-Zamani. With Harkha's story alive between us, who can say that Hindu blood is different from Muslim? An ancient Rajputani-Mughal queen could well teach us, in modern India, a lesson or two in secular politics and syncretic culture!

40 | Jahanara: Fakira Begum

1614–1681, Agra and Delhi

Jahanara's ambitions were sky-high: she inscribed herself within the imperial firmament, in letter of gold. Yet, she called herself 'fakira'—a woman detached from worldly concerns. One of the wealthiest and most powerful individuals in the world, at points she chose privation over luxury, for the sake of spiritual merit and filial loyalty. For decades, she played her role as Padshah Begum (first lady of the empire) to perfection, displaying a rare equanimity in personal and public relations. This was achieved through arduous effort, as she confronted the many challenges life threw at her.

Losing her mother at age 17 was difficult enough, but Jahanara had to handle her father Emperor Shah Jahan's insuperable grief, and care for her younger siblings—Dara Shikoh, Shah Shuja, Roshanara, Murad, Aurangzeb and Gauharar. Mumtaz Mahal died in birthing Gauharar, her fourteenth child. The mantle of empress fell on Jahanara: she advised her father on myriad matters, and took independent decisions. She issued *firmans* and kept the royal seal. She organized ostentatious weddings for her brothers, though she herself never married. Her role in the Mughal court was crucial, and a marriage would likely upset the balance. If she felt any inner turmoil, she did not let it affect her efficiency.

Her twentieth year onward, she trod the Sufi path. Before

she turned 30, Jahanara had penned two philosophical books, *Risalah-i-Sahibiyah*—an autobiographical treatise passionately describing her spiritual journey and *Munis-al-Arvah*—a biography of Moinuddin Chishti. She wrote: 'I decided to follow what my pir requires, to die before death, to not wait for death to extinguish me, to become one with the divine...'[67] Her *pir* Mullah Shah Badakshi spoke highly of her devotion and spiritual achievements: 'She has attained so extraordinary a development of mystical knowledge that she is worthy of being my representative if she were not a woman.'[68] She recorded that:

> In our family no one took the step on the path to seek God
> or the truth that would light the Timurid lamp eternally.
> I was grateful for having received this good fortune and
> wealth. There was no end to my happiness.[69]

During 1640, Jahanara took time out from her onerous duties, to lead an austere life in Mullah Shah's hermitage in Kashmir, meditating, immersing herself in the teachings, and serving her *pir* (including cooking and regularly sending *naan* and *saag* to him). Jahanara returned to Agra 'with a spiritually heavy heart'. In Agra, she interceded with Shah Jahan to get the Jami Masjid built. On the grand mosque these words were prominently inscribed: '...built by her order who is high in dignity... illuminated as her wisdom, veiled with chastity, the most revered of the ladies of the age, the pride of her gender, the princess of the realm... the chosen of the people of the world, the most honoured of the issue of the head of the Faithful, Jahanara Begum.'[70] There is a zenana section to the mosque used, to date, for devotional Sufi rituals. She helped Shah Jahan plan the Taj Mahal, and saw it come up, stone by marble stone.

One day, in 1643, the fine muslin of Jahanara's kameez caught the flame of a lamp in the palace at Agra Fort; two maids died trying to save her. With severe burns all over her body, Jahanara hovered between life and death, taking eight months to recover. In gratitude, she constructed a pavilion exclusively for female devotees, Begumi Dalan, at Moinuddin Chishti's dargah in Ajmer.

When the city of Shahjahanabad was built, Jahanara designed Chandni Chowk, the ethereal central boulevard where moonlight shimmered on the waters, and bazaars and artisans flourished. She built a mansion overlooking the Yamuna; the enormous garden, Sahiba ka Bagh, laid out with fruit trees, flowering bushes, ponds and fountains; and a caravanserai unmatched in size and elegance, with the hope that: 'The wanderer who enters its courts will be restored in body and soul and my name will never be forgotten.'[71]

The 1650s, spent in Shahjahanabad, were years of peace and prosperity. Jahanara continued playing a role in politics, handling many tasks and influencing her father wherever she thought fit. She was active as a trader too, and owned the port of Surat as well as a ship, *Sahibi*, which carried goods made at her karkhanas; she earned colossal profits, boosting her annual income of three million rupees.

Shah Jahan cherished Jahanara and Dara Shikoh, but repeatedly insulted Aurangzeb. Finally, Aurangzeb, the successful warrior, struck back, assisted by Roshanara, the vivacious younger sister who detested living under Jahanara's shadow. Aurangzeb brutally deposed Shah Jahan; Jahanara's efforts to work out a compromise failed. Aurangzeb imprisoned their father in Agra Fort and assassinated Dara Shikoh. Despite their differing proclivities, Aurangzeb always held Jahanara in great respect. He wished for her to stay on with full honour at Shahjahanabad, but she chose to be with their sick, sad father, caring for him until his death eight years later.

After Shah Jahan passed away, Jahanara agreed to Aurangzeb's plea. She rode into Delhi on an imperial elephant, and settled in an independent mansion overlooking the Yamuna. Roshanara held a high position in Aurangzeb's court, but Jahanara's was far higher, as Padshah Begum—still. She decorated her haveli with exquisite paintings, bright curtains and priceless carpets, and extended hospitality to visiting scholars, poets, physicians, soldiers, artists, astrologers and religious teachers. She held musical salons, and became the foremost woman patron of literature and the arts in Shahjahanabad.

Jahanara showered affection on Jahanzeb Banu, her beloved brother Dara Shikoh's daughter. In 1669, she arranged Jahanzeb's marriage to Aurangzeb's son, Azam—the first imperial wedding in Aurangzeb's reign. Jahanara interceded with the emperor on behalf of minor rajas and others who came to her with grievances and gifts. Although she could not prevent Aurangzeb's increasingly rigid views, his ban on music and dance, and imposition of jizya, Jahanara influenced his daughters—Zebunissa and Zeenat. She bequeathed most of her wealth, jewels and property to her nieces.

In 1681, Jahanara built a simple open-air enclosure within Nizamuddin Auliya's dargah, with delicate lattice-work walls. She died within the year, and was buried as she had desired, within this white marble structure. Her words were inscribed on a tablet: 'Let nothing cover my tomb save green grass, for grass suffices well as a covering for the grave of the fakira.' Pilgrims strew rose petals over the green grass; many believe this place heals disturbed women. The cool marble interior usually has a few troubled women, sitting disconsolate, seeking Jahanara's intercession. The Fakira lives on, her spirit strong, and soothing.

41 | Zebunissa: Hidden Rebel

1638-1702, Daulatabad and Delhi

Zebunissa learnt the Quran by heart when she was seven years old. When she grew up, she wrote verse in quite a different strain:

> Zealots, you are mistaken—this is heaven
> Never mind those making promises of the afterlife
> Join us now, righteous friends, in this intoxication.
> Never mind the path to the Kaaba: sanctity resides in the heart.
> Squander your life, suffer! God is right here.
> Oh excruciating face! Continual light!
> This is where I am, thrilled, right here
> There is no book anywhere on the matter.
> Only as soon as I see you do I understand.
> If you wish to offer your beauty to God, give Zebunnisa
> A taste; Awaiting the tiniest morsel, she is right here.[72]

In beautiful Persian, she narrated the story of her human heart:

> Heart like a mercurial fountain is filled with life this evening,
> This is the time to ask for wine, bid farewell to sense this evening...

She adopted the pen name 'Makhfi'—the hidden one. As Aurangzeb's daughter, Zebunissa was expected to be pious above all else; passion and zest were unacceptable. One day, walking in the garden, she composed aloud: 'Four things are necessary to make me happy—wine, flowers, a running stream and the face of the Beloved'. Suddenly she saw her father, and fearing he may have heard her, she deftly changed her tune, now reciting: 'Four things are necessary for happiness—prayers, fasting, tears and repentance!'

Despite the necessary concealment, she was a prolific writer. In addition to *Diwan-i-Makhfi*, a collection of nearly 5,000 verses, she wrote *Monis-ul-Roh*, *Zeb-ul-Monsha'at* and *Zeb-ul-Tafasir*.

Zebunissa was born in Daulatabad, to Dilras Bano Begum, a Safavid princess and Aurangzeb's first wife. Zebunissa's younger sisters were Zeenat, Zubdat, Badrunissa and Mehrunissa. They learnt Arabic, Persian, astronomy and arithmetic. When seven-year-old Zebu became a Hafiz, her proud father celebrated by gifting her 10,000 gold coins, holding a feast for the army and distributing gold coins to the poor. When Aurangzeb became emperor and the family moved to Shahjahanabad, he would often discuss political matters with 21-year-old Zebunissa.

Over time, of course, her Sufi and liberal views clashed with her father's increasing orthodoxy and intolerance. She wrote— sacrilegious to the dogmatic mind:

> Whether it be in Mecca's holiest shrine,
> Or in the Temple pilgrim feet have trod,
> Still Thou art mine,
> Wherever God is worshipped is my God.

Equally subversive was the following verse:

> No Muslim I, but an idolater,
> I bow before the image of my Love, and worship her

No Brahmin I, My sacred thread I cast away,
Around my neck I wear her plaited hair instead.

She disowned her father's legacy, critical of the fratricide he indulged in and the cruelty shown towards his own father, Shah Jahan; she chose to reject his ways for a peaceable path: 'I am the daughter of a King, but I have taken the path of renunciation, and this is my glory, as my name Zebunissa, being interpreted, means that I am the glory of womankind.'

Shah Jahan, her grandfather, had got Zebunissa engaged to Dara Shikoh's son, Sulaiman Shikoh. Aurangzeb did not allow the marriage; nor did he accept other proposals that came her way, including from Mirza Farukh, prince of Persia. She immersed herself in reading and writing, her library well-stocked, and employed scholars to produce literary works at her bidding. She once visited Lahore, and laid out a beautiful chauburgi, four-towered garden, in the Nawa Kot locality. Back in Shahjahanabad, she helped widows and orphans, and continued her sequestered life. She wore white, a string of pearls around her neck and a garment of her own invention, the Angya Kurti, a modified form of the dress of her Turkic ancestors.

Zebunissa's younger brother Mirza Akbar made a bid to depose Aurangzeb, and she supported him. Aurangzeb crushed the rebellion and discovered revelatory correspondence between brother and sister. Enraged, he confiscated her property, nullified her annual pension and imprisoned her in Delhi's Salimgarh Fort. Her younger sister Zeenat, always loyal to their father, was appointed Padshah Begum. Zeenat, calm and equable, continued as Padshah Begum after Aurangzeb died (1707), for seven emperors in all, until she passed away in 1721.

Day after lonely day, Zebunissa longed for freedom, awaiting the day her brother Mirza Akbar would win the throne, and release her. The days stretched into years, and she lost hope:

So long as these fetters cling to my feet
My friends have become enemies, my relations strangers
to me.
Why seek any more to keep my name unblemished
When friends seek to disgrace me?
Seek not relief from the prison of grief, O Makhfi,
No hope of release hast thou until the Day of Judgment
come.

Night after endless night
I sat in lonely grief remembering thee;
Tears fell into my heart disconsolate
Ho'w long have I, in striving to be free
Broken my bleeding nails, but never quite
Untied the knot of fate!
Stronger my love shall grow:
Bearing the bonds of sorrow for thy sake.
More patient and more proud my heart shall grow
Like the imprisoned bird who tries to make
His cage a garden, though his wild heart break
He never shall be free.

Long is thine exile, Makhfi, long thy yearning
Long shalt thou wait, thy heart within thee burning
Looking thus forward to thy home-returning
But now what home hast thou, misfortunate?
The years have passed and left it desolate.

I have experienced such cruelty and harshness in this
land of Hind,
I shall go make myself a home in some other land.

She died at Salimgarh Fort, she was 64 years old; her father
Aurangzeb had her buried with royal honours. In the twentieth

century, her remains were moved from Delhi to Akbar's mausoleum at Sikandara.

In Lahore, an alternative story circulates: Aurangzeb banished Zebunnisa to Lahore, where she fell in love with a Khan, lived in a humble dwelling within a garden at Nawa Kot, and ran a free kitchen for the needy. Khan gave up position and wealth to dwell with her. When Aurangzeb heard of that, he got the Khan boiled in a cauldron in front of Zebunissa, and imprisoned her in the same place, where she eventually died, and was buried in the same garden. There is no historical evidence for this story; and yet Zebunnisa has become, in Lahore, a potent symbol for political dissent. And do we not need her, in India too?

42 | Umayamma: Attingal Amazon

?-1698, Kerala

Umayamma was the most powerful queen of Attingal—one in a long lineage of queens. Umayamma Asvathy Thirunal waged wars, made alliances with neighbours, signed treaties and efficiently ran the administration of Travancore as well as Attingal. Since 1305, women had ruled the tiny principality of Attingal; while their sons were rulers of the far larger state of Travancore. The Attingal Senior Rani automatically held the title 'Rani of Travancore'; the reigning king of Travancore was invariably her son, nephew or brother. In the case of Umayamma, her nephew Ravi Varma was a minor when crowned Raja of Travancore; Umayamma thus took charge of the state of Travancore as his regent, in 1677.

An obscure law banned Attingal Ranis from crossing into Travancore, but Ummayama, with characteristic confidence, crossed over, and lived and ruled in Travancore, quelling all opposition. A Dutchman who met her noted that she commanded an army of 30,000; and was

> of such noble and manly conduct that she is both feared and respected by everyone... She not only rules Attingal but Travancore itself, within whose bounds no princess may set foot according to their laws... but this young Amazon has

lately violated those customs and made even the king fly before her.[73]

Umayamma was Junior Rani of Attingal at the time that she became regent at Travancore. The minor king, Ravi Varma, was son of the Senior Rani of Attingal, Umayamma's elder sister Makayiram Thirunal. In 1678, Makayiram Thirunal died, and Umayamma became Senior Rani of Attingal. She was a warrior queen: like all Attingal Ranis, she worshipped Goddess Tiruvirattukkavu Bhagavati, whose legends were replete with rage and righteous wars. Umayamma's army repelled a military coup against her by chieftains of Nedumangad and Kottarakara, a terrible attack by Muligan, an invader from the North, in 1684, and confronted repeated invasions by Madurai.

She was a capable administrator:

> Queen Umayamma came to prominence by the management of Travancore. Her first task was to improve the finances of the state. There were no proper accounts. Arrears accumulated, collections disappeared, and debts increased. She ordered the preparation of the accounts of every village in Trippappoor [Travancore]. By insisting upon proper accounts and strict collection of all arrears and current dues, she converted the deficit into a surplus, and provided regular income for Trippapoor. All those who had misappropriated public money were compelled to refund it, and punished according to the gravity of their offence.[74]

Ravi Varma was crowned ruler of Travancore in 1685, when he turned 16, but Umayamma continued to dominate Travancore. The Dutch regarded the Travancore Raja as a vassal of the Attingal Rani, and described her thus:

... She had a guard of above seven hundred Nair soldiers about her, all clad after the Malabar fashion; the queen's attire being no more than a piece of calico wrapped around her middle, the upper part of her body appearing for the most part naked, with a piece of calico hung carelessly round her shoulders. Her ears, which were very long, her neck and arms were adorned with precious stones, gold rings and bracelets and her head covered with a piece of white calico. She was past her middle age, of a brown complexion, with black hair tied in a knot behind, but of majestic mien, she being a princess who showed a great deal of good conduct in the management of her affairs.[75]

As European traders scrambled for trade rights, Umayamma negotiated with them and kept close watch on terms of trade and the behaviour of traders. She granted the English factory sites at Valiyathura and Vizhinjam, and allowed construction of a fort at Anchuthengu: 'Because the English I called hither have always been obedient to me, I do hereby grant unto them the following privileges: I give unto them the hill that is at Anchuthengu, to fortify with stone and to abide there forever.' Under the contract, the English were to purchase all the pepper Attingal produced, and pay Umayamma 75 Venetian sequins, 2.5 per cent on all imports and exports, and 50 per cent of booty from any shipwrecked vessels. The English promised to 'obey her Highness' and carry on trade 'without any manner of impudence'. They did not live up to their promise; as she noted, they 'were troublesome to my people and therefore I ordered that they should go from there and make no more contracts in my land'. When they disobeyed her, Umayamma led a force to evict them, declaring she would not rest 'until every stone of Anchuthengu Fort had been tumbled down', but her army was defeated by

English cannons in 1697. In 1695, finding the Dutch behaving impudently, Umayamma destroyed their fort at Thengapattanam.

Little is known about Umayamma's personal life. We know that Attingal Ranis married men from select royal houses, who became their consorts, but never became kings. There is no reliable record of her earlier life, before she took charge of Travancore. There is a mention of her having six sons, five of whom drowned; but this theory is generally debunked. There was speculation, however, on her sexual life: she invited 'whom and as many as she pleases to the honour of her bed... The handsomest young men about the country generally compose her seraglio'.[76] If there was a nugget of truth in these statements, the sexual freedoms Umayamma enjoyed were impressive indeed.

Umayamma died in 1698. With her passing, the power of the Attingal Ranis declined. The English ignored the next Rani and approached Raja Ravi Varma directly: 'It is highly doubtful if the English would have dared to open direct contacts with the Rajah if the present Queen was as strong as the old Queen.'[77] The English established monopoly over the pepper trade, stationed troops at Anchuthengu, and were rude and cruel to the populace. In retaliation, in 1721, some 150 Englishmen were massacred, purportedly led by Gouri Parvati Bayi, Rani of Attingal. In 1729, however, Raja Marthanda Varma of Travancore got the then Rani of Attingal to sign a treaty by which Attingal Ranis lost all political power. Ironically enough, it was Umayamma who had laid the sound administrative foundation on which Marthanda Varma built 'modern' Travancore.

43 | Ahilya:
Rare Peace

1725-1795, Madhya Pradesh

Ahilyabai Holkar, ruler of Indore state for some three decades, created an oasis of peace and stability, while wars raged all around. Although an able warrior, she was not interested in territorial expansion, nor were her territories attacked. Focusing on the welfare of her people, she held darbar daily from 2.00 to 6.00 p.m.:

> [She] heard every complaint in person; and... was always accessible. So strong was her sense of duty on all points connected with the distribution of justice, that she is represented as not only patient but unwearied in the investigation of the most insignificant cases... With the natives of Malwa... her name is sainted and she is styled an avatar or Incarnation of the Divinity. In the soberest view that can be taken of her character, she certainly appears, within her limited sphere, to have been one of the purest and most exemplary rulers that ever existed.[78]

She moved from Indore to charming Maheshvar, where her cell-like bedroom overlooked the Narmada, her lifestyle frugal. Ahilyabai encouraged local employment, art and crafts such as weaving of exquisite Maheshvari handlooms in subtle and bright colours. Her architectural and philanthropic works stretched across the country: Kashi-Vishvanath temple and Ahilya ghat in Varanasi, Panchkuian (five wells) in New Delhi, countless rest houses, dharamsalas, wells, shrines, bridges, roads and temples, from Badrinath to Rameshwaram, Puri to Somnath. She worked as a duty and responsibility without arrogance, her name was not inscribed on her constructions.

Ahilya was born in rural Maharashtra in the Dhangar caste— traditional shepherds, cowherds and wool weavers. Her father, Mankoji Shinde, was village *patil*. Malhar Rao Holkar, ruler of Indore state, halted at Chaudi village en route to Pune, and thought the serious little girl would be just right for his somewhat wayward son, Khande Rao. The two children, aged eight and nine, were soon married. They grew up together, under the care of Ahilya's mother-in-law Gautamabai and younger mother-in-law, Harkubai.

Some 12 years later, Ahilya bore a son, Male Rao, and three years later a daughter, Muktabai. In 1754, Khande Rao was killed in the battle of Kumbher. Ahilya and his other wives prepared to commit sati. The others plunged into the flames, but her father-in-law managed to dissuade Ahilya, whom he greatly respected. He knew how capable she was—she frequently advised him on weighty matters. During the next decade, Malhar Rao increasingly entrusted her with administrative and military responsibilities, which she grew proficient at handling.

In 1766, Malhar Rao died on the battlefield. Male Rao came to power, but he was mentally unstable, and soon fell ill and died. His wives Maina and Peerta committed sati, although Ahilya tried her level best to prevent them. When Maratha warrior Raghoba marched towards Indore to contest Ahilya's accession, she rode out with a small army of women, to the banks of Shipra, where Raghoba was camping, and sent him a letter warning of the dishonour that awaited him should he choose to fight women!

This brilliant stratagem averted a disastrous war and her reign began on a peaceful note.

Facing a problem from 'plunderers' on her borders, she announced she would marry her daughter Muktabai to the person who could bring an end to the trouble. Yashwant Rao Phanse managed to capture the gang leaders and brought them to Ahilyabai. Rather than punish them, she settled matters amicably by granting them hilly tracts, with the right to collect duty on goods passing through.

Muktabai duly married Yashwant Rao and they had a son, Nathyba. Ahilyabai cherished Nathyba, her putative heir. Her life ran on an even keel, as did the state. The capital, Maheshvar, became a major centre for literature, music, industry and trade. Merchants and cultivators prospered. Ahilyabai kept taxes low, and used her personal wealth and land holdings for charitable works. She ensured that widows inherit their husbands' wealth, and were allowed to adopt sons.

Ahilyabai won the respect of other Maratha rulers for her able governance and political acumen:

> Ahilyabai Holkar, the 'philosopher-queen' of Malwa, was an acute observer of the wider political scene. In a letter to the Peshwa in 1772, she warned against association with the British and likened their embrace to a bear-hug: 'Other beasts, like tigers, can be killed by might or contrivance, but to kill a bear is very difficult. It will die only if you kill it straight in the face. Or else, once caught in its powerful hold, the bear will kill its prey by tickling. Such is the way of the English. And in view of this, it is difficult to triumph over them'.[79]

Nathyba, a promising youth, fell ill and passed away in 1789; two years later, Yashwant Rao died of cholera. Muktabai insisted on committing sati. For Ahilyabai, this was the greatest shock, and extreme irony. But Muktabai was adamant, and the tragic event took place. Ahilyabai continued her active lifestyle, though she was sad and broken. Often she walked by the Narmada, a solitary figure. She designated trustworthy Tukoji Holkar, who had served Indore state over decades, her successor, thus ensuring smooth transfer of power after her death.

Over a century later, Annie Besant wrote of her reign:

The poor, the homeless, the orphaned were all helped according to their needs... Hindu and Musalman alike revered the famous Queen and prayed for her long life... Ahilya Bai was seventy years old when her long and splendid life closed. Indore long mourned its noble Queen, happy had been her reign, and her memory is cherished with deep reverence unto this day.[80]

44 | Muddupalani: Art of Love

1739–90, South India

Muddupalani's *Radhika Santwanam* (Appeasement of Radhika) was a most unusual retelling of the Krishna-Radha love story: for it was conceived from the perspective of Radha. It was an epic poem in Telugu in the 'sringaraprabandham' genre, whose leitmotif was sringara rasa or erotic pleasure. Works in this genre were popular, but written exclusively by men—she was the one exception. Her writing was subtle and sophisticated, exploring emotion, desire and agency, stemming from a woman's mature awareness of the art of love. *Radhika Santwanam* was acknowledged as a literary masterpiece.

There was no coyness about Muddupalani, but rather frank acknowledgement of facts. In the introduction to her 584-verse epic, with poise and self-assurance, she described herself thus:

Which other woman of my kind has
Felicitated scholars with gifts of money?
To which other woman of my kind have
Epics been dedicated?
Which other woman of my kind has
Won such acclaim in each of the arts?
You are incomparable,
Muddupalani, among your kind.

A face that glows like the full moon
Skills of conversation, matching the countenance
Eyes filled with compassion,
Matching the speech.
A great spirit of generosity,
Matching the glance.
These are the ornaments
That adorn Palani,
When she is praised by kings.[81]

She described her lineage—elucidating what 'women of my kind' meant—her mother Rama Vadhuti and grandmother Tanjanayaki were both devadasis, like herself, and accomplished poets and bearers of refined culture. Devadasis were also known as *nagara shobhinis*—the pride of the city. Muddupalani grew up in a household immersed in music and scholarship. Proficient in Tamil, Telugu and Sanskrit, she drew her confidence and competence from the female fraternity around her—writers, composers, singers, dancers, women of independent means. As an adolescent she translated Andal's *Tirupavvai* into Telugu. King Partapsimha, a patron of the arts, invited her to the Thanjavur court; in time, she became his consort.

In *Radhika Santwanam*, Muddupalani tracks a strong Radha, who is Krishna's aunt as well as lover, a very human Krishna, and Ila, his young bride. The story begins with Radha's amusement as Ila witnesses her relationship with Krishna. Radha then prepares the young woman, counselling her on love and sexuality; she also counsels Krishna:

Move on her lips
The tip of your tongue
Do not scare her by biting hard,
Place on her cheeks

A gentle kiss
Do not scratch her with your sharp nails,
Hold her nipple
With your fingertips
Do not scare her by squeezing it tight,
Make love
Gradually
Do not scare her by being aggressive,
I am a fool to tell you all this.
When you meet her
And wage your war of love
Would you care to recall
My dos and don'ts, Honey?[82]

The poem dwells on Radha's subsequent emotional turmoil, and Krishna's attempts to placate her. Ila's feelings are almost mirror images of the elder woman's, both experience love, loss, jealousy and anger. Krishna is subordinate to both women—he is torn between the two, careful not to annoy either, tries to please both, and is no divine being!

The story is, at root, autobiographical, transmuted through myth and art. Tanjanayaki, Muddupalani's grandmother and a celebrated court musician, had long been the king's consort. Muddupalani displaced her, but a few years later, the king renewed his attentions to the older woman. In *Radhika Santwanam,* Muddupalani empathizes equally with Radha and Ila—both are, like the poet herself: sensitive, beautiful, willful and passionate, and both experience betrayal.

Radha's anger and assertion of right are dominant motifs. She refers to men as inconsistent and unreliable, and berates Krishna for abandoning her. When he implores forgiveness, she literally hits out; he woos her tenderly, claiming eternal devotion:

Honey,
Why did I stamp on Kali?
The snake seemed to
Rival your lovely plait.
Why did I break Kamsa's bow?
It seemed to
Rival your shapely brows.
Why did I uproot Govardhan?
The mountain seemed to
Rival your firm breasts.
Why did I hurt Kuvalayaspida?
The elephant seemed to
Rival your graceful gait.
Do ask yourself, then,
If it's fair that you
Treat me shabbily?

Radha eventually accepts Krishna's entreaties, and allows herself to be placated. Radha is assertive, actively expresses her desires and demands reciprocity. After they revive their relationship, we have him mock complaining:

If I ask her not to kiss me,
Stroking my cheeks
She presses her lips hard against mine.
If I ask her not to touch me
Stabbing me with her firm breasts
She embraces me.
If I ask her not to get close
For it is not decorous
She swears at me loudly.
If I tell her of my vow not
To have a woman in my bed

She hops in, and begins the game of love.
She lets me drink from her lips,
Fondles me, talks on,
Makes love again and again.
How could I
Stay away from her?[83]

Muddupalani was radical in her unwavering expression of women's right to pleasure. Writing *Radhika Santwanam* might have helped Muddupalani come to terms with some of her own complicated feelings; 'Radha', in her case, was her own grandmother. Reflecting on the situation from each one's point of view may have helped calm her turbulent emotions. It is noteworthy that nowhere in the epic do Radha or Ila direct resentment against one another. They remain closely bonded, for each understands what the other is going through.

∽

Bangalore Nagaratnamma, a learned devadasi of the twentieth century, traced Muddupalani's original palm-leaf manuscript, and published a complete edition of *Radhika Santwanam* in 1911. She wrote in the preface: 'I find the work immensely beautiful... brimming with rasa. However often I read this book, I feel like reading it all over again... As it has been composed, not only by a woman, but a woman of our community, I felt it was necessary to publish the proper work.' The British banned the book on charges of obscenity. Many littérateurs opposed the order; Nagaratnamma questioned double standards whereby erotica written by men was appreciated, while women who wrote sensuous poetry were called immoral and their books banned. The administration seized and destroyed copies of the book, but it continued to circulate secretly. The ban was withdrawn in 1947 by the chief minister of Madras, and a new edition brought out in 1952.

Muddupalani's *Radhika Santwanam* has ridden the waves of time! As denizens of the twenty-first century reclaim the right to name and experience pleasure, and explore desire in its rainbow colours, we find an ally across the ages in Muddupalani, the devadasi littérateur.

45 | Onake Obavva: Indomitable Courage

?-1770, Karnataka

Onake Obavva was a Dalit woman of humble means, who defended her people from enemy assault—with no weapon save the humble pestle! Obavva was all alone when she confronted grave danger. Displaying amazing presence of mind, she managed to strategically kill a large number of armed soldiers with her wooden pestle. Her act of incredible heroism has entered the annals of Kannada history and folklore.

Obavva lived within the magnificent Chitradurga Fort. They were Holayas, a traditional agriculturalist community; her husband, Hanumappa, had taken up employment as a soldier, with Ling Madakari Nayaka V. The Nayaka rulers had built the Chitradurga Fort to protect their kingdom. Hanumappa was posted as one of the guards to keep vigil, and defend the fort. Set in hilly terrain, the fort walls were of sheer rock, covering a perimeter of eight kilometres. Nineteen gates led into the fort at various points, each with ascending access through a narrow winding corridor. Guards were posted at all gates, and at each of the 2,000 watchtowers, 35 secret entrances and four invisible passages. Inside the 1,500-acre expanse lived thousands of people, and there were water reservoirs, tanks, warehouses and stores to ensure food, water and military supplies, sufficient to endure even a long siege.

Hyder Ali attacked Chitradurga Fort multiple times from 1760 onwards, but failed in his initial attempts since the fort was virtually impenetrable. In 1770, he posted spies around the fort; one day his spies noticed somebody entering the fort through a crevice in the rocks, halfway up the hill. The crevice was barely visible, but an adult could just about squeeze through it. Hyder Ali laid a plan—his soldiers would use this secret passage to gain entry into the fort. They would first crawl up the hillside, and then squeeze in through the crevice, one at a time.

This crevice was guarded by just one individual: Obavva's husband. A conscientious worker, he worked long hours at his duty-post. He took a lunch-break in the afternoon, and returned within the hour—a fact that Hyder Ali's spies duly observed.

One day when Hanumappa went home for lunch, enemy troops lined up and began crawling up the hillside, each man creeping towards the crevice, intending to surreptitiously enter the fort.

Meanwhile, it so happened that as Obavva's husband sat down to his meal, Obavva decided to go fetch some drinking water. She walked towards the pond, which was situated near the crevice. While filling water in her pitcher, she heard muted sounds of people outside the fort walls. In a flash, she gauged the situation.

There was no time to lose. In this moment of enormous crisis, she had only herself to rely on. Glancing around, Obavva saw an *onake* (long pestle for pounding paddy) lying nearby. She hatched a bold plan and immediately acted upon it. Armed with the onake, she stood beside the crevice, alert. When she heard the first soldier squeezing his way through, she positioned herself to attack the instant he appeared. The moment the man emerged through the crevice, she gathered all her strength and dealt him a massive blow. Landing on the skull, the blow proved fatal. The soldier collapsed in a heap. Obavva quickly dragged his corpse some distance away, moving silently, so the soldiers outside would not suspect anything.

Then she came and stood again by the crevice, in attack stance. When the second soldier emerged, he met the same fate at her hands. She dragged aside his corpse, and waited for the third... and then the fourth... and the next... she lost count, yet carried on, as if in a trance. The task was excruciating and drew upon all her strength of mind and body. Some sources state that she killed about 10 men; others put it at over a hundred.

Obavva's husband returned after lunch, and was stunned to see her standing by the crevice, blood-stained pestle in hand, surrounded by enemy corpses. Hanumappa could not believe his eyes, for what she had achieved seemed superhuman. He heard enemy soldiers still swarming outside, and immediately blew his bugle. Several soldiers rushed to the spot, and a large number ran outside, to battle with the invaders clinging to the hillside—decimating them in no time.

Obavva was left alone, the stench of death all around her. She was exhausted beyond words, but immensely relieved that the invaders were being dealt with. Amid all the commotion and confusion, one of Hyder Ali's soldiers managed to get in through the crevice when she was least suspecting it. One version surmises that Obavva died of sheer exhaustion, but others say the enemy soldier stabbed her. She was discovered later that day, dead. Many wept for her. She saved them all, but herself slipped away unprotected.

Chitradurga Fort remains inextricably linked with the legend of Onake Obavva. She occupies a special place in the hearts of local people. Visitors travel to the well-preserved fort, and the particular crevice in the fort is today called 'Onake Obavva Kindi'. People come to see the kindi, and pay their tribute to

Obavva. In Chitradurga, her statue stands proud amid major government offices; and the city stadium is named 'Veera Vanithe Onake Obavva Stadium.' Citizens' groups have been demanding that she be declared a national hero; at a protest to press their demand in 2017, women carried pestles, dressed as Onake Obavva, shouted slogans and asked, 'Why don't we celebrate Onake Obavva Jayanti? She killed soldiers in order to protect our land!'

46 | Velu, Kuyili, Udaiyal: Comrades-in-Arms

Eighteenth Century, Tamil Nadu

Velu Nachiyar the queen, Kuyili her army commander and Udaiyal a patriotic village girl—from three different backgrounds, these women knit a common tapestry. Courageously, they struggled to retain self-respect against creeping British imperialism. Velu created an army of women and strategically won back her kingdom; Kuyili was the first 'suicide bomber' we know of, who crafted Velu's victory; Udaiyal sacrificed her life rather than betray the cause.

Velu Nachiyar (1730–96) was queen of the Tamil kingdom of Shivagangai. Born in 1730, the only child of Chellamuthu Sethupathy and Rani Sakandhimuthal of Ramnad, she learned archery and martial arts like silambam, valari and varmakalai, from childhood onwards. She was fluent in Tamil, Telugu, French, English and Urdu. At the age of 16, she married the Raja of Shivagangai, Muthuvaduganathar Thevara. The story goes that once in the forest of Courtallam, a tiger attacked her husband; Velu caught hold of its tail, jumped on its back and killed the tiger.

In 1772, the English along with Nawab of Arcot attacked Shivagangai. Troops stormed Kalaiyar Kovil temple, killing Muthuvaduganathar Thevara and Gowri Nachiyar, Velu Nachiyar's co-wife. The town of Shivagangai was ravaged and occupied. Velu was in nearby Kollangudi, with her small daughter, Vellachi. Taking along her trusted advisors, Thandavarayan Pillai and the Maruthu brothers, Velu escaped to Virupakshi, Dindigul. She vowed to avenge her husband's death and reclaim her kingdom. Enemy troops pursued them, and en route questioned a simple peasant girl, Udaiyal, who was grazing the cows, about Velu's whereabouts. Udaiyal refused to give them any clues as to whether they had passed that way. Determined not to let on the queen's route, to every question, she firmly replied in the negative. Enraged, the British soldiers tortured her, but when she still declined information, they shot her dead. When Velu heard of this atrocity committed on a simple, patriotic young woman, she was incensed and sorrowful.

Velu knew she needed allies if she was to fight the British. She wrote a letter to Haider Ali asking for support, and met him in Dindigul Fort. When he entered the hall, he saw only men; taking off her turban, Velu revealed her identity. Her command over Urdu helped her build a rapport with Haider Ali. He promised to support her when the time was ripe. In the meantime, she stayed on at Virupakshi Fort.

Velu created an army of women, named 'Udaiyal Padal'—in honour of the brave young cowherd. Another intrepid Dalit, Kuyili, became *dalavai* or commander-in-chief of the women's army. Addressed as Veerthalapathy (The Brave Commander), Kuyili belonged to the Arunthathiyar caste. Her father, Periyamuthan, was a cobbler; her mother Raku had died protecting their fields from a wild bull. Periyamuthan raised Kuyili relating many of Raku's inspiring deeds. Kuyili became Velu's personal bodyguard as well. Once when an intruder tried to murder Velu while she slept, Kuyili dealt him a fatal blow. On another instance, Kuyili discovered that her own silambam teacher was an enemy spy, and immediately killed him.

In 1780, Velu decided to launch an attack to win back Shivagangai. At that time, Haider Ali was battling the British on various fronts, and it seemed the right time for Velu to strike out. By now, her daughter Vellachi had also joined the army. The women's army, buttressed by a few troops from their allies, marched more than 100 kilometres, and reached the outskirts of Shivagangai. Velu and Kuyili planned to infiltrate and enter the fort—a hazardous undertaking. They carefully laid their plan. It was Vijayadashami, a day women were allowed to enter the fort for celebrations at the temple and palace. Velu's soldiers dressed as civilians, mingled with the crowd of women and entered, unnoticed by British guards who were swarming around the fort. When sufficient women soldiers had gathered in the palace complex, Velu gave the signal. Her soldiers drew out swords and daggers from their flower and fruit-baskets, and attacked, shouting, 'Vetrivel! Vetrivel!' ('victory to the sword'—an ancient battle cry).

The British were caught unawares. However, though initially nonplussed, they were confident of defeating Velu, using sophisticated artillery. They trained guns on the women soldiers, preparing to decimate them. Kuyili then acted upon a plan that she and Velu had made for just this contingency. At their command, Kuyili's companions poured ghee and oil, meant for lighting lamps, upon her. Thus soaked, Kuyili rushed into the storeroom of British arms and ammunition, and set herself afire. She thus detonated the British arsenal—and blew up along with the ammunition. The British army was now easily defeated. Velu and her army of women took charge. They rang the temple bells and flew her flag, signifying victory, and informing everyone of the momentous event.

Velu was crowned queen of Shivagangai. The populace rejoiced. Velu got made a temple for Udaiyal in nearby Ariyakurunji village, where devotees still flock to worship Udaiyal in the form of Kali, the demon-devouring goddess.

Velu ruled through the next decade as regent for her daughter, Vellachi. The Maruthu brothers, however, staged a coup against Velu. They manipulated Vellachi's marriage to Vangam Periya Udaya Thevar, who was under their thumb. When Vellachi became ruler of Shivagangai in 1790, Velu was removed from the scene of power. According to some descendants of the royal family, Velu had been unwell with a heart problem, and in 1791, travelled to France for medical treatment; she returned to India in 1793, to find that Vellachi had died in childbirth. We do know that Vellachi passed away in 1793.

Velu's son-in-law Vangam Periya Udaya Thevara usurped the kingdom. Velu had an unhappy end, having lost her daughter as well as her kingdom. She moved back to Virupakshi Fort, and three years later, passed away.

Though Velu died in obscurity, the Veeramangai Velu Nachiyar Memorial at Shivagangai, inaugurated by Jayalalithaa in 2014, honours her memory. Udaiyal is held sacred at the Kali temple at Ariyakurunji, and Kuyili is today respected as a brave Dalit martyr.

47 | Nangeli: Defending Dignity

1768–1803, Kerala

Nangeli rebelled against an exploitative regime, in Travancore state, which charged exorbitant taxes from the common people: in particular a tax called Mulakkaram, which was levied on all Dalit women, in particular those who wore clothing covering their breasts. Nangeli was Dalit, from the Ezhava community. She spoke up not only for herself but for all labouring Dalit women. Her protest helped light the spark of rebellion in her area.

Nangeli and her husband Chirukandan lived in Cherthala, a small coastal village. They worked as agricultural labourers and collected sap from coconut trees. Travancore Rajas ruthlessly extracted some 110 kinds of levies from Dalit people—on the fisherman's net, ornaments worn, a moustache sported and so on. A general tax was levied on men called Talakkaram, literally 'head tax'; Mulakkaram literally means 'breast tax'.

Anyone of Ezhava or Nadar caste was expected to appear bare-torso in the presence of Brahmins, royalty or generally anyone of higher caste. Traditionally, it was common for men and women of various castes to be bare-chested—and no shame attached to women's bare chest. By the late eighteenth century however, clothing, especially women's upper-cloth or blouse, took on pronounced symbolic significance as a marker of social identity.

Among women, chest-covering was permitted only to those from high castes. Mulakkaram began to be collected from *all* Ezhava women—beginning from puberty onward. The parvarthiyar, a local official, would collect Mulakkaram, going from door to door in Dalit neighbourhoods.

Anger was brewing against the unjust tax. Nangeli felt keenly the injustice her community was subjected to. The burden of taxes left them with hardly a handful of rice to eat at day end. They worked to the bone, yet there was always some tax to be paid; a blanket of fear covered them, and so life carried on.

Nangeli knew the parvarthiyar would soon arrive to collect Mulakkaram. Born of intense anger, her resolve was building up over the years. She decided she would not pay Mulakkaram that day, or ever again. She could not win against state brutality by any of the usual tactics. Nangeli thought of something unprecedented, a dramatic act that would draw attention to the tyranny being enacted in Travancore.

When the parvarthiyar and his men came to collect Mulakkaram, Nangeli asked them to wait. They waited, relieved that she was quiescent, and would soon bring them the tax in the usual form, that is, rice. They were accustomed to collecting taxes thus: rice placed on banana leaves.

Nangeli indeed had two long green banana leaves ready. She had sharpened her sickle too. All her life she had worked in the fields, and was adept at handling the sickle. She now picked up the tool, and in one smooth motion, slashed off one of her own breasts. The searing pain was unbearable; the wound bled on her body like a fountain. She carried on like one possessed—another deadly stroke. Placing both breasts on the banana leaves, hardly any strength left in her mutilated body, she went out to the waiting officials. Nangeli offered them her two breasts, mangled flesh that had, a minute ago, formed an integral part of her beautiful body.

Before she bled to death, Nangeli saw, to her great satisfaction, the stricken look on the faces of the parvarthiyar and his men, horror and panic writ large, as well as urgent recognition. She knew in that moment that her sacrifice was not in vain. The state official recognized her sacrifice, and wordlessly acknowledged the wrong done to Nangeli and all Dalits. Nangeli the fighter, passed away knowing that word of her brave deed would spread like wildfire. It would make a difference.

As Nangeli collapsed in a heap, the parvarthiyar fled, leaving the severed breasts lying next to her corpse. Neighbours gathered, and someone ran screaming to fetch Chirukandan. Grief-stricken, he joined his beloved wife. In protest against the unjust regime, the story goes that he jumped into her funeral pyre, and burned to death.

Nangeli's protest sent shock waves throughout the state. The next day, Sreemolam Thirunal, king of Travancore, issued a proclamation revoking Mulakkaram, fearing an agitation. The area she lived in came to be known as Mulachiparambu (land of the breasted woman). However, Dalit women were still prohibited from wearing top clothing when in the presence of upper castes.

Maaru Marakkal Samaram, or Channar Lahala (revolt) of Dalit women burgeoned in the state a decade later—a collective revolt of Dalit women fighting for the right to wear upper-body garments. Nadar and Ezhava women campaigned to be allowed to cover their breasts. The British passed an order permitting Christian women to wear upper cloth in Travancore, but withdrew it after the Raja's council objected that this would obliterate caste differences. Nadar women were forbidden to wear upper-body cloth, but could wear a short jacket called *kuppayam*. Ezhava and Nadar women continued the struggle, and were violently opposed by upper castes. Travancore royalty issued a proclamation in 1829, denying Nadar women the right to wear upper cloths.

As the agitation raged, in 1859, the Travancore Raja granted Nadar women the right to tie cloth around their upper body, but only in a specific way.

By the late nineteenth century, Dalit women's struggles on the issue succeeded in Travancore. In Cochin and Malabar, where similar practices prevailed, struggles carried on well into the twentieth century.

Nangeli's protest is hardly mentioned in official history; even in Cherthala, most people have forgotten her. Her humble hut has long vanished; no memorial was built to commemorate her. Local leaders like C. Kesavan and K.R. Gowri Amma recall her courage. Her great-great-granddaughter, Leena, retells her story with pride. A new generation draws inspiration from her incredible story, and the contemporary Dalit movement continues the struggle for an end to exploitation, and the establishment of social justice.

48 | Joanna:
Lady of Sardhana
1752–1836, Uttar Pradesh, Delhi and Haryana

Joanna kept reinventing herself: crossing boundaries and taking on new names, even as she grew ever more powerful. Her birthname is lost to history; she became Begum Samru when she was 14 (from the corruption of 'Sombre', her partner's moniker); Joanna Nobilis (modelled on Joan of Arc) when she converted to Christianity; Farzand-i-Azizi (Farzana for short) after she saved the Mughal emperor's life in battle; and Zebunissa ('jewel among women') when she once again saved the emperor's life. A tawaif's daughter, Joanna commanded an army, and owned a flourishing jagir at Sardhana, where she built a magnificent Italianate cathedral, the Basilica of Our Lady of Graces. This intrepid lady, less than five feet tall, was ambitious, fearless and a survivor.

Joanna was born in Kutana, near Delhi, her mother was Kashmiri, and father Latif Khan, of Arabic descent. When Latif Khan died, she and her mother were tortured by his son (from an earlier wife). Forced to leave, penniless, they travelled to Delhi. Broken by misfortune, the mother gave 10-year-old Joanna to well-known tawaif Khanum Jan, and passed away. The orphaned girl grew up learning music, dance and poetry, living in Bazaar-e-Husn (Chawri Bazaar); and soon began performing in mehfils to entertain wealthy men.

Walter Reinhardt Sombre, an Austrian, came to the kotha, and struck a deal with Khanum Jan: he took 14-year-old Joanna as his mistress. Thirty years older than her, Reinhardt owned a private militia, which he deployed for different masters; he was dubbed 'Butcher of Patna' for slaughtering 150 Englishmen while serving Mir Qasim.

Quick-witted Joanna settled into her new life with aplomb. Her ability to make friends helped win the couple popularity in the Mughal court; she was as lively as Reinhardt was gloomy! Reinhardt helped Mughal emperor Shah Alam II quell the Jats, and was rewarded with a jagir—Sardhana, near Meerut. In 1778, Reinhardt passed away.

Joanna immediately established sway over Reinhardt's troops, becoming commander-in-chief of the army of 4,000 Indian and nearly 100 European men. The emperor granted her the jagir of Sardhana, overruling the claim of Zafaryab Khan, Reinhardt's son (from Badi Bibi, Reinhardt's first wife). Joanna converted to Christianity, partly perhaps to buttress her claim to being Reinhardt's legal wife and rightful heir. Blending diverse cultures, Joanna evolved a unique way of life, dress and religious beliefs. Occasionally observing parda, she often joined mixed gatherings unveiled.

She led her troops to battle, and proved to be a consummate diplomat. In 1783, when a Sikh army camped at Tis Hazari, planning to conquer Delhi, Emperor Alam Shah II requested her to intervene. She negotiated a peaceful settlement, with the Sikhs permitted to build eight gurudwaras in Delhi. In 1787, Joanna defeated Najaf Quli Khan, saving the emperor's life. He honoured her with the title 'Farzand-e-Azizi', beloved daughter. Joanna also enjoyed fiefdom of Jharsa-Badshahpur (in present-day Gurugram), where she stationed her cavalry, and built an Islamic-style palace-cum-fort. In 1778, Rohilla chieftain Ghulam Qadir occupied Delhi, and captured and blinded the emperor. Joanna arrived with her troops, and rescued Shah Alam II. The grateful emperor conferred upon her the title 'Zebunnisa'.

Rumour linked Joanna to two of her officers: Irishman George Thomas, popularly called Jahazi Mahal, who headed her troops (1787 onwards); and Frenchman Le Vaisseau, whom she secretly married. Zafaryab and her own troops opposed the match, leading to a scuffle in which Le Vaisseau was killed. Joanna quickly re-established authority over her army, and placed Zafaryab under house arrest unto his death in 1807.

Joanna sent five battalions to the Battle of Assaye (1803). While the rest of the Maratha forces were driven away in disarray, her army withstood a cavalry charge by the British, and marched away from the battlefield in good order. Many believed Joanna was a witch who destroyed enemies by throwing her magic cloak over them! Later that year, however, the British won Delhi, and threatened to annexe Sardhana. Pragmatically, Joanna surrendered. Eventually, Lord Cornwallis confirmed her control over Sardhana, but she was forced to lend troops to the British; she lost the status of an independent commander.

Joanna turned her attention to philanthropy, education and the care of her properties. She established several schools, colleges, churches and seminaries in Sardhana, Meerut, Agra, Calcutta and Madras. Her jagir flourished, with an upright administration, and concern for the welfare of inhabitants: 'Her fields look greener and more flourishing, and the population of her villages appear happier and more prosperous than those of the [East India] Company's provinces. Her care is unremitting and her protection sure.'[84]

Joanna built a palatial residence in Sardhana, and a kothi in Meerut. Emperor Akbar Shah gifted her prime land in Shahjahanabad, in 1806, where she built a grand mansion, with Greek columns and extensive gardens along the cypress-lined avenue from Chandni Chowk. She ran a salon there, supporting poets and musicians, commissioned paintings and decorative art, and entertained lavishly with elaborate cuisine, dancing and fireworks. British officials, European ladies and Mughal royalty were among her guests—Delhi's elite as well as visiting dignitaries. Joanna smoked the hookah, redolent of pleasure and enchantment, adding to her charisma. She adopted David Ochterlony Dyce Samru (Zafaryab's grandchild) as her son and heir.

Joanna constructed an elegant cathedral in Sardhana, designed by Reghelini, an Italian architect who served in her army. The domes and columns resemble St Peter's Basilica in Rome, while the marble altar with pietra dura resonates with the Taj Mahal. In 1834, Joanna wrote to the Pope, requesting a Bishop for the church, which: 'I am proud to say, is acknowledged to be the finest, without exception, in India.'[85]

She died at a ripe old age, and lies buried within her cathedral. David commissioned a marble sculpture by Tadolini of Bologna, got it shipped to Calcutta, then down the Ganges and by bullock-cart to Sardhana. It was fixed beside the altar: a life-size Joanna sitting regally, draped in a Kashmiri shawl, smoking her hookah; beneath her stand European and Indian courtiers. Bas-relief panels depict her commanding troops in battle; an inscription announces: 'Her Highness Joanna Zebanissa the Begum Sombre.'

49 | Mahlaqa Bai Chanda: Dancer-Diplomat
1768-1824

Mahlaqa Bai Chanda—poet, singer, dancer, diplomat, philanthropist and builder—rose to power as a courtesan in the court of the Nizam of Hyderabad. Her diwan of beautiful ghazals, *Diwan-i-Chanda,* ensured her a place in literary history. She sponsored *Tarikh-i-Dilafruz*[86], an important chronicle of the history of Hyderabad state. In its preface, the writer, Jauhar, extolled his patron's talents in poetry, music, horse riding and wrestling, and praised her as a woman of cultural finesse from an illustrious family. In 1815, she was honoured with the title 'Mahlaqa' (angelic face like the moon), by Asaf Jah III, Nizam of Hyderabad. Well into her 50s, she continued to grace elite gatherings, where she was adept at 'blending political diplomacy with performance'.[87]

Chanda's ghazals were a means of expressing multiple desires: using tropes of romance and sensual love, she sought diverse ends such as land, property, political patronage and spiritual blessing. In many ghazals she addressed Maula Hazrat Ali, whom she, a devout Shia'ite, revered:

Will you keep inventing new oppressions every day
You will ruin countless lovers' hearts in this way
Will you release me from your net? But then
You will make someone else your captive prey

Will you truly think only of me, even if
You will entertain other lovers for display?
Will you ever make a heart happy? It seems
You will keep aloof letting hearts in sorrow stay
Will you accept a hundred loves like Chanda's,
Maula Ali?
You will help her sacrifice, for this alone
She will pray.[88]

A ghazal, addressed to the prime minister of Hyderabad state, articulated a request for 'charity land':

Let Nauroz bring forth ever increasing pleasure and
spring
By your fortune, flowers are strewn in the garden
everywhere for eternity
Don't let anyone end the pleasure and luxury in his reign
With whose grace each and every house is prosperous
and has companion for wine
Aristu Jah oh fortunate, beautiful-faced and learned one,
Whose abundant beneficence is known throughout the
world,
This is a prayer from Maula Ali for charity land
Let Maula Ali keep you under his love and care always
Nothing adorns the moon better in this world
And whatever is visible on Chanda is for you.[89]

It was in the court of Aristu Jah, the Nizam's prime minister, that Chanda gave her first dance performance at the age of 15. She was well-trained by her family of closely allied women. It seems they were not traditional performers—rather, over a couple of generations, they had completely reinvented themselves.

Chanda's grandmother, Chanda Bibi, had struggled to survive. Chanda's grandfather, Khwajah Hussain, embezzled money from his employer the Nawab of Gujarat, and fled the scene. The Nawab placed Khwajah Hussain's wife Chanda Bibi under house arrest in Ahmedabad, along with her five children. They managed to escape, and wandered homeless, until taking shelter with a troupe of dancer-singers in Deolia town. The three daughters— Nur, Polan and Mida—became performing artistes, and renamed themselves Burj Kanwar Bai, Polan Kanwar Bai and Raj Kanwar Bai, respectively. Raj Kanwar became for a while a concubine of Salim Singh, ruler of Deolia, and had a daughter, Mehtab, but left his harem after an attempt on her life. Chanda Bibi having passed away, the three sisters hit the road again with little Mehtab, and reached Burhanpur. In Burhanpur and Aurangabad, they became popular within the armies of Asaf Jah II, Nizam of Hyderabad. They moved from camp to camp with their patrons, becoming deredar tawaifs (the best of the courtesans). When the Nizam shifted his capital to Hyderabad, they moved too. Raj Kanwar cohabited with Bahadur Shah Turki, a soldier in the Nizam's army, and bore a child: Chanda.

Mehtab took in Chanda—her half-sister—and brought her up. Mehtab was by now in a position of power due to her liaison with Nawab Mohammad Yar Khan. Mehtab provided Chanda with an all-round education, appointing the best of tutors. Chanda learnt the intricacies of khayal and thumri, Kathak and Persian poetry, and her talents began to be noticed and appreciated. When Raj Kanwar passed away in 1792, she was secure in the knowledge that her last born, Chanda, was on the path to exceptional achievement.

Chanda established herself as a public performer. She was employed by the Nizam's court, and the courts of Aristu Jah, Nawab Mir Alam (prime minister after Aristu Jah), Raja Chandu Lal (a patron of the arts) and Raja Rao Rambha Sahib (a high official). She had a busy schedule as star entertainer at small, select gatherings of the local elite and European officials. Chanda usually recited and sang her own ghazals, accompanied by music and dance. After performing, she would mingle with the men, and engage in conversation. She was learned in the arts, and knowledgeable about politics. She used such occasions to further her own ends, networking to win powerful allies. For instance, during a dance performance at Mir Alam's house, in 1799, she gifted a copy of her diwan to John Malcolm, an official of the East India Company.[90]

Chanda received a salary from each court where she performed. The Nizam granted her land, guards, her own troops, palanquin with palanquin bearers and a drummer to announce her arrival. Thrice she went to the battlefield with the Nizam and his army. As a reward for her services to the state, in battle and civilian life, she received a number of jagirs including Hyderguda, Chanda Nagar, Syedpalli and Adikmet. She lived in her own palace, Khas Haveli, with some 300 attendants helping run her establishment, and manage her properties. She maintained a vast library, patronized writers and employed calligraphers to prepare original works—including several copies of her own diwan. She bequeathed her enormous wealth to charities for the education and shelter of homeless women and orphan girls.

Chanda built an *ashurkhana* (prayerhouse); a guesthouse for pilgrims during urs and a mausoleum complex for her mother, Raj Kanwar: a magnificent tomb with exquisite carvings, set within a beautiful garden called Chandabagh, at the foot of Maula Ali Hill. Within the compound she built a mosque. Next to Raj Kanwar's tomb, Chanda marked out space for her own burial; she was laid there after her death in 1824. On carved teak wood is an inscription in Urdu:

When the tidings of the advent of death arrived from
God
She accepted it with her heart, and heaven became her
home.
Alas! Mahlaqa of the Deccan departed for heaven 1240
A.H.

Chanda's residence in Nampally, Hyderabad, is now a girls'
college. Osmania University stands on land that was once her
jagir. Chandabagh, and the mausoleum with twin tombs of
Mahlaqa and her mother, were recently renovated—debris
cleared, water channels rebuilt and trees, bushes and buildings
restored. Chanda's legacy may not have got the attention it
deserves, but neither has it been completely forgotten.

50 | Chenamma: Freedom First

1778–1829, Karnataka

Rani Chenamma resisted British onslaught on the fort of Kittoor, against tremendous odds. One of the first Indian rulers to launch an armed struggle against British imperialism, she fought fiercely, and won twice. She continued to fight for liberty, refusing to compromise and survive by signing a treaty with the East India Company. Chenamma is remembered as one of the foremost Indian freedom fighters, and in Kittoor, 23 October 1824 is celebrated as 'Women's Day'—the day on which the queen of a small state defeated powerful British invaders with skill, strategy, determination and a fearless heart.

Chenamma was born to Padmavati and Thulappagowda Desai, in Kakati, a tiny jagir held by her family. She grew up learning Kannada, Marathi, Urdu and Persian, as well as horse riding and sword fighting. One day, 14-year-old Chenamma was out hunting when Mallarudra Sarja Desai, king of Kittoor, happened to be in the same forest. As the legend goes, both aimed at the same tiger, came up to their common prey and disputed one another's claim over it. Mallarudra was enamoured of Chenamma; soon, they were married.

Kittoor was a principality of 280 villages in north Karnataka (in present-day Dharwad and Belgaum) under Maratha suzerainty. It was a prosperous kingdom, with business in precious stones;

its treasury held much gold. Chenamma began assisting the king in affairs of state, touring with him and taking specific decisions, such as support for rebuilding a mosque at Amatur, and permitting African ex-slaves (escaped from the Portuguese) to settle in Kittoor. She gave birth to a son, Shivabasavaraj. With his senior wife, Rudramma, Mallarudra had two sons, Shivalingarudra and Veerarudra. Chenamma involved herself with educating the three boys. Her son was married to a young girl called Janakibai. However, he did not live to adulthood; neither did Veerarudra.

In 1813, Peshwa Baji Rao II imprisoned Mallarudra in Poona, and kept him semi-starved. Released three years later, Mallarudra somehow reached Kittoor, but died soon after. Shivalingarudra, still a minor, became king, with Chenamma as regent. In 1818, Shivalingarudra signed a treaty with the British under which he paid an annual tribute, and inheritance was guaranteed to his male descendants. Shivalingarudra was married to a young girl, Viramma.

A few years later, Shivalingarudra fell ill with tuberculosis, and adopted a small boy, Shivalingappa. On 12 September 1824, Shivalingarudra passed away. The British agent, Thackeray, arbitrarily declared that Shivalingappa's adoption was a fraud. The royal family now consisted only of Chenamma, 16-year-old Janakibai and 11-year-old Viramma. The British thought they could easily grab the kingdom. Thackeray asked the governor, Elphinstone, to take over the kingdom under paramountcy, using a doctrine formalized in 1848 by Dalhousie, the infamous Doctrine of Lapse.

In a clear act of provocation, Thackeray set his seal on Kittoor's treasury and posted guards around it, and at the main gates of the fort. He refused to release funds even for routine religious celebrations. Chenamma wrote letters of protest to senior British officials, but got no reply. On 18 October, she called her ministers and asserted: 'These Britishers...do not know that the people of Kittoor love freedom more than life... Kittoor will fight to the last man on its soil. They would die rather than be slaves of the British.'[91]

Anticipating armed conflict, Chenamma had strengthened the fort, put her army on the alert and prepared a roster of trained fighters who could be requisitioned, if need be. On 21 October, Thackeray instructed his men to storm the fort. The Kittoor army succeeded in driving them out and capturing 40 British soldiers, along with some women and children. Chenamma imprisoned the soldiers and kept the women and children in comfort.

On 23 October—Dussehra day—Thackeray and his troops arrived at Kittoor Fort and ordered Chenamma's guards to open the gates within 24 minutes. When the gates did not open, British artillery opened fire and blew up the gates. Chenamma's soldiers burst forth, surging forward in a fierce surprise attack. Within moments they captured British guns, killed about a hundred soldiers and threw the rest into disarray. Chenamma directed the attack from the fort ramparts, astride her horse, sporting helmet and armour. At her order, the warrior Balappa shot Thackeray dead. Kittoor troops arrested two army commanders: Stevenson and Elliot.

This was a resounding victory. Chenamma demanded that Thackeray's attack on Kittoor Fort be investigated, justice duly established and Kittoor respected as an independent state. But the British assembled forces from Sholapur, Mysore and Bombay, preparing to mount a fresh assault. Chenamma warned them that if they attack Kittoor, her people will fight to the end, and the English prisoners will be put to death. Thereupon, Elphinstone issued a proclamation announcing that the Company would take over governance of Kittoor, pardon Chenamma, make a suitable allowance for her and other women of the family, and restore her treasury and private property.

Chenamma and the people of Kittoor refused to accept these conditions; she reiterated that the kingdom must be restored, and her people were not willing to surrender under any circumstances. As a gesture of goodwill, she released all the prisoners except Stevenson and Elliot. But during the last week of November, some 25,000 British troops surrounded Kittoor Fort. On 2 December, Chenamma was assured that if Stevenson and Elliot were set free, the British would not attack the fort. To prevent a bloodbath, she released the two: they described the courtesy and consideration with which Chenamma had treated them and recommended that her demands be met. But the British went back on their word and, on 3 December, stormed Kittoor Fort. Some 200 heavy guns fired continuously, fierce fighting ensued over three days. Shelling from Kittoor's guns was weak because cow dung and millet had been treacherously mixed with their gunpowder. Kittoor troops were defeated; on 5 December, Chenamma, Viramma and Janakibai were captured by the British, and forced to sign a document relinquishing their hold on Kittoor. They were then imprisoned in Bailhongal Fort.

Her trusted allies such as Sangolli Rayanna (disguised as an ascetic) would meet Chenamma in Bailhongal jail, and discuss how to continue the struggle to free Kittoor. For over five years, the countryside was rife with rebellion. The British captured Rayanna, and executed him by hanging from a banyan tree in Machigad village. Having lost hope of victory and freedom, Chenamma breathed her last in February 1829; Janakibai and Viramma passed away a few months later. Their memory is very much alive, preserved in folk stories, legends, songs, books and a feature film such as *Kitturu Chenamma*.

51 | Baiza:
Starting Point of Revolution
1784–1863, Madhya Pradesh and Maharashtra

Baiza Bai challenged British imperialism—in her roles as queen, financier and fugitive freedom fighter. Her groundwork during the first half of the nineteenth century helped lead the way to the massive uprising of 1857. Historical accounts indicate that Baiza was 'a formidable force… a remarkable political figure…who occupied a central place in the politics of early nineteenth-century Malwa and north India, to which she bequeathed a strong anti-British ideology'.[92] There is evidence for 'tracing the genesis of the Revolt to Baiza Bai', confirming 'the popular view in which the Bai was seen as the starting-point of the contemporary resistance to British rule'.[93]

The extraordinary story begins with 14-year-old Baiza marrying Daulat Rao Scindia, ruler of Gwalior, and moving from Kagal village, Maharashtra, to cosmopolitan Ujjain. Her father Sarje Rao Ghatge left the post of Deshmukh at Kagal, and joined as Scindia's Dewan. Baiza, when 18, battled alongside her husband in the Battle of Assaye (1803): 'a lance in her hand and an infant in her arms.'[94] Her father being a fierce opponent of British intervention in Gwalior, the Company wanted Scindia to expel him; in 1809, Ghatge was murdered. Baiza, pregnant at the time, was terribly distressed.

Baiza was strong-minded and clear about opposing the

Company. She urged Scindia to support Baji Rao II's battle against the British; while he vacillated, she unilaterally commenced marching towards the Deccan. She also used her financial acumen to develop clout as a banker, and earn huge amounts through speculation, moneylending and bills of exchange.

Through all this, Baiza gave birth to several children, of whom only two—Jija Bai and Chimna Bai—survived to adulthood; Jija Bai too died in 1820, leaving behind three small daughters. Scindia died in 1827. Before his death, he adopted an 11-year-old boy, Jankoji. Baiza took charge as regent, and proved to be an exceptionally competent monarch: 'a ruler who afforded protection for the weak against the extortions of their superiors.' Observers acknowledged: 'Scindia's domains were better governed by her than by any of the other members of the house.'[95] Trade prospered, and copper coins were minted with the legend 'Baijabai'. Confident of her rights, Baiza communicated to the British Resident: 'during my lifetime, I should be allowed to retain supreme control of the affairs and the administration of the Government in my own hands, as it was held by the late Maharajah.'[96]

The Company called on her for a loan of ₹10 million; she actually lent them ₹8 million, in 1827. The Company avoided repayment, upon which Baiza initiated a cash crackdown. All bankers refused to lend money to the Company which therefore, finally, repaid Baiza's loan. The Company planned to ask her for another whopping loan to pay for its wars in Burma; Baiza pre-empted this by requesting the Governor-General for a loan of ₹1 million—thus seeking to convince the British that she was impoverished!

The British favoured the young Jankoji over her; her independence of mind irked them. Baiza was suddenly ousted in 1833, an army coup adding to the confusion. Fearing for her life, she fled to Agra with a large retinue. Her daughter Chimna Bai died due to exposure and anxiety, which grieved Baiza at least as much as the loss of her kingdom. A granddaughter, Gujia Raje (Jija Bai's daughter), accompanied Baiza. They moved constantly the next few years, trying to gather support for deposing Jankoji, who proved to be a puppet in British hands.

In Farrukhabad in 1835, Welsh traveller Fanny Parkes visited Baiza and found her 'seated on her gudee of embroidered cloth, with her granddaughter the Gujia Raje Sahib by her side'. She was dressed in simple silk with few ornaments, her voice sweet and manner pleasing, 'a freedom and independence in her air that I greatly admire'.[97] The two struck up a friendship. Baiza was puzzled by British women riding side-saddle, 'all crooked', and challenged Fanny to dress and ride the correct way, astride a horse. Fanny did so, after changing into 'Mahratta dress'—sari drawn between the legs, giving it 'the effect both of petticoat and trousers'. The two women conversed on many things, including injustice towards women in the laws and customs of England and India.

In 1840, Baiza moved to Nasik, where she helped sow seeds of resistance to colonial rule, and saw a new consciousness grow, particularly among soldiers. When the Company uncovered a rebellion near Pune, in 1842, Baiza was reported to have funded it. The Governor-General warned her of 'the necessity of the most guarded conduct on her part to prevent any further similar reports'. She countered, feigning innocence: 'Is it possible that I, who have no other engagements than the worship of God, shall now in my old age engage myself in intrigues?'

After Jankoji's death in 1843, Gwalior witnessed an anti-British uprising. Soldiers fought pitched battles, initially successfully, but later defeated by sheer numbers and superior fire-power. Baiza reiterated her claim to state power, reminding British authorities:

'my late husband in the enjoyment of sound good sense made over to me the whole of the household property, the affairs of the state, the right of inheritance and the management of the Government.'[98]

Incredibly, Baiza managed a spectacular comeback—through a carefully calibrated matrimonial alliance. Jankoji's adopted son, nine-year-old Jayaji, was ruler of Gwalior. Shrewdly, Baiza proposed marriage between Jayaji and her own great-granddaughter, six-year-old Chimna Raje (Gujia Raje's daughter). She couched her proposal to sound like a family rapprochement, but the terms of the deal were clear: Baiza would will her entire wealth to Jayaji, and Ujjain would come under her direct control. The carrot she dangled—wealth worth several crores—was too tempting to refuse. Baiza attended Jayaji and Chimna Raje's wedding in Gwalior, and triumphantly resettled in Ujjain, nearly half-a-century after she had first come there as a bride. British political agent S.C. Macpherson commented, in 1854, that Baiza's influence in Gwalior came 'from her great wealth, from the Maharaja being her expectant heir, from the presence of her grandchildren in his Palace, from her veteran skill in plots'.[99]

In 1856, she moved back to Gwalior; British records noted: 'Baiza Bai's asserted proceedings and speeches during the early period of the mutiny were the subject of much remark.'[100] When Gwalior was occupied in June 1858, Jayaji went into British protection; Baiza too was escorted out by armed guards. Tatya Tope, Lakshmi Bai and Nana Saheb wrote to Baiza Bai, requesting her to lead an indigenous government. She made no response. If the cost of survival was compromise, Baiza, now over 70 years old, chose to keep her own counsel.

Sitaram Baba, an ordinary participant in the uprising, disclosed: 'Baiza Bai was the person who commenced this conspiracy about twenty years ago', while in Nasik, 'she continued plotting at

Ujjain'. Later, Nana Saheb became the lead organizer.[101] Baiza's groundwork in laying the foundations for the great uprising was well known to participants and local people, but usually eclipsed in subsequent historical accounts.

Baiza lived on another five years in Gwalior. Dowager queen, she kept an eye on affairs of state, and no doubt influenced her great-grandchildren and their children, with colourful stories from her dramatic past.

52 | Qudsia and Sikander: Nawab Begums

Nineteenth Century, Bhopal

The Nawab Begums of Bhopal, a remarkable quartet, ran the state for well-nigh one century (1819–1926). Qudsia set a pattern of good governance, which the others followed, each in her own way. Both Qudsia and her daughter Sikander had to fight for their right to rule. Qudsia further witnessed the reign of her granddaughter Shah Jahan; and saw her great-granddaughter Sultan Jahan grow to womanhood. All four Nawab Begums were widely acknowledged as capable and far-sighted, prompting Sultan Jahan Begum to conclude: 'administrative capacity is more inherent in women than in men, and...nature specially intended them to be rulers.'[102]

Qudsia (1800?–1881) had been married less than three years when her husband, Nazar, was accidentally killed by a gunshot by her eight-year-old brother. During the death ceremonies, Qudsia stunned relatives, friends and British officials by declaring her two-year-old daughter Sikander heir to the throne. Nobody dared contradict her—she became the queen regent.

Qudsia took charge of a kingdom which already had a history of illustrious women. Dost Muhammad Khan, an Afghan, founded the kingdom in 1709; his daughter-in-law Maimola Bai, became regent for her stepsons Faiz (in 1754) and Hayat (in 1777), was popular and continued to rule for some 40 years.

Qudsia's father, Ghaus Mohammed (Hayat's son), ruled after Maimola, but was weak and ineffective, while Qudsia's mother, Zeenat, displayed sterling qualities of head and heart. Ghaus's cousin Wazir displaced Ghaus, and was followed by his son, Nazar Mohammed.

In 1817, Qudsia married her cousin, Nazar; they got along well. Nazar signed a treaty with the British, in 1818, whereby he and his descendents would rule Bhopal, and provide military support to the British. At the third-day rites after Nazar's death, Qudisa got everyone present to sign an oath of allegiance to the infant Sikander, Nazar's rightful heir. By her public declaration and quick action, Qudsia outsmarted several ambitious relatives, including her own brothers. She got the document ratified by the state Kazi, Mufti and British officialdom. Qudsia was pregnant during this time, but due to grief and stress, she miscarried.

Qudsia was a people's queen, attentive to their needs. Though unlettered, she established her authority and created a system of trustworthy advisors. She set up waterworks with free piped water for the citizens of Bhopal, an extraordinarily prescient welfare measure. Clean drinking water helped wipe out cholera in the city. She managed state finances well, and lived frugally, meeting her personal expenses from a small cottage industry she ran within the palace.

She constructed mosques and rest houses for pilgrims, the Jama Masjid and a palace, Gohar Mahal, with a garden called Nazar Bagh. She had a bell placed in the garden that anybody could ring for justice, and every evening sat under a tree in the palace garden, accessible to the public. Qudsia and Sikander (when she grew old enough) moved around incognito to gauge how people lived, and whether the state administrators were following instructions properly.

Around 1834, Qudsia gave up parda because it interfered

with her duties—noting that the Prophet's wives wore no veils. She learnt to ride for the first time, and grew adept at riding not only horses, but also elephants and camels. She picked up military skills, went hunting and commanded her troops. Yet, her male relatives represented their case, pleading that Islam does not countenance women as rulers. The British consequently passed a law by which a female heir in Bhopal must relinquish the right to rule in favour of her husband.

Qudsia brought up Sikander with diligence, and a rich education. But the British threatened to imprison mother and daughter, unless Sikander married her cousin Jahangir. Sikander and Jahangir were betrothed when both were eight years old, but where Sikander grew up bright and energetic, Jahangir was sloppy and wayward. Sikander was loath to marry, but realizing its inevitability, got Jahangir to sign an agreement under which he would not take another wife, would honour Qudsia as his mother and always be obedient to her. They duly married, and power was transferred to Jahangir.

The British declared that Qudsia must henceforth have no say in state affairs. Qudsia, just 37 years old, moved to the majestic Islamnagar Fort, in what looked like permanent retirement. In fact, she was mentally agile, and hoped to reclaim Bhopal for her daughter. Sikander, an active, strong-willed woman, loved riding, fencing and swordplay, and had discarded parda. She was deeply interested in the economy of the state and the welfare of its people. Jahangir and Sikander, husband and wife, were ill-matched and perpetually at loggerheads. One night when Sikander was lying down, Jahangir attempted to kill her. She managed to escape, and went straight to Islamnagar Fort. Here, she gave birth in July 1838, to their daughter, Shah Jahan.

British agent, Wilkinson, was constrained to observe: 'The people of Bhopal say that they lived in peace and comfort under the protection of the Nawab Qudsia Begum, who was a widow, but under the present Nawab, who is a man, they live in terror and misery.' Soon Jahangir brought matters to a head, by drinking himself to death.

Seven-year-old Shah Jahan was declared ruler of Bhopal. The three Begums—Qudsia, Sikander and Shah Jahan—rode back to Bhopal triumphantly, in 1844, and reoccupied the palace. Qudisa was provided a jagir, and enjoyed being dowager mother—close to the seat of power, her cherished daughter holding the reins. The two often discussed important matters of state. Qudsia loved walking in the city, meeting and chatting with ordinary folks; she also enjoyed entertainments and singing.

Sikander Begum (1817–1868)

Sikander Begum ruled as regent for her daughter Shah Jahan. Devoted to the job, Sikander drew up new administrative units, centralized the tax system, toured the state and was attentive to the conditions of the people. She reshaped judicial and legal systems, inspected district offices and courts to ensure things ran smoothly, commanded and modernized the army, and took progressive measures in public health, agriculture and industry.

Sikander invited Islamic scholars of diverse schools to Bhopal, initiating religious reforms and creating a multilingual literary culture. She founded schools and technical centres, especially for girls, both Hindu and Muslim. In madrasas, she refurbished syllabi, introducing Urdu, Persian and English along with Islamic studies. At home, she made sure her daughter and granddaughter too learnt English well.

Qudsia and Sikander kept up a steady volley of petitions to revoke the unjust law which dispossessed female heirs. They argued that Islam accepted women rulers, citing the Prophet's wife Ayesha and the Queen of Sheba. Queen Victoria, too, was ruling an empire which included millions of Muslims! The Quran, they asserted, nowhere bans women from leadership positions. Rather, in the name of Islam, powerful men impose double standards, denying opportunities to women. In 1855, the British revoked the order—a signal victory for the Begums.

Qudsia and Sikander arranged Shah Jahan's marriage, against her wishes, to an elderly court minister. In 1857, Shah Jahan had a daughter, Sultan Jahan, whom Sikander adopted and doted upon.

During 1857–58, Sikander contributed troops to the British. Bhopal remained virtually unaffected while the uprising raged in central and north India. Securing the goodwill of the colonial masters, she maintained her position as a figure of indigenous authority, and continued to mould Bhopal into an early welfare state.

In 1860, Shah Jahan was old enough to take charge of the state. In an unprecedented move, guided by Qudsia, Shah Jahan abdicated in favour of her mother. Sikander Begum now ruled in her own right—not regent. Ignoring kingly traditions of fratricide and patricide, these royal women created a paradigm of logic, justice and solidarity. An experienced ruler, widely acknowledged for her progressive policies, continued in saddle; her daughter would take over after she died.

In 1861, the British decorated Sikander as Grand Commander of the Order of the Star of India (the only woman, apart from Queen Victoria, to bear this rank at the time). The same year, Sikander persuaded the British to open Delhi's Jama Masjid again; it is said she washed it herself and was the first person to pray in it. Over a couple of years, the British had parked horses in the Jama Masjid as part of their ravaging of Shahjahanabad.

Qudsia and Sikander went on hajj, starting from Bhopal, in the summer of 1861. Sikander was the first Indian ruler to make the pilgrimage. She recorded the experience, vividly describing Jeddah and Mecca, local customs, houses and sanitation systems, religious rites and interesting encounters.[103] Qudsia, always lavish in her generosity, gave out gold mohurs and gifts to all and sundry; consequently, they were besieged by mobs of fakirs, and had to ask for the Sherif's protection. Unfazed, Qudsia carried on distributing largesse. In Mecca, Sikander advised local officials to make arrangements for washing pilgrims' clothes, which would teach people to keep clean, rather than the unkempt appearance they now displayed. She decided against travelling to Medina, a route on which robbers would certainly ambush them, news of Qudsia's riches having spread far and wide. The party returned to Bhopal, in little over a year.

Sikander continued her good governance, and also created a rigorous daily schedule—including studies, sports and prayer—for her adoptee, Sultan Jahan. When Sultan Jahan was eight, Qudsia and Sikandar carefully selected an eight-year-old boy of proper lineage, betrothed Sultan Jahan to him, and brought him to live in the palace so the two could study and play together.

In 1868, Sikandar died of a kidney ailment—leaving Qudsia grief-stricken and 11-year-old Sultan Jahan bereft.

Shah Jahan ascended the throne. Her husband had died the previous year; a few years later, she married the scholar Siddiq Hasan Khan of Kannauj, a marriage Qudsia disapproved of. For several decades, the royal family was rife with tension. In Shah Jahan's reign, Qudsia became persona non grata. Shah Jahan never invited her grandmother for any functions, official or personal—not even Sultan Jahan's wedding, though Sultan Jahan greatly loved her great-grandmother.

Qudsia continued funding charities and good works, for instance, contributing ₹15 lakh towards the Great Peninsular Railways. In 1876, at the Great Durbar in Delhi, the British invested Qudsia with the Order of the Crown of India.

Qudsia breathed her last in 1881. She had ruled well and wisely, inaugurating a century of women's rule: marked by benevolence and modernity, education and openness to change. The Begums' rule in Bhopal led to the rise of a unique culture, syncretic and cosmopolitan.

53 | Jindan: Revolutionary Lion Queen
1817–63, Punjab

Maharani Jind Kaur laid the groundwork in and around Punjab for insurrection against British imperialism, mobilizing sepoys, sadhus and Sardars. Fearful of her influence and determined to annexe the prize territory, the British tortured, exiled and jailed her. The indefatigable rebel escaped, incredibly, from a high-security prison; warrants for her arrest were posted far and wide. She travelled incognito all the way to Nepal, sought refuge in Kathmandu, from where she continued guiding rebels in north India. Towards the end of her life she was reunited with her son, whom British imperialists had snatched away as an eight-year-old child; she inspired in him a sense of history and resistance.

Jindan's father was employed in the palace at Lahore—where her beauty and ringing laughter caught the eye of Maharaja Ranjit Singh. Not yet 20, she married the 57-year-old king and became his favourite wife. In 1838, she had a son, Duleep Singh, but the following year, death snatched away her husband. The British declared Duleep Singh as heir, in 1843, with Jindan as regent, assuming that annexing Punjab would now be a cakewalk. But if Ranjit Singh had been the Lion of Punjab, Jindan proved herself Lion Queen. Throwing aside her parda, she challenged the soldiers to fight, rather than faint-heartedly succumb. Officers and troops swore on Maharani Jindan, took an oath of loyalty to Maharaja Duleep Singh and resolved to save the Khalsa.

Governor-General Ellenborough realized: 'It would not be so easy to deal with Maharani Jindan...she is a woman of determined courage.'[104] In 1845, Governor-General Hardinge noted: 'the Maharani...in concurrence with the Army, governs in person... She has shown much spirit and energy on more than one occasion.' And Lord Dalhousie noted: '...having watched the defiant Maharani's conduct during the past few years, I am firmly of the opinion that she is the only person of manly understanding in the Punjab.'

In 1845, the British moved troops into Punjab, declared authority over territories across the Sutlej, and severed diplomatic relations with the Khalsa Durbar. The Sardars panicked, but Jindan made a spirited war speech: 'You spoke forcefully about conquering London and Delhi... Now either move to the front and redeem your pledge or retire to the barracks in Lahore!' She dispatched a detachment to Buddowal to capture the Company's ammunition train, and fought the battles of Pherushehr, Mudki and Sobraon with great valour. Hardinge admitted that Punjab had 'brought into field warlike resources on a more perfect system of military organization than any by which our arms have hitherto been opposed'.

The British annexed large swathes of Punjab, slapped a war indemnity of ₹1.5 crore and occupied Lahore (February 1846). Maharani Jind sent emissaries throughout Punjab, mobilizing resistance. Sardars of Anandpur, Kharar, Sialbah, Nabha, Ladwa, Jasrota, Nurpur, Kulu and Manali expressed loyalty to her, as did ex-soldiers and some sepoys of British regiments at Lahore and elsewhere. Her maidservant, Jawai, went to Multan ostensibly to fetch *aak*, a medicinal plant, but in fact secured the support of Multan's Diwan, Mul Raj. Hardinge instructed Maharani Jind to write a letter requesting continuation of British troops in Lahore; she wrote suggesting that the troops be limited to one artillery, two infantry and one cavalry regiments. Hardinge accused her of wanting to manage British intervention, to which she responded with sarcasm: 'the Lord Sahab wants the keys of the palace to be handed to him!'

The British systematically decimated her power, dismissing loyal courtiers, cooking up salacious gossip and charging her with 'profligacy'. Finally, they made eight-year-old Duleep sign a document relinquishing sovereign status, and in January 1847, forced Jind Kaur to sign a treaty wherein she gave away her son. They confined her to her apartment, and shut all palace gates except Hathi Gate, where British personnel stood guard. She wrote to the Resident, alleging he had made her a prisoner in her palace, 'while putting the people of the whole of Punjab to the sword!'

On 19 August 1847, Jindan was dragged out of the palace—struggling, crying and cursing—pushed into a palanquin and taken to Sheikhupura Fort, 40 kilometres off Lahore. She protested her incarceration, sent lawyer Jiwan Singh to Calcutta to represent her case, but was informed that her confinement was irrevocable. In England, an opposition Member of Parliament (MP) asked why no 'formal trial of the Queen Mother of a friendly state under British guardianship was held, affording her opportunity for self-defense', and why 'a good deal of abuse' was being heaped upon her; but the abuse carried on.

From her prison cell, Jindan prepared for a massive uprising. She dispatched a stream of letters, through personal attendants and the family priest, Shiv Dayal. In a letter written in Gurmukhi, 'Bibi Sahiba' wrote to Shiv Dayal and Umrao Singh: 'I have received your letter and understood its contents... Work quickly, delay not, make much of a few words.'

Kahan Singh Mann wrote to her: 'All the respectable officers in the regiments have told me to write to the Mai Sahib... They say when we have killed the Europeans, we will release her... This will turn out well for you.' The Khalsa army issued an appeal: 'The Khalsa may once more unite and relieve the Maharaja and his mother from the thralldom of Sahib log.'

Thirty letters are preserved in the National Archives of India, from the nine-month period of Jindan's incarceration at Sheikhupra; there must be many more that are now lost. Her trusted lieutenants fanned out, and the countryside became rife with the belief that 'soon the Europeans will be driven out of Punjab'. Shiv Dayal informed her about support from sepoys in Ludhiana, Ferozepur, Ambala and Meerut cantonments, and requested money for further mobilization; she sent a bill for ₹50,000. Umrao Singh wrote to 'Mai Sahiba' assuring support of Sheikh Jung Ali and Khaleefa from Doobasun Regiment, Bidijo Singh, Luchum Singh, Ungud and Hyder Khan of 73rd Regiment, Bhagwan Singh, Ujoodhya Singh, Gya Deen, Omran Shhokur, Dunya Singh Jamadar and Shookhanundan of Kareetun and 52nd Regiments, Shiv Churn Tewaree of the Brurdwan-ki-Paltan, and so on.

Dewan Mul Raj informed her about Kahan Singh and others moving around disguised as fakirs, adding: 'Whatever orders you may send I will obey... If the affair is to be accomplished by money, spend freely. Be confident.' She provided access to funds and properties to finance the movement. Kahan Singh wrote to 'Hazoor Sree Bibi Sahiba', noting: 'If the present moment should pass away, it will be too late. In future you are master... This is no child's play. If the scheme does not answer, the fall will be into the abyss and one's life will be the forfeit.'

The assassination of British officers Agnew and Anderson in Multan, in April 1848, alerted the British. In May, Kahan Singh and Ganga Ram were sent to the gallows on charges of conspiracy against the British. Ganga Ram, who was Jindan's confidential Vakil, confessed: 'the Mooltan murders were premeditated.' He revealed Maharani Jind Kaur had masterminded the plot to kill Agnew and Anderson. The British noted in a memorandum (December 1848):

> [T]he intention of an insurrection, with a view to getting rid of the British from the Punjab, had been constantly agitated since the very hour of signing the treaty. From the time of the Maharanee's residence at Sheikhoopoora, intrigues had been constantly afoot.

Maharani Jind was sent into exile, to Banaras, with a few female and male household staff. Though ordered not to talk to anybody, she alighted often from her palki, unveiled, and talked to people. When British officer Mr Cox approached, she dropped her palanquin parda and refused to unveil for identification. The cavalcade reached Banaras on 2 August. She was imprisoned in an apartment in the fort, supervised by Agent MacGregor. Gulabo, Hargo, Ratni, Mago, Badami and several others female attendants stayed with her, four male attendants took in her meals, and Munshi Ram Kishan managed her official work. Pen and paper were banned to prevent her sending out letters. Sixty sepoys stood vigil outside the fort, a Havaldar at her door. MacGregor and another officer came daily, but Jindan firmly refused to let any Englishman see her, claiming her rights as a queen to maintain strict parda with alien men.

Jindan engaged Newmarch, a lawyer at Calcutta High Court, to fight her case, demanding a chargesheet and impartial investigation. Obtaining pen and paper, she wrote several letters. A letter to Sher Singh:

The first thing to be done is to root out the feringees. Use the same wiles that they have used and expel them from Lahore! Exert yourself to the utmost in ways you think best, by soft words or by force whichever appears best suited for destroying our enemies. Above all, be confident... If you require funds, send your people to Sheikhupura, you will find in a well outside the house, a crore and sixty lakh rupees... I shall return. My thoughts night and day are fixed on Punjab.

She wrote to Diwan Mul Raj,

By the grace of Satguru I am well and pray for your welfare... You have settled matters well with the British. They have lost their ascendancy. They tremble with fear, have abandoned food, and their tongues falter. Be confident and firm... Give the British whom you have taken prisoner, one hundred blows daily, blacken their faces, parade them on donkeys through your camp. Cut off their noses. Soon not one Britisher will be left on the land. Proclaim by beat of drum—all who enter the Maharaja's service will be rewarded. Collect 1–2,000 able-bodied men, disperse them as fakirs and send them across the Sutlej. Instruct them to watch the British during day and kill them at night. The British have hardly 1–2,000 men in this part of the country, and at night they sleep with no one near them.

She added: 'They do not molest me at all, being afraid to do so.'

Jindan planned a daring escape. She experimented: one day, Hargo disguised herself as a servitor, and managed to leave the fort. When inquiries were made, Jindan claimed she learnt of Hargo's absence only during morning prayers. Hargo was found and brought back. But the next day, Jindan was sent to Chunar

Fort, a state prison, with 17 maidservants. When they reached the magnificent fort by the Ganga, she refused to show her hand for identification. Captain Rees came daily to the fort, and exchanged a few words with her, across a screen. She requested permission for a tailor, and the seamstress came often (from 5 April 1849).

On 15 April, Rees found the Maharani's voice huskier than usual; she had a cold. Two days later, he informed MacGregor about the changed voice. Another two days later, female attendants screamed through prison bars that the Rani was missing. Disguised as the seamstress, she had left the fort; a Punjabi boatman awaited her by the river, and she had made good her escape!

The Britishers in-charge of her incarceration couldn't identify her since they had never set eyes upon her. Lt Nelson noted, 'It was a ruse which the Maharani deftly played.' A letter was found near the gate of Chunar Fort:

> I committed no crime yet you put me in a cage and locked me up... For all your locks and sentries, I got out by my magic. You will want to punish my attendants, but they knew nothing... I got harsh treatment and have borne it. Now we will see how Punjab will be finally settled... I shall never again encounter your wiles.

A warrant was issued for her arrest and sent throughout north India, but the queen was untraceable. Her perfectly executed escape was a moment of triumph for the rebels, and extremely discreditable to the British. Dalhousie was only thankful she had not escaped Sheikhupura Fort, for 'her presence among the Sikhs, as the widow of Ranjit Singh, would have roused their enthusiasm and greatly encouraged and strengthened them during the kingdom-wide revolt'. MacGregor noted that her attendants were 'superior persons who can read and write, treated by her with consideration, and doubtless proved useful aides in carrying out her various plans'. They were sent back to Punjab.

Jindan travelled dressed as a jogin, calling herself Parvati, traversing fields and forests, sleeping in temples and dharamsalas. On 21 May, she crossed into Nepal, with pilgrims to Pashupatinath temple. In Kathmandu, she met the royal family, old friends of her late husband. The Rana granted her asylum and a residence in Kathmandu. She met the British Resident and appealed for personal attendants Gulabo and Ratni to be restored to her; of course, they never were. The Resident discouraged the Rana from interacting with 'this restless and intriguing lady'. Dalhousie instructed the Rana to 'not permit the Maharani to carry out any intrigue', calling her 'a bitter enemy of the British'. He offered to 'extend clemency' to her should she return to India as a loyal subject of the British government.

Jindan continued her subversive activities. Parsu Ram and Sitaram, co-conspirators, went regularly between Nepal and Allahabad; they compiled lists of soldiers for mobilization at Allahabad, Kanpur and Lucknow cantonments. She wrote to Gurdial Singh, to raise men in preparation for rebellion at Peshawar, and sent similar instructions to Narain Das in Banaras and Isree Singh in Calcutta. She instructed Kahan Singh's son in Amritsar, to 'make known in the Manjha country that in the month of Kooar when the insurrection breaks out at Peshawar you must also rise'. She wrote to Raja Lal Singh of the Khalsa Durbar, asking him to urge Barukzai chief Mohammad Khan to rise against the British. She wrote to Raja Sher Singh: 'I, who am a woman, escaped from the Fort of Chuanar. You are a man, better make good your escape by bribing the guards.' To Buta Singh and Lal Singh, prisoners in Allahabad jail, Jindan wrote, 'Let your mind be at ease. We are not sitting idle. Bagha will explain the steps we have taken. It is hoped we will be crowned with success, in a few days.'

In September 1850, the British intercepted some letters; and ordered the Nepal Durbar to curb the Maharani's activities. A few Sikhs were caught coming to meet her; she tried to pass on ₹2,000 to them. The Rana warned Jindan against continuing anti-British activities. She considered moving to Jammu and Kashmir, but her correspondence with Maharaja Gulab Singh, who agreed to ally with her, was intercepted, and the Governor-General issued a statement: 'If Maharani Jind Kaur tries to enter British territories, she will be seized and imprisoned more severely than was done earlier.'

Jindan contributed tirelessly to building revolutionary consciousness in north India. During 1857–58, she remained in touch with the rebels. The Punjab Commissioner described her ex-attendant Chet Singh as 'a known rebel', who travelled between Punjab and Nepal 'at the height of the Mutiny'. But with the crushing of the uprising, Jindan's hopes for free Punjab were snuffed out.

She fervently desired to meet her son, Duleep Singh, and finally the government agreed. She travelled to Calcutta, where he too came. She had nursed the image of a Sikh warrior-king, and was shattered to see cropped hair; she resolved to draw him back to his history and culture. They sailed off, reaching London in June 1861.

Initially she was not allowed to live with him; she lived alone, meeting Duleep twice a day. An acquaintance, Lady Login, found Jindan 'prematurely old, well-nigh blind, broken but not subdued in spirit'. Duleep requested permission to take her to his estate in Yorkshire. There, she educated him on their joint heritage, injustices wrought by the British and explained the Gurbani. These revelations had a profound impact on the young man, who had been dispossessed, transplanted and kept ignorant of the history of his people. Duleep became a crusader against British imperialism.

Jindan died in August 1863. A few months later, Duleep came to India, but was denied entry into Punjab. He immersed his mother's ashes in the Godavari, near Nasik, and built a small memorial. Sixty years later, his daughter, the suffragette Sophia Duleep Singh, reinterred Jindan's remains next to Ranjit Singh's at Lahore, just as her grandmother had wished.

Maharani Jind Kaur was a magnificent fighter, whose sacrifices and spirited strategems kept the lamp of liberty burning. Tragically, we barely remember her, and the immeasurable contributions she made, paving the way to ultimate victory. The colonial government violently crushed her. Surely we, who are free due to efforts such as hers, need to reclaim and honour her legacy of great courage.

54 | Avanti:
Lodestar and Youth Icon
1831-58, Chhattisgarh and Madhya Pradesh

Avanti Bai Lodhi fought to protect Ramgarh as well as neighbouring states of central India against British takeover. She ruled as a capable and popular queen for four glorious months, in liberated parts of central India. But the colonizers, aggressive and unprincipled, gathered forces and returned with a vengeance. Avanti Bai engaged in guerilla warfare in the forested hills and valleys she knew well, and died fighting, not yet 30 years old. She is celebrated, especially by the Lodhi community, as a fierce revolutionary, a lodestar who guided others with her leadership and a youth icon.

Avanti was born in Mankedi, a tiny village on the banks of the Narmada, in present-day Dindori district of Madhya Pradesh. Her father Jujhar Singh was zamindar of 187 villages. She grew up learning horse riding, sword fighting and hunting in surrounding thick jungles. At 18, she married Vikramjeet Singh, whose father Lakshman Singh was Raja of Ramgarh, a state established in the seventeenth century by Gar Singh Lodh. A year later, her father-in-law passed away and Vikramjeet became ruler. The couple had two children, Amaan Singh and Sher Singh.

When Vikramjeet fell grievously ill in 1851, Avanti took charge of the administration. In September 1851, Dalhousie brought Ramgarh under the Court of Wards, declaring Vikramjeet unfit to rule, and refusing to accept Amaan or Sher Singh as heirs. When Vikramjeet died, rather than accept Avanti governing in her own name or as regent for her son Amaan Singh, the East India Company appointed two administrators, and dismissed Avanti with a meagre pension.

In Ramgarh and the rest of the Jabalpur Garha-Mandla range, signs of insurrection appeared in January 1857, in the form of small chapatis sent secretly from village to village, a message to mobilize. In June, a soldier in Jabalpur attacked and killed a British officer. Avanti Bai allied with soldiers, peasants, zamindars and rulers of neighbouring kingdoms to defeat British imperialism. Key rebels included Raja of Garha-Mandla Shankar Shah, his son Raghunath Shah, Saryu Prasad of Vijay-Raghavgarh, Khuman Singh Gond of Mukam and Rajas of Sohagpur, Hirapur, Kothi-Nigwani, Sukhri-Buragi and Shahpura. In July 1857, Avanti Bai and her allies won Suhagpur and Shahpura; the British faced ignomionous defeat, Captain Washington fleeing from the front.

In September, the British government arrested Shankar Shah and Raghunath Shah on charges of sedition, and executed them— by tying them to cannons which were blasted. Shankar Shah's brutal slaughter further incensed the public. The 52nd Regiment revolted in Jabalpur the same night, rebellion spread to Patan and Sleemanabad cantonments, and intensified in Ramgarh: 'When news of Shankar Shah's execution reached Mandla District, the Rani of Ramgarh broke into rebellion, drove the British officials from Ramgarh, siezed Ramgarh and took over its governance in the name of her son.'[105]

The commissioner of Jabalpur ordered Avanti Bai to meet the Mandla deputy collector. Instead, she prepared for war. She strengthened walls and ramparts of the fort of Ramgarh, and circulated small prasad packets among the people, each containing two black bangles and a hand-written note: 'Raise your swords and prepare to battle against the invaders, or wear these bangles and stay home.' Secret meetings were held all over.

The commissioner of Jabalpur reported:

> Under the able leadership of widowed Rani Avantibai of Ramgarh and young Raja Saryu Prasad, 4000 rebels, enraged and insulted by the death of Raja Shankar Sahi, have gathered and are prepared for armed revolt. They have gathered in the area north of Narmada River.

Avanti Bai and her comrades registered victory after victory. Her army commander captured Bhua Bichiya, Avanti Bai captured Ghughri and her allies captured Ramnagar. Except for Mandla town, the entire area was liberated. The rebel forces camped at Kheri village, just east of Mandla. Soldiers from Khadadevra joined them, and from Shahpura and Mukam. In the Battle of Kheri (November 1857), the British were vanquished. Deputy Commissioner Waddington and other officials fled from Mandla, terrified. The entire Mandla district and Ramgarh state were liberated.

Avanti Bai ruled both Mandla and Ramgarh, from early December 1857. The region enjoyed the benevolent rule of its queen, albeit for a short time. This will forever be recalled as a glorious chapter in the history of central India. Having freed Ramgarh and Mandla from the oppressive power of alien rulers, she established autonomous and independent government.

The British, determined to recover territories and reputation, marched towards Ramgarh with Nagpur Infantry, 52nd Native Infantry and local police. On 26 March 1858, they attacked and took control of Vijay-Raghavgarh. Raja Saryu Prasad escaped and went underground. On 31 March, the British occupied Ghughri, and thereafter trounced the revolutionaries in Narayanganj, Patan and Sleemanabad.

On 2 April 1858, they launched a massive attack on Ramgarh Fort in a pincer formation. Avanti Bai and her troops fought back fiercely, but it was a lost battle due to sheer numbers and arms and ammunition on the British side. When there was no hope left, Avanti Bai and her family escaped and rode towards the thickly forested hills of Deohargarh. The British plundered and destroyed Ramgarh.

In Deohargarh forests, living in caves amid wild animals, Avanti Bai gathered her scattered army. When Waddington heard, he requisitioned troops from the Raja of Rewa, and attacked Rani Avanti Bai's guerilla fighters. On 9 April 1858, fierce battle raged in Deohargarh forest, on one side colonial invaders, on the other a revolutionary guerilla army. Avanti's small band of brave fighters used guerrilla warfare tactics, defending and attacking, and plunged the enemy camp into chaos. However, their spirit and strategy could not withstand brute strength. Her soldiers sacrificed their lives, not one fleeing from the arena.

Faced with the prospect of defeat, Avanti Bai Lodhi, like Rani Durgavati two centuries earlier, stabbed and killed herself rather than surrender.

Avanti Bai is remembered in local folklore, and claimed today as an important icon among youth, women, Dalits as well as Rajputs. Her history has taken on mythical proportions in popular culture; historians are scrambling to catch up, and provide well-researched accounts of her life and contributions.

55 | Jhalkari, Lakshmi: Twin Warriors

Mid-Ninteenth Century, Jhansi, Central India

Jhalkari Bai led the Durga Dal, the women's wing of Rani Lakshmibai's army. Her striking resemblance to Lakshmibai led to a clever military strategy. During 1857–58, Lakshmibai and her troops fought courageously, but could not match British artillery. When Lakshmibai escaped from Jhansi Fort, Jhalkari replaced her, thus distracting the British forces and allowing Lakshmibai to speed away, so as to continue the struggle. Lakshmibai and Jhalkari Bai are immortalized in folk songs and legends of Bundelkhand. Throughout India, Lakshmibai is synonymous with courage; Jhalkari Bai, in contrast, is little known.

Lakshmibai (1835–58) was born in a Bramhin family in Varanasi. Her mother Bhagirathi died when she was small; her father Moropant Tambe took her to Peshwa Baji Rao II's palace in Bithoor, where she studied, and learnt horse riding, sword fighting and mallakhamb (wrestling). She married Raja Gangadhar Rao of Jhansi in 1841; her father too moved to Jhansi, later remarrying a young woman, Chimabai.

Gangadhar Rao was 21 years older than Lakshmi, and more interested in art than administration. Lakshmi familiarized herself with state governance, and often rode out from the fortified palace to meet people in different neighbourhoods of the city. In 1851, she had a son, who lived only four months. Gangadhar Rao fell ill; before his death in 1853, they adopted five-year-old Damodar Rao. The British, unreasonably, refused to accept Damodar Rao as a legitimate heir. In March 1854, British Agent Ellis announced annexation of Jhansi. Lakshmibai, from her throne at one end of the Diwan-e-Khas, behind a fine screen, declared in ringing tones, '*Main apni Jhansi nahin doongi* [I will not give my Jhansi].' She was ejected from the fort and relegated to a Rani Mahal, with a pension. Her letters arguing and petitioning against the annexation went unanswered. The entire populace felt humiliated. The British imposed heavy taxes on farmers, and drove artisans to pauperization.

On 4 June 1857, soldiers of artillery and infantry divisions of the Company's army in Jhansi declared mutiny. Officers, their wives and children took refuge in a fortress, Star Fort. Lakshmibai advised them to shift to nearby Sagar or Datia, since Jhansi was utterly unprotected. Four days later, rebel soldiers killed all 66 people within Star Fort. Unconscionably, Governor-General Canning blamed Rani Lakshmibai for this massacre.

They referred to Lakshmibai as the 'Rebel Queen', yet allowed her to govern Jhansi while they confronted the wider conflagration. From June 1857 to March 1858, Lakshmibai ruled Jhansi:

> She proved herself a most capable ruler. She established a mint, issued currency, fortified the strong places, cast cannon, raised fresh troops. Into every act of her government she threw all the energy of a strong and resolute character. Possessing considerable personal attractions, young, vigorous, and not afraid to show herself to the multitude, she gained a great influence over the hearts of her people. It was this influence, this force of character, added

to a splendid and inspiring courage that enabled her some months later to offer to the English troops, a [remarkable] resistance.[106]

After the Rani occupied the fort in June 1857, normal life was restored and the people of Jhansi rejoiced, even as they prepared for battle. Lakshmibai recruited thousands of citizen-soldiers, and strengthened the city's defences. She replaced the Union Jack with her own blood-red flag. In her army, she included Dalits, despite opposition from 'upper' castes, and women, though opposed by patriarchal forces. Members of her women's brigade, Durga Dal, included Kashi, Sundari, Mandari, Heera Korin, Juhi, Motibai Natakwali, Gangubai and Jhalkari Bai Korin.

Jhalkari Bai (1830–58) was born in Bhojla village, near Jhansi, and learnt weaving from her parents Jamna and Sadova Kori. People of the area say that one day, a tiger attacked Jhalkari while she was gathering wood in the forest. Her friends, the boys Channi and Ramchi, froze with fear, but Jhalkari struck the tiger dead with an axe blow on its forehead. Another time, assaulted by ruffians while walking with a girlfriend, Jhalkari dealt them fatal blows. Her reputation spread to Jhansi city, and Pooran Kori's family approached her parents. She married Pooran, a weaver like herself, and, with him, practised martial arts.

Lakshmibai heard of Jhalkari's bravery, and invited her to join as commander of the Durga Dal. Lakshmibai trained women recruits every morning, while Jhalkari continued the training during the afternoon. They honed their skills in archery, sword fighting and mallakhamb, and learnt how to fire pistols and ignite cannons. They practised horse riding in surrounding forests and fields. Dalit women joined in large numbers, as well as some Kshatriyas and Brahmins. The appeal to women's patriotism was stark: '*Churi forwai ke nevta, sindoor pochwai ke nevta* [Invitation to smash your bangles, and wipe vermilion off your foreheads].'

Koris, Kolis, Lodhis, Telis, Jatavs and others were included in the Jhansi army. Pooran was in the army, as was Jhalkari's father, Sadova. Lakshmibai faced massive opposition for her inclusive policy, as did Jhalkari: they were accused of destroying culture and tradition. While training women soldiers, once Jhalkari accidentally shot a Brahmin's cow in the leg. The owner hid his cow, and accused Jhalkari of having killed it; the panchayat imposed a boycott on Jhalkari and her family. Lakshmibai held a trial, in which Jhalkari Bai was exonerated—justice prevailed.

One day, dacoit Sagar Singh and his men surrounded Jhalkari. When he realized who she was, he apologized, and at Jhalkari's behest, gave up dacoity. Lakshmibai appointed him in the army, where he served honourably. People of Bundelkhand sing of the Rani in folk songs:

> She made soldiers out of soil,
> And swords out of wood
> She picked up mountains and made horses,
> And off she rode to Gwalior.

In the words of Rahi Masoon Raza:

> Suddenly there was silence, here comes the Rani
> The army was the oyster, the pearl was the Rani

In the words of Makhmoor Jallundhari:

> Laxmibai the sword and shield in your hands
> Is your jewelry, your string of pearls

In March 1858, British forces attacked Jhansi. On 20 March, they surrounded Jhansi Fort. To Jhansi's 30 cannons, they had more than 120, yet Jhansi answered fire with fire. Fierce battle raged; women clad in Pathan outfits were part of the fighting forces. Jhansi's troops valiantly defended the fort, and inflicted heavy damages. Rose, commander of the force, later wrote: 'It was clear that the people have plunged into this struggle of resistance with a strong determination which is apparent everywhere. Politically, it could be said that the leaders knew fully that the rebellion in central India would end as soon as Jhansi, the wealthiest Hindu city and the strongest fort, fell.'

By evening, cannons caused cracks in the walls; at night Lakshmibai's masons, draped in black, repaired the cracks. Rose decided his soldiers would enter the fort by scaling the walls, using ladders. They arrived at dawn and fixed rope ladders, but suddenly torches lit up the fort, the Rani's bugle sounded, Durga Dal warriors poured large vats of hot oil and rained arrows on the invading soldiers. The women's contingent strategically repulsed the attack, twisting the rope ladders around enemy soldiers' necks, injuring and killing many, while others ran helter-skelter. The British stratagem proved an utter failure.

However, Rose concocted another plan, which involved bribing the guard stationed at the fort's south gate. Thus his troops deceitfully breached the city's defences, forced their way in and stormed the city. Every step of the way they faced resistance from soldiers and ordinary citizens.

Amid the mayhem, Lakshmibai's advisors, including Jhalkari, persuaded her to leave the fort. Lakshmibai knew that so long as she remained alive, people would have some hope. With her son Damodar Rao strapped to her mare Sarangi, she rode off swiftly towards Kalpi. Kashi and Mandar fled with her, a few officers and 400 soldiers. They fooled three layers of British soldiers, saying they were riding from Orchha to aid the British.

Jhalkari, meanwhile, swung into action. She changed into the Rani's clothes, donning armour, jewellery and royal turban. Thus disguised, she emerged from the royal chambers and went out of the fort to fulfil her unique mission. Jhalkari knew that if the British got a whiff of Lakshmibai's escape, they would be hot in pursuit. By distracting them, she won precious time. Fearless, she rode into the British encampment towards Rose's tent. He was confabulating with Dulhaju, a traitor, when suddenly the 'Rani' rode right up to his tent. In great confusion, Rose stepped out. He roared: 'Put down your arms! Consider yourself captive!' She chastised him sharply: 'Do you foreigners have no manners? Do you not know how to address a queen? Is this your civilization and culture?' Thus rebuked, Rose sobered down.

Sergeant Stuart rushing up, leering at her: 'O, she is beautiful!' She turned upon him: 'Is this how you treat women? No man talks thus to us!' British soldiers were awe-struck. The enemy queen was dazzling, courageous and self-respecting

Jhalkari said: 'I have come to surrender. In exchange, you must pardon the citizens of Jhansi.' Rose tried to extract sundry information from her; she conversed readily, confusing the officers with meaningless talk, throwing the camp into disarray. Time elapsed and she was relieved knowing that every minute counted for the Rani to make good her escape. Then Dalhaju came out, and shouted: 'This is not the queen! This is Jhalkari Bai, who looks like the queen.'

Rose ordered his men to capture and kill Jhalkari. She brandished her double-bladed sword, and killed soldiers who came up. The perplexed general asked: 'What punishment shall I give you?'

She replied, 'Death by hanging!'

Some folk stories say that after discovering the impersonation, the British shot Jhalkari dead; or imprisoned her for several years. Other versions claim that Rose, overwhelmed by her courage, let Jhalkari go, and she rode back to the fort. Pooran had already died fighting; she too was martyred later that day. Yet another version tells us that Jhalkari survived the war, and lived on in Jhansi for another three decades.

∽

Rose's troops plundered the city and looted the palace, burnt houses, and killed unarmed civilians. They massacred over 10,000 people and reduced the flourishing city to rubble. He sent soldiers in pursuit of Rani Lakshmibai. At Bhandir, they engaged in battle. Lakshmibai struck an officer, Dowker, with her sword, knocking him off his horse. She lost 250 soldiers but escaped, and joined Tatya Tope at Kalpi. Her father Moropant and a few others rode out in another direction, but were captured; he was hanged on 19 April.

Lakshmibai and Tatya Tope together attacked and occupied Gwalior Fort—an incredible victory. The Company summoned massive forces to re-establish control over Gwalior. On the scorching summer morning of 16 June 1858, Lakshmibai led a countercharge with what remained of her Jhansi contingent. She fought her last battle on 17 June 1858, in Kotah-ki-Sarai at the outskirts of Gwalior:

> Amongst the fugitives in the rebel ranks was the resolute woman who, alike in council and on the field, was the soul of the conspirators. Clad in the attire of a man and mounted on horseback, the Rani of Jhansi might have been seen animating her troops throughout the day. When inch by inch the British troops pressed through the defile, and when reaching its summit Smith ordered the hussars to charge, the Rani of Jhansi boldly fronted the British horsemen... A hussar close upon her track, ignorant of her sex and her rank, cut her down. She fell to rise no more. That night her devoted followers, determined that the

English should not boast that they had captured her even dead, burned the body. Rose reported that she was interred 'with great ceremony under a tamarind tree beneath the Rock of Gwalior'.[107]

Her name has been synonymous ever since with courage; her twin too is emerging from the shadows.

56 | Uda, Hazrat Mahal: Sharpshooter, Guerrillera

Nineteenth Century, Avadh, UP

Uda Pasi displayed exemplary courage on the battlefront of Lucknow. Known as a sharpshooter, she was a leading member of the battalion of women formed by Begum Hazrat Mahal during the 1857 Rebellion. Hazrat Mahal, with her army, challenged the might of the Company and kept up the longest resistance, resorting—after Lucknow was finally lost—to guerilla warfare over one year. Uda's role was little known until recently, and even the astonishing contributions of Hazrat Mahal need to be better understood.

Uda (?– 1847) was a Pasi, from Ujriaon village, near Lucknow. She was known also as Jagrani—appropriately enough, for she was a leader among the common people. Her husband, Makka Pasi, was also a soldier in the struggle against British imperialism. He was killed while fighting at the battle of Chinhat, in June 1847. Her husband's martyrdom added an extra edge of grief and fury to Uda's commitment to oust the British.

Uda was also keen to avenge the oppression faced by Pasis at the hands of the Company. In Avadh, Pasis were traditionally employed as chowkidars, but the British removed them from their posts and thus snatched away their income. After defeating the British and taking charge of the state in July 1857, Begum Hazrat Mahal announced at a public meeting, 'Pasis know that guarding every town and city is their ancestral duty. But the British appointed others in place of the Pasis, and so deprived them of their livelihood. This will not be repeated.'

We have only one specific account of Uda—her participation in battle in November 1857. Recorded in history, this became the defining moment of her life and work. She was a combatant in one of the fiercest battles of the uprising—the Battle of Sikandar Bagh. Sikandar Bagh, a walled garden, was occupied by thousands of Indian soldiers. Commander Campbell was sent to rescue Europeans besieged in the Residency. Sikandar Bagh fell on his route, and he planned to capture it on his way to the Residency. A pitched battle ensued.

As the story goes, British soldiers were taken by surprise to find bullets raining down, apparently from the heavens. In fact, a revolutionary soldier, perched atop a tall pipal tree, was firing from that height. This was Uda Devi, well hidden by dense foliage! Taking aim unerringly, she killed many unsuspecting soldiers, fighting on the ground. Meanwhile, one soldier spied her, and one of his shots found its target—she was killed.

Only later did the British discover that the person shooting so accurately was a woman, identified as Uda Devi. An officer wrote:

> She was armed with a pair of heavy old-pattern cavalry pistols, one of which was in her belt still loaded, and her pouch was still about half full of ammunition, while from her perch in the tree, which had been carefully prepared before the attack, she had killed more than half-a-dozen men.[108]

Some accounts say she killed over 30 soldiers.

Some 2,000 Indian soldiers were killed in Sikandar Bagh that day; it was the beginning of the end for the Indian revolutionaries. The British recognized the courage of Indian patriots. It is said that even Campbell respectfully bowed his head over the dead body of Uda Devi. Today, the brave woman warrior's statue stands proud in the square outside Sikandar Bagh.

Uda Devi was one of many brave women soldiers in Hazrat Mahal's army. When male soldiers started losing morale, the women's unit took up the gauntlet and infused new energy into the First War of Independence. Women in Hazrat Mahal's army were from diverse backgrounds—Dalits, Muslims and Hindus of various castes. Some armed with rifles and others with muskets, they were tough and intrepid:

> *Koi unko habsin kehta, koi kehta neech achchut,*
> *abla koi unhein batlaye, koi kahe unhe majboot.*

Some called them Africans, others dubbed them lowly untouchable,
Some said they were defenceless, others called them tough and strong.[109]

Hazrat Mahal (1820–79), named Mohammadi Khanum at birth, was the child of a tawaif and a slave, Umber. She learnt music and dance, and her parents sold her as a young girl to Wajid Ali Shah, to serve as a personal attendant to one of his Begums. He soon promoted her to the status of 'Pari' and inducted her into his 'Parikhana'. He called her 'Mahak Pari' (Fragrant Fairy), and for a while was infatuated with her. In his harem's hierarchy, a 'Pari' stood lower than a wife.

When Mahak Pari became pregnant, Wajid Ali had her placed in parda. She gave birth to a son, Birjis Qudr, in 1845, and he bestowed upon her the title 'Hazrat Mahal', and raised her to the position of Begum. Subsequently, at some point, she was divorced from Wajid Ali, but continued to live in the harem.[110] She was interested in the politics of the day, while he was immersed in dance and music. The British declared Wajid Ali incapable of managing the state, and the Resident at Lucknow proposed a treaty by which Avadh would be annexed.

Hazrat Mahal managed to persuade Wajid Ali to resist the treaty. At his refusal, in March 1856, the British deposed and forcibly removed him to Calcutta. His mother and three wives (including Khas Mahal and Akhtar Mahal) accompanied him, but most wives were left behind, along with nine divorced women including Hazrat Mahal.

Hazrat Mahal took charge of the state. Determined to check British imperialist designs, she mobilized forces. Disbanding the Nawab's troops had released 30,000 soldiers, many of whom were angry and inclined to rebellion. On 7 May 1857, two platoons of the British army at Musa Bagh, Lucknow, refused to obey their commander's orders. Avadh was in ferment: Hazrat Begum's allies included Raja Jailal Singh of Azamgarh, Sarafad-daulah, Maharaj Bal Krishna, Mammu Khan, Rana Beni Madho Baksh of Baiswara, Raja Drig Bijai Singh of Mahona, Ahmadshah of Faizabad and Raja Man Singh.

On 30 June 1857, troops led by Ahmadshah attacked the British forces in Chinhat. Joint slogans of 'Allah-o-Akbar' and 'Jai Bajrang Bali' rent the air. Indian forces won a spectacular victory. The city was under siege, and most British officers, women and children took refuge in the Lucknow Residency.

During the 30-week siege of Lucknow, from July to November 1857, Hazrat Begum effectively ruled as regent for her minor son. On 5 July, she declared her son, 11-year-old Birjis Qudr, heir to the throne of Avadh, under Mughal suzerainty. She held a coronation ceremony for Birjis in Baradari, Qaiserbagh Palace, and sent a message to Bahadur Shah Zafar heralding the end of British rule. On 16 July 1857, her forces opened fire on Beligarad. The British had lost control of the city.

Hazrat Mahal made Begum Kothi her army headquarters,

and strengthened the armed forces. She appointed capable administrative officers, both Hindu and Muslim, raised soldiers' salaries and built the women's brigade, training them well. Her firmans instilled energy and enthusiasm in the people of Avadh. A British officer wrote: 'This Begam exhibits great energy and ability. She has excited all Oudh to take up the interests of her son, and the chiefs have sworn to be faithful to him. The Begum declares undying war against us.'[111]

She mocked the British claim of allowing freedom of worship: 'To eat pigs and drink wine, to bite greased cartridges and to mix pig's fat with sweetmeats, to destroy Hindu and Mussalman temples on pretense of making roads...with all this, how can people believe that religion will not be interfered with?'

The British gathered their forces and mounted attack on Lucknow. On 21 September 1857, Hazrat Mahal's troops engaged in pitched battle at Aalambagh. Four days later, the British captured the Residency. However, they were unable to wrest Lucknow: Hazrat Mahal continued her reign as regent. She had the largest army of all the forces that fought during the First War of Independence; her troops fought for Jaunpur, Azamgarh and Allahabad, where the British faced defeat in various battles.

She laid a plan to ambush Fort William in Calcutta, where Wajid Ali was captive; however, the plan could not materialize. Wajid Ali, highly appreciative of Hazrat Mahal's fighting spirit, wrote:

> Calamity befell houses in the morn, my bazaars were
> looted, Hazrat Mahal,
> You alone are a source of comfort, o comforter of the
> poor, Hazrat Mahal.

The British refurbished their arms, ammunition and troops, and the tide began to turn. In February 1858, Ahmadshah was grievously injured, and Lucknow's prime minister, Balkrishna Rao, died fighting. In early March, British forces, under Campbell and Outram, attacked Hazrat Mahal's troops in Lucknow. Fierce battle raged for 10 days, 6–15 March. On 16 March, the British captured Begum Kothi and Qaisarbagh, and on 21 March, established their rule over the entire city.

With this began a new revolutionary saga of guerrilla warfare. Hazrat Mahal escaped into the countryside and, with some 6,000 soldiers, continued war. They sheltered in ruins and caves, ferried across rivers and canals, traversed hillocks. They smashed police posts, and attacked stray enemy soldiers. Among her allies were Nana Sahib, the queen of Tulsipur and Raja Devibaksh of Gonda. Hazrat Mahal and Nana Saheb rescued Ahmadshah, though subsequently he was killed treacherously.

The British burnt entire villages, captured revolutionaries and supporters, and ruthlessly executed them. Hazrat Mahal and her trusted allies kept up the resistance against incredible odds. Villagers sheltered and fed them, for which they were punished brutally, if caught. For over a year, Hazrat Mahal remained underground and kept up the insurgency. By November 1859, her forces were worn and depleted. The British had hunted down her troops, and planted their flag over most of Avadh. She was a fugitive, one of the most wanted persons; she was also utterly exhausted and despairng.

Hazrat Mahal crossed over to Nepal to rejuvenate her energies. She still hoped to strike at an opportune moment, and reclaim Lucknow. Birjis Qudr was with her. The British offered truce thrice, but she challenged their sincerity. Troops loyal to her took refuge in places around the Indo-Nepal border. In Kathmandu, the Rana granted her asylum, and she built a residence, Barf Bagh, with a masjid and imambara in the precincts.

Hazrat Mahal longed to fight for a free Avadh, but lived

the rest of her life in exile. She died in April 1879, and was buried in the compound of her house. Her tomb has this couplet inscribed on it:

Ai bad-e-saba aahista chal
Yahan soee hui hai Mahak Pari.

O' zephyr, blow sweet and calm
Here lies in slumber Mahak Pari.

In 1962, Victoria Park in Lucknow was renamed Begum Hazrat Mahal Park. At a gathering to commemorate her, the organizers noted: 'Never forget how the entire city united under the leadership of Begum Hazrat Mahal to stand up against the British.' Birjis Qudr moved to Calcutta; he passed away in 1893. Hazrat Mahal's great-grandson Kaukub Qudr Mirza, taught Urdu at Aligarh Muslim University, his daughter Manzilat Fatima studied in Aligarh, and now lives in Kolkata, where she educates people on Avadhi cuisine. When someone asked whether she received a recipe book as family heirloom, she replied: 'No! ... my great-great-grandmother, Hazrat Mahal, was a queen who was fighting the British, not writing cookbooks.'[112]

Thankfully, between her family and the public of Lucknow, Hazrat Mahal's memory is robust and alive.

57 | Saguna, Savitri, Fatima, Mukta, Tara: 'The Future Is Ours'

Ninteenth Century, Maharashtra

Savitribai Phule (1831–97) is known as India's first female teacher. She was not alone: her colleagues Sagunabai Ksheersagar and Fatima Sheikh, too, were pioneers in girls' education, and education of Dalits. Indeed, the three were drivers of radical social change; their student Muktabai Salve, and associate, Tarabai Shinde, wrote powerfully on gender and caste.

Sagunabai Ksheersagar worked as an ayah in a British household, where she learnt to speak English. She was a child widow, and Jyotirao Phule's cousin. After Jyotirao lost his mother in childhood, Saguna nurtured him within the joint family. Saguna arranged for Jyotirao's studies in a missionary school, and inspired in him a love for education.

At the age of 13, Jyotirao married nine-year-old Savitri, who left her parents Lakshmi and Khandeji Nevase in Naigaon village, and settled with her in-laws in Poona. Saguna became a mother-figure to her too. An unusual activity soon occurred: Savitri and Saguna began learning to read and write from Jyotirao. Both proved to be excellent pupils.

Five or six years later, Savitri enrolled in a school run by American missionary Cynthia Farrar, in Ahmednagar. Cynthia was an inspiring teacher, a single woman from Boston, who had travelled to Bombay in 1827 and, as superintendent of Girls' Schools, had enrolled more than 400 Indian girls in her schools by 1829; she worked in India until her death in 1862. Savitri, along with Sagunabai, also studied in the Normal School at Pune, a teacher training institution for girls run by Britisher Mrs Michelle. Savitri passed the fourth-year exam in 1847.

Fatima Sheikh, a classmate of Savitri's at the Normal School, became a close friend. In 1848, Saguna, Fatima, Savitri and Jyotirao Phule opened a school in Bhidewada, Pune, beginning with nine girls, from various castes and communities. The number soon grew to 25. No fees was charged; Fatima, Savitri and Saguna taught with great commitment, and no remuneration.

Fatima and Savitri walked from door to door, persuading people to send their children to school, discussing how education could improve their lives. Orthodox forces were furious at these efforts to educate girls, especially from 'untouchable' communities. When Savitri walked to school, people threw stones and cow dung at her. Fatima experienced similar harassment. They braved terrible persecution, and continued to work enthusiastically.

Members of the Mali caste, to which the Phules belonged, were enraged. They accosted Jyotirao's father, Govindrao Phule, who then issued an ultimatum—Jyotirao and Savitri must discontinue their work with Mahars and Mangs (Atishudras), or leave home. Savitri and Jyotirao left home, forsaken by family and community. Fatima Sheikh and her brother Usman Sheikh opened their home to them. The Phules lived with the Sheikh siblings in Mominpura, Ganj Peth, for several years (1849–57). Within the Sheikhs' *wada* (building), they started a school for adults.

Fatima Sheikh faced opposition both from Hindus, dominant in Pune, and orthodox Muslims. Muslims were broadly divided into elite Ashrafs, Ajlaf (backward caste) and Arzal (Dalit

Muslims). For a Muslim woman to step out across caste, class and religion, into the homes of 'untouchables', and teach their children, was unacceptable.

Savitri and Fatima kept their energies focused on teaching well. Their school curriculum included grammar, maths, geography and history. In 1852, Jyotirao and Savitribai were felicitated by the British government for their efforts for girls' education, and Savitribai was felicitated as the best teacher. A report in *The Poona Observer* (29 May 1852) noted:

> The number of girl students in Jotirao's school is ten times more than the number of boys studying in government schools. This is because the system for teaching girls is far superior to what is available for boys in government schools. If this situation continues, then the girls from Jotirao's school will prove superior to the boys from government schools.

Mukta Salve (1841–?) hailed from the Mang community. Her education began at the age of 11, in 1852, when Savitribai and the rest started their third girls' school at Vetal Peth. At the age of 14, Mukta wrote an essay, 'Mang Maharanchya Dukhavisatha' (About the Grief of Mangs and Mahars). She clearly stated that Brahminical religion cannot be the religion of the untouchables; and described the exploitation and miseries of Dalit women within caste-patriarchal society. Mukta's critique was spirited, and scathing:

> The Creator is the one who created the Mangs, Mahars and also brahmins and He is the one, who is filling me with wisdom to write... O learned pandits, wind up the selfish prattle of your hollow wisdom and listen to what I have to say.

...The brahmins have degraded us so low; they consider people like us even lower than cattle. Under Bajirao's rule, if any Mang or Mahar happened to pass in front of a gymnasium, they would cut off his head and play 'bat and ball' with their swords as bats and his head as a ball. When we were punished for even passing through their doors, where was the question of getting education, getting the freedom to learn?

...Nobody gives us employment because we are untouchables. We have to endure grinding poverty... When our women give birth to babies, they do not have even a roof over their heads. How they suffer in the rain and cold!

...Mang and Mahar children never dare to lodge a complaint if brahmin children throw stones and injure them seriously. They suffer silently because they know they have to go to the brahmin's house to beg for leftover food.

...Oh, the Mahars and Mangs, you are poor and sick. Only the medicine of knowledge will cure and heal you. People who treat you like animals, will not dare to anymore. So please work hard and study. Get educated...

Mukta's essay won a prize, and she read it out at a well-attended function. When Major Candy of Pune University presented the prize, she said: 'Sir, give us a library, not toys and goodies.'

The same year, Mukta's essay was published in *Dnyanodaya,* a Marathi periodical. This one essay has won her a special place in literary, feminist and Dalit histories.

Mukta lived in Mithgunj, near Ganj Peth. Her grandfather Lahuji Salve, a freedom fighter and wrestler, ran an akhara at Ganj Peth where Jyotiba would sometimes practise martial arts and discuss socio-political issues. Lahuji, along with Ranoji Mahar, urged Mangs and Mahars to send their children to school.

Later Lahuji joined the Satyashodhak Samaj. However, no further record of Mukta Salve is available.

∽

Savitribai's book, *Kavya Phule*, was published in 1854. She was one of the first modern, radical Marathi poets; her verses lyrical and thought-provoking:

Pledge

A smooth round rock with a coat of oil and saffron
And lo, behold, it becomes one of the Gods of the
pantheon
Buffaloes and what not, such terrifying Gods
Yet people believe them to be their Lord...
...If rocks can answer prayers and grant them children
What's the need for marriage between men and women?

Should They Be Called Humans?

The woman from dawn to dusk does labour
The man lives off her toil, the freeloader.
Even birds and beasts labour together
Should these idlers be called humans at all?

The Butterfly and the Bud

He shatters her beautiful form
And ravages her like a storm
Sucks her dry of all nectar
Lifeless, wasted he discards her...
Which flower bud?—he conveniently asks,
Forget the old and search anew is his task
Ways of the world, deception and promiscuity
I am aghast!—says Savitri

Meaning of the Word 'Shudra'

The word shudra in truth, connoted a native
But the powerful victors made shudra an invective
The ultimate victors, over the Iranis and Brahmins
Over Brahmins and British, the most radical were the
natives.
Wealthy were they, the original inhabitants
They were known by the name 'Indians'.
Such heroic people were our ancestors, see,
The descendants of such people are we.

Savitribai's poetry was rich in ideas. Jyotirao Phule's *Gulamgiri* (1873), published two decades after *Kavya Phule*, echoed many of the same ideas. It is a moot point whether Savitribai was the original source of several ideas which Jyotirao later developed, or perhaps they generated these ideas in tandem. Another collection of Savitri's poems, *Bavan Kashi Subodh Ratnakar* (The Ocean of Pure Gems), was published in 1891, and a collection of her speeches in 1892.

Savitri and Jyotirao had an unusual relationship—comrades, along with being a couple. Fatima and Savitri too shared a relationship of mutual respect, support and trust. Savitri once went to her mother's home in Naigaon, to recover from an illness. She wrote to Jyotirao, in October 1856:

> …my brother said, 'You and your husband have rightly been excommunicated because both of you serve the untouchables…' I told him, 'Brother, your mind is narrow, and the Brahmins' teaching has made it worse. Animals like goats and cows are not untouchable for you, you lovingly touch them… But you consider Mahars and Mangs, who are as human as you and I, untouchables… My husband

is a god-like man... Yes, we both teach girls, women, Mangs and Mahars. I get immeasurable joy by doing such service...' My brother finally came around, repented and asked for forgiveness. Mother said, 'Savitri, your tongue must be speaking God's own words. We are blessed by your words of wisdom.'...We shall overcome and success will be ours in the future. The future belongs to us.

While Savitri was away, Fatima handled the responsibility of running the schools. Savitri wrote: 'I know my absence causes Fatima so much trouble but I am sure she will understand and won't grumble.' When Savitri returned, Fatima's load lightened, and they worked with their customary synergy. In all, Savitri and her colleagues opened 18 schools, including a night school for peasants and labourers.

Savitri and Jyotirao built a house in Ganj Peth, where they shifted in 1857. They opened the well in their house to Shudras and Atishudras. To help destitute, exploited widows, they set up a shelter, Balhatya Pratibandhak Griha (Anti-Infanticide Protection Home)—where women stayed, delivered their babies and found care and counselling. Hundreds of women, mostly Brahmin, gave birth in this shelter; many may otherwise have killed themselves or their infants. In 1873, the Phules adopted a child, Yashwant, born at the shelter to one such widow.

Jyotiba and Savitribai started the Satyashodhak Samaj in 1873, to intensify social reform. Savitribai initiated 'Satyashodhak weddings' with no priest, and minimal cost; the bridegroom took an oath promising education and equal rights to the bride. In 1889, their son Yashwant married Radha Sasane in this manner. Prior to the wedding, Savitribai invited Radha to stay at their home, so that the young couple could get better acquainted. After Jyotirao's demise, in 1890, Savitri lit his funeral pyre—an unprecedented act.

She also took charge of the Satyashodhak Samaj.

In 1896, famine struck Maharashtra, and next year, the bubonic plague wreaked havoc in Pune. Savitri engaged in relief work throughout. Yashwant, a doctor, started a hospital for plague victims. One day, Savitribai carried an infected child from a Mahar settlement to the hospital. She herself contracted the disease and, on 10 March 1897, breathed her last.

∽

Tarabai Shinde (1850–1910), when young, was influenced by the current of radical thought represented by the Phules, and their colleagues. In 1882, she wrote a powerful treatise, *Stree Purush Tulana* (Comparison between Men and Women).

Tarabai was a member of the Satyashodak Samaj, and engaged with the schools as well as the work with widows. Hailing from a high-caste Maratha family, her father, a clerk in Buldana town, taught her Marathi, Sanskrit and English; he too was interested in the Satyashodhak Samaj. Tara was married young, her husband moved in with her family—an unusual arrangement. Even more unusually, she decided to have no children, a choice she actively defended. The details of her life are obscure.

Tarabai's book was a no-holds-barred, perceptive critique of gender arrangements. In Surat, a widow, Vijayalakshmi, was sentenced to death for undergoing an abortion, and journals castigated women's 'new loose morals'. Tarabai observed that society ought to stop treating all women as criminals, and making their lives a living hell.

She delineated atrocities committed against widows and wives, argued for ending child marriage and caste-based marriages and exposed double standards: 'But do men not suffer from the same flaws that women are supposed to have?' She set out the flaws commonly attributed to women and refuted each, pointing out that men displayed those same faults in more gross ways. She broadened the scope of analysis to include the entire ideological fabric of patriarchal, caste-based society.

Tarabai presented robust social commentary; boldly she questioned dominant religion: 'Let me ask you something, Gods! You are supposed to be omnipotent and freely accessible to all… Then why did you grant happiness only to men and brand women with nothing but agony?' She revealed inherent patriarchy in Hindu scriptures and rituals, and asserted that women everywhere were oppressed.

Five hundred copies of *Stree Purush Tulana* were printed in 1882. The reception was hostile: local newspapers ridiculed the work and condemned the writer. Jyotirao referred to her work in the Satyashodhak journal *Satsaar* (1885), suggesting that she was condemned because the men she criticized included those who wrote and published newspapers. The treatise fell into oblivion until its republication in 1975. It is possible that those vicious diatribes extended into her personal life, and perhaps she was forced into silence.

Stree Purush Tulana is today celebrated as India's first modern feminist text. Tarabai is dubbed one of the foremost 'makers of modern India'[113], and so indeed she was; but not in isolation—rather, as one in a long chain of women, who together have been a force in the making of India. Tarabai fought with words, sharp as a sword. Savitri, Saguna, Fatima, Mukta and Tara fought in different, multiple ways, supporting one another as best they could. Their vision of a truly democratic society is yet to be fulfilled; their dreams are still alive in countless hearts and minds. Recently (2019–20), a Fatima Sheikh Savitribai Phule Library was set up at Shaheen Bagh, a site of democratic protest for equal citizenship waged by women of all ages, including university students and homemakers from diverse religious backgrounds.

Their solidarity traces a marvelous trajectory from those subversive women of the past.

Yes, the future is ours. There are, and will be, more stories of life and liberty, subversion and solidarity.

Acknowledgments

I thank Rudra Narayan Sharma of Rupa Publications for approaching me, out of the blue, to write this book—a book I have always wanted to write. Although I could devote only late-night hours to working on it, the 'Rupa book' had me in its grip, the incredible women I was profiling kept me on track, and a continuous trickle of words emerged on paper (or rather the computer screen). My students were integral to the journey during 2017–18. While teaching them about gender during sociology and political science post-graduation classes, I would often discuss the lives and contributions of women in history, and clearly they were enthralled.

I was in Agra at the time, to be with my intrepid, nonagenarian father. Up to the end, he was immensely pleased that I write books, and his enthusiasm encouraged me. I am grateful to my mother for the firm feminist that she was. Decades ago, she wrote and directed a dance-drama called *She* (in Delhi University), where she brought alive several wonderful women through lively tableau. I absorbed ideas and inspiration while still a schoolgirl. Feminist storytelling is a powerful legacy. Our foremothers stretch back across time, and their stories are blessings that we carry forward from one generation to the next.

My friends had little choice but to hear various stories that I would narrate in spurts; my sister and brother-in-law took time out to read several of the stories. Brinda Balakrishnan read the manuscript at several stages and gave valuable suggestions; and my daughter was supportive at every stage.. A residency in 2019 at the Rockefeller Center, Bellagio, nurtured the writer in me.

I owe a debt of gratitude, of course, to each of the women profiled, for the lives they led, the resistance they waged, and the nurturance and inspiration they provide across the span of time. I would also like to thank the many awesome women whose stories I could not include—the exclusions are many, and are due entirely to my own limitations of language, time and space, sources and resources. I am painfully aware that some constituencies are under-represented, and some of the most powerful stories yet unrecorded, or inaccessible to me. I trust that other writers will continue to bring out many stories from different regions and contexts.

And finally, I would like to thank the editorial and design team at Rupa for their support and cheerful cooperation.

Notes

1. The 'Global Gender Gap Report' (World Economic Forum, March 2021) ranks India 140 out of 156 countries on the basis of economic participation and opportunity, health and survival, political empowerment and educational opportunity. Women's labour force participation and political participation rates are both low and declining, while violence against women is high and rising.

2. Mahabharata, Section CCCXXI, pp. 52–72, https://www.sacred-texts.com/hin/m12/m12c020.htm.

3. Vanita, Ruth. 'The Self Has No Gender: A Female and a Male Scholar Debate Women's Status in the Mahabharata', *Gandhi's Tiger and Sita's Smile: Essays on Gender, Sexuality and Culture*, Yoda Press, 2005, pp. 14–34.

4. Adapted from the following sources: Sri Aurobindo, *Rigveda: Samhita and Padapatha—Translations and Commentaries*, http://sri-aurobindo.in/workings/matherials/rigveda/01/01-179.htm; Doniger, Wendy. *Rigveda*, Penguin Classics, pp. 250–52; and Stephanie W. Jamison and Joel P. Brereton. *The Rigveda: 3-Volume Set*, Oxford University Press, 2014, pp. 379–84.

5. Susie Tharu and K. Lalita. *Women Writing in India: 600 BC to the Present. Volume 1: 600 BC to the Early Twentieth Century*, Oxford University Press, 1995, pp. 68–69.

6. Susan, Murcott. *First Buddhist Women: Poems and Stories of Awakening*, Parallax Press, 1991, p. 31.

7. *Therigatha: Poems of the First Buddhist Women*, translated by Charles Hallisey, Murty Classical Library of India, Harvard University Press, 2015, pp. 113–15. All the poems in this chapter are from this source: p. 67, pp. 72–75, pp. 113–15.

8. Ibid. 67, 72–75, 113–15.

9. McLoughlin, Margo. 'The Verses of Ambapali', *Parabola*, 2016, https://parabola.org/2016/11/08/the-verses-of-ambapali-by-margo-mcloughlin/.

10. *Therigatha: Poems of the First Buddhist Women,* translated by Charles Hallisey, Murty Classical Library of India, Harvard University Press, 2015, p. 268.

11. Falk, Nancy Auer. 'The Case of the Vanishing Nuns: The Fruits of Ambivalence in Ancient Indian Buddhism', *Unspoken Words: Women's Religious Lives,* edited by Nancy Auer Falk and Rita M. Gross, Wadsworth, 2001, pp. 196–206.

12. Chakravarti, Uma. 'The Rise of Women as Experienced by Buddhism', *Manushi*, November–December 1981.

13. *Therigatha: Poems of the First Buddhist Women,* translated by Charles Hallisey, Murty Classical Library of India, Harvard University Press, 2015, pp. 64–65.

14. Bodhi, Bhikkhu. *The Connected Discourses of the Buddha*, Wisdom Publications, 2000.

15. *Therigatha: Poems of the First Buddhist Women,* translated by Charles Hallisey, Murty Classical Library of India, Harvard University Press, 2015, pp. 78–79.

16. Ramanujan, A.K. *Poems of Love and War*, Oxford University Press, 2006, p. 55, p. 183, pp. 169–70.

17. Pechilis, Karen. *Interpreting Devotion: The Poetry and Legacy of a Female Bhakti Saint of India*, Routledge, 2012. Other poems in this chapter are from the same source.

18. McGlashan, Alastair. *The History of the Holy Servants of the Lord Siva—A Translation of the Periya Puranam of Cekkilar*, Trafford Publishing, 2006.

19. Sayed Ahmed and Farid Ahmed. 'The Maxims of Khona: A Contextual Study of Sustainability over Vernacular Architecture Practice of Bangladesh', *Journal of Modern Science and Technology*, 2015.

20. Sengupta, Mallika. 'Amra Hasya Amra Larai', transalted by Amitabha Mukerjee.

21. Raman, Sita Anantha. *Women in India: A Social and Cultural History*, Praeger, 2009, p. 178.

22. Dehejia, Vidya. *The Body Adorned: Dissolving Boundaries Between Sacred and Profane in Indian Art*, Mapin Publishing, 2009, pp. 140–41.

23. Priya Sarukkai Chabria and Ravi Shankar. *Andal: The Autobiography of a Goddess*, Zubaan, 2015, pp. 158, 165.

24. Dalrymple, William. 'In Search of Tamil Nadu's Poet-Preachers', *Financial Times*, 10 July 2015, https://www.ft.com/content/a01a138c-20b2-11e5-ab0f-6bb9974f25d0.

25. *Kalhana's Rajatarangini,* translated by Ranjit Sitaram Pandit, South Asia Books, 1990. *Rajatrangini* was written in 1149 (twelfth century). Kalhana chronicled the kings and several queens of Kashmir, including Yashovati of ancient times; Amritaprabha (sixth century), who hailed from Assam; and Sugandhadevi, who accompanied her husband Shakaravarman on military expeditions and, upon his death, ruled as regent for her son Gopalvarman (904–906); her coinage refers to her as 'Srisugandha Deva', and she was popular among her subjects.

26. Rabbani, G.M. *Ancient Kashmir: A Historical Perspective*, Gulshan Publishers, 1981.

27. Sitaram Pandit, Ranjit, *Kalhana's Rajatarangini*, South Asia Books, 1990.

28. Susie Tharu and K. Lalita. *Women Writing in India: 600 BC to the Present. Volume 1: 600 BC to the Early Twentieth Century*, Oxford University Press, Delhi, 1995, p. 79.

29. Ramanujan, A.K. *Speaking of Siva*, Penguin Classic, 1973, p. 134.

30. Ibid. 129.

31. Susie Tharu and K. Lalita. *Women Writing in India: 600 BC to the Present. Volume 1: 600 BC to the Early Twentieth Century*, Oxford University Press, Delhi, 1995, pp. 79–80.

32. Ramanujan, A.K. *Speaking of Siva*, Penguin, 1973, p. 135.

33. Chakravarty, Uma. 'The World of the Bhaktin in South Indian Traditions—The Body and Beyond', *Women in Early Indian Societies,* edited by Kumkum Roy, Manohar, 2015.

34. Minhaj-us-Siraj Juzjani. *Tabakat-i-Nasiri,* Sang-e-Meel Publications, 2006.

35. Khosro, Amir of Delhi. *Duval Rāni Khezr Khān* (Persian), edited by M.R.A.S. Ansari and K.A. Nezāmi, Delhi, 1988, p. 49.

36. Battuta, Ibn. *Rehla* (Arabic), translated Mahdi Hussain, 1964; *The Rehla of Ibn Battuta (India, Maldive Islands and Ceylon)*, Oriental Institute Baroda, 1976, pp. 34–35.

37. Venkateshwarlu, K. 'Two Sculptures of Rudrama Devi Shed Light on her Death', *The Hindu,* 5 December 2017, https://www.thehindu.com/news/two-sculptures-of-rani-rudrama-devi-shed-light-on-her-death/article21268201.ece#:~:text=VIJAYAWADA%3A%20Two%20sculptures%20depicting%20Rani,in%20Warangal%20district%20of%20Telangana.

38. Marco Polo. 'Chapter 19', *The Travels of Marco Polo*, Book 3.

39. The ballads or 'Vadakkan Pattukal', an oral storytelling tradition, often narrate legends of brave Kalaripayattu fighters.

40. Susie Tharu and K. Lalita. *Women Writing in India: 600 BC to the Early Twentieth Century—Vol. 1*, Oxford University Press, 1997, p. 82–84.

41. Sellergren, Sarah. 'Janabai and Kanhopatra: A Study of Two Women Sants', *Images of Women in Maharashtrian Literature and Religion,* edited by Anne Feldhaus, State University of New York Press, 1996, p. 221.

42. Susie Tharu and K. Lalita. *Women Writing in India: 600 BC to the Early Twentieth Century—Vol. 1*, Oxford University Press, 1997, p. 83.

43. Raman, Sita Anantha. *Women in India: A Social and Cultural History*, Praeger, 2009, pp. 175–76, p. 183. The next poem is from the same source, p. 182.

44. Didamari, Khwaja Muhammad (Azam). *Waqiat-i-Kashmir* (Persian), Urdu translation by Munshi Ashraf Ali, Delhi, 1846.

45. Mattoo, Neerja. *The Mystic and the Lyric: Four Women Poets from Kashmir,* Zubaan, 2019, pp. 1–82. The Vakhs quoted next are from the same source: p. 41, p. 16, p. 70, p. 64, p. 49, pp. 32–33, p. 56, p. 36.

46. Hoskote, Ranjit. *I, Lalla: The Poems of Lal Ded,* Penguin, 2013, p. 148.

47. Susie Tharu and K. Lalita. *Women Writing in India: 600 BC: to the Present–Vol. I: 600 BC to the Early Twentieth Century*, Oxford University Press, 1991, pp. 85–86; the poem later in this chapter is from pp. 86–87.

48. Sellergren, Sarah. 'Janabai and Kanhopatra: A Study of Two Women Saints', *Images of Women in Maharashtrian Literature and Religion* edited by Anne Feldhaus, 1996, SUNY Press, pp. 227–28.

49. Adapted from Sandhya Mulchandani, *For the Love of God: Women Poet Saints of the Bhakti Movement* (Penguin Viking, 2019).

50. Adapted from Susie Tharu and K. Lalita. *Women Writing in India: 600 BC to the Present–Vol. I: 600 BC to the Early Twentieth Century*, OUP, 1991, pp. 95–96; all poems in this chapter are from the same source: pp. 94–98.

51. Martin, Nancy M. 'Mirabai Comes to America: The Translation and Transformation of a Saint', *The Journal of Hindu Studies*, Vol. 3, No. 1, 1 April 2010, pp. 12–35.

52. Gulbadan Begum, *Humayunama*, translated by Annette Beveridge, Mushiram Manoharlal Publications, 2001, p. 109.

53. Ibid. 116.

54. Ibid. 127–28.

55. Ibid. 142.

56. Ibid. 178.

57. Ibid. 198–99.

58. Ibid. 201.

59. Ibid. 112.

60. Ibid. 130–31.

61. Ibid. 189–90.

62. Monserrat, Antonio. *Commentary—On His Journey to the Court of Akbar*, Humphrey Mildord, Oxford University Press, 1922.

63. Mubarak, Abul Fazl Ibn. *The Akbarnama of Abul Fazl*, translated from the Persian by H. Beveridge, The Asiatic Society, 2000; reprint edition.

64.   Valle, Pietro Della. *The Travels of Pietro Della Valle in India, Letters Vol. 2,* edited by Edward Grey, from an old English translation of 1664, Hakluyt Society, pp. 306–43

65.   Her real name was Harkha Bai, Harkhan Champavati or Hira Kanwar. Popular imagination knows her as Jodha Bai but this is entirely an error, introduced by James Tod in the *Annals and Antiquities of Rajasthan* (early nineteenth century); in fact, Jagat Gosain, another wife of Akbar's, was Jodha Bai, daughter of Raja Udai Singh, ruler of Jodhpur.

66.   Mukhoty, Ira. *Daughters of the Sun: Empress, Queens and Begums of the Mughal Empire,* Aleph Book Company, 2018, p. 130. She quotes an unnamed 'English agent'.

67.   Jahanara, *Risalah-i-Sahibiyah,* cited in Ira Mukhoty, *Heroines: Powerful Indian Women of Myth and History,* Aleph Book Company, 2017, p. 106.

68.   Bukhari, Afshan. 'Masculine Modes of Female Subjectivity', *Speaking of the Self: Gender, Performance and Autobiography in South Asia,* edited by Anshu Malhotra and Siobhan Lambert-Hurley, Zubaan, 2017, pp. 165–202. She is citing Tawakkul Beg, *Nushkah-i-Ahwal-i-Shahi,* p. 181.

69.   Jahanara, *Risaliyah,* cited in Afshan Bukhari, 2017, p. 179.

70.   Ibid. 187–88.

71.   Balabanlilar, Lisa, *Imperial Identity in the Mughal Empire,* I.B. Tauris, 2012.

72.   Mukherjee, Soma. *Royal Mughal Ladies and Their Contributions,* Gyan Publishing House, 2011. She is citing Zeb-un-Nissa, *Diwani-i-Makhfi.* All Zebunissa's verses quoted are from the same source: p. 182–87.

73.   Gupta, Archana Garodia, *The Women Who Ruled India–Leaders Warriors Icons,* Hachette India, 2019, citing Hendrik von Rheede, an administrator in the Dutch East Indies.

74.   Ayyar, K.V. Krishna. *A Short History of Kerala,* Pai & Company, 1966.

75.   Nieuhoff, Johann. *Voyages and Travels to the East Indies (1653–70),* Oxford University Press, 1988.

76. Grose, John Henry. *A Voyage to the East Indies*, S. Hooper, 1766.

77. More, Leena. *English East India Company and the Local Rulers in Kerala: A Case Study of Attingal and Travancore*, Institute for Research in Social Sciences and Humanities, MESHAR, 2003.

78. Malcolm, John. *A Memoir of Central India*, Cambridge University Press, 2011. (First published in 1823)

79. Keay, John, *India: A History*, Grove Press, 2000, p. 425.

80. Besant, Annie. *Children of the Motherland*, Nabu Press, 2012. (First published before 1923)

81. Susie Tharu and K. Lalita, *Women Writing in India: 600 BC to the Early Twentieth Century - Vol. 1*, Oxford University Press, 1997, pp. 116–17.

82. Ibid. 218–19.

83. Ibid. 219.

84. Major Archer. *Tours in Upper India, and in Parts of the Himalaya Mountains; With Accounts of the Courts of the Native Princes*, Palala Press, 2015.

85. Lall, John. *Begum Samru—Fading Portrait in a Gilded Frame*, Roli Books, 2005.

86. Jauhar, Ghulam Hussain. *Tarikh-i-Dilafruz*, Salar Jung Library Collections, 1819, pp. 149–52.

87. Jha, Shweta Sachdeva. 'Tawaif as Poet and Patron: Rethinking Women's Self-Representation', *Speaking of the Self: Gender, Performance and Autobiography in South Asia,* edited by Anshu Malhotra and Siobhan Lambert-Hurley, Zubaan, 2017, p. 151.

88. Kugle, Scott. 'Mah Laqa Bai and Gender,' GulzarI Mah Laqa, Nizam al-Matabi, 1906, p. 368.

89. Jha, Shweta Sachdeva. 'Tawaif as Poet and Patron: Rethinking Women's Self-Representation', *Speaking of the Self: Gender, Performance and Autobiography in South Asia,* edited by Anshu Malhotra and Siobhan Lambert-Hurley, Zubaan, 2017, p. 153 (translation by Shweta Sachdeva Jha of ghazal 9, in Azmi, Rahat, *Mah Laqa: Halat-i-Zindagi: Mah-i-Diwan*, Urdu Academy Andhra Pradesh, 1998.*)

90. This copy of the diwan is now in the British Library, London.

91. Gupta, Archana Garodia. *The Women Who Ruled India: Leaders. Warriors. Icons,* Hachette, 2019, pp. 241–42.

92. Farooqui, Amar. 'From Baiza Bai to Lakshmi Bai: The Sindia State in the Early Nineteenth Century and the Roots of 1857', *Issues in Modern Indian History,* edited by Biswamoy Pati, Popular Prakashan, 2000, p. 47.

93. Ibid. 69.

94. Parks, Fanny. *Wanderings of a Pilgrim in Search of the Picturesque During Four-and-Twenty Years in the East; with Revelations of Life in the Zenana,* 2 volumes, Pelham and Richardson, 1850.

95. R. Shakespear, Resident at Gwalior, cited in Amar Farooqui, 'From Baiza Bai to Lakshmi Bai: The Sindia State in the Early Nineteenth Century and the Roots of 1857', *Issues in Modern Indian History,* edited by Biswamoy Pati, Popular Prakashan, 2000, p. 64.

96. Ibid. 51.

97. Parks, Fanny. *Wanderings of a Pilgrim in Search of the Picturesque During Four-and-Twenty Years in the East; with Revelations of Life in the Zenana,* Pelham and Richardson, 1850, pp. 2–4.

98. Farooqui, Amar. 'From Baiza Bai to Lakshmi Bai: The Sindia State in the Early Nineteenth Century and the Roots of 1857', *Issues in Modern Indian History,* edited by Biswamoy Pati, Popular Prakashan, 2000, p. 59.

99. Ibid. 67.

100. Ibid. 68.

101. Ibid. 69.

102. Begum Sultan Jahan. *An Account of My Life, Vol. 1,* translated by C.H. Payne, John Murray, 1912.

103. Sikandar Begum, *A Pilgrimage to Mecca,* translated by E.I. Willoughby-Osborn and William Wilkinson, W.H. Allen, 1870.

104. Ahluwalia, M.L. *Maharani Jind Kaur,* Singh Brothers, 2001. All other quotations concerning Jindan are from the same source.

105. Wills, C.U. *The Raj-Gond Maharajas of the Satpura Hills: A Local History Based Mainly on Mahomedan Authorities,* Central Provinces Government Press, 1923.

106. John Kaye and George Bruce Malleson. *Kaye's and Malleson's History of the Indian Mutiny of 1857–8: Volume 1,* Cambridge University Press, 2010.

107. Ibid.

108. Forbes-Mitchell, Willaim, *Reminiscences of the Great Mutiny 1857–59 Including the Relief, Siege and Capture of Lucknow*, Echo Library, 2010.

109. Varma, Ram Dayal. *San 1857 ki Shaheed Virangana Uda Devi,* Manoj Printers, 2004.

110. Llewellyn-Jones, Rosie. *The Last King in India: Wajid Ali Shah*, Random House India, 2014.

111. Russell, William-Howard. *My Indian Mutiny Diary*, Cassell, 1957.

112. Ghosh, Paramita. 'Fatima and Fatima', *Hindustan Times*, 26 February 2019, https://www.hindustantimes.com/india-news/fatima-and-fatima/story-abpJ85mOQAJEyiY0VfDaON.htmlf.

113. Guha, Ramachandra. *Makers of Modern India*, Penguin, 2012.

Bibliography

'Baiza Bai: The Banker-Warrior Queen of Gwalior', *Madras Courier,* 19 July 2017, https://madrascourier.com/biography/baiza-bai-the-banker-warrior-queen-of-gwalior/.

'Chandanbala', https://en.encyclopediaofjainism.com/index.php/Chandanbala.

'Karaikkal Ammai in Tamil Temples', glorioustamils, 27 October 2019, https://glorioustamils.com/2019/10/27/karaikkal-ammai-in-tamil-temples/.

'Mata Khivi Ji', All About Sikhs, https://www.allaboutsikhs.com/biographies/great-sikh-women/mata-khivi-ji/.

'Mata Khivi', The Sikh Encyclopedia, https://www.thesikhencyclopedia.com/biographical/famous-women/khivi-mata/.

'Queen Mallika', Myanmarpedia, http://myanmarpedia.wordpress.com/2007/09/27/queen-mallika/.

'Rudrama Devi, the First Woman Ruler of Andhra', The Hans India, 25 February 2014, https://www.thehansindia.com/posts/index/Parenting-and-Kids/2014-02-25/Rudrama-Devi-the-first-woman-ruler-of-Andhra/87355.

'Tarabai Shinde: The Life of a Pioneer (1850–1910)', https://artsandculture.google.com/exhibit/tarabai-shinde-zubaan/LgKymlfRaYmiLw?hl=en.

'Visakha, Great Female Supporter', *Buddhist Studies, The Life of the Buddha, (Part Two)*, Buddha Dharma Education Association and BudhhaNet, http://www.buddhanet.net/e-learning/buddhism/lifebuddha/2_4lbud.htm. 2019.

Abida Sultaan. *Memoirs of a Rebel Princess*, Oxford University Press, Pakistan, 2013.

Ahluwalia, M.L. *Maharani Jind Kaur,* Singh Brothers, 2001.

Ahmed, Nazeer. 'Razia, Sultana of Delhi (1205–1240)', History of Islam, https://historyofislam.com/contents/the-post-mongol-period/razia-sultana-of-delhi/.

Aklujkar, Vidyut. *'Between Pestle and Mortar: Women in Marathi Saint Tradition', Goddesses and Women in the Indic Religious Tradition,* edited by Arvind Sharma, Brill, 2005.

Allen, Charles. *Ashoka: The Search for India's Lost Emperor,* Hachette, 2012.

Aranha, Jovita. 'The Untold Story of the Brave Maratha Warrior Queen Ahilyabai Holkar', *The Better India,* 17 October 2017, https://www.thebetterindia.com/119761/queen-ahilyabai-holkar-maratha/.

Archambault, Hannah L. 'Becoming Mughal in the Nineteenth Century: The Case of the Bhopal Princely State', *Journal of South Asian Studies,* Vol. 36, No. 4, 2013, pp. 479–95.

B.S. Chandrababu and L. Thilagavati. *Woman, Her History and Her Struggle for Emancipation,* Bharathi Pustakalayam, pp. 155–56.

Basavaraja. 'Anti-British Rebellions in Karnataka of the Nineteenth Century', *The South Indian Rebellions (Before and After 1800),* edited by S. Gopalakrishnan, Palaniappa Brothers, 2007.

Bedi, J.S. 'She Rose to Be a Heroine', *The Tribune,* 20 October 2001, https://www.tribuneindia.com/2001/20011020/windows/slice.htm.

Bhandare, Shailen. 'Historcal Study of the Satvahana Era—A Study of Coins', Phd Thesis.

Bhattacharyya, Uday. *Khanar Bachan,* Blurb Publications, 2021.

Bihari, Nepram. *Cheitharol Kumbaba: The Royal Chronicle of Manipur,* Spectrum Publications, 2012.

Bode, Mabel. 'Women Leaders of the Buddhist Reformation', *Journal of the Royal Asiatic Society,* 1893, pp. 517–62.

Bukhari, Afshan. 'Masculine Modes of Female Subjectivity', *Speaking of the Self: Gender, Performance and Autobiography in South Asia,* edited by Anshu Malhotra and Siobhan Lambert-Hurley, Zubaan, 2017, pp. 165–202.

Chakravarti, Uma. 'The World of the Bhaktin in South Indian Traditions—the Body and Beyond', *Women in Early Indian Societies,* edited by Kumkum Roy, Manohar, 2015, pp. 299–321.

Chakravarti, Uma. 'The Rise of Women as Experienced by Buddhism', *Manushi*, November–December 1981.

Chowdhury, Mahfuz Ul Hasib. 'Value of "Khona's Parables" in Bengali Folklore', *Daily Asian Age*, 8 June 2017, https://dailyasianage.com/news/66423/value-of-khonas-parables-in-bengali-folklore.

Craddock, Elaine. *Siva's Demon Devotee: Karaikkal Ammaiyar*, State University of New York Press, 2010.

Crossette, Barbara, 'Sanghamitta,' *Tricycle*, Fall 2001.

Dehejia, Vidya. *The Body Adorned: Dissolving Boundaries Between Sacred and Profane in India's Art*, Mapin Publishing, 2009,

Devadhar, C.R. 'The Identity of Rudrakumaradevi with Prataparudra of the Kakatiya Dynasty', *Annals of the Bhandarkar Oriental Research Institute*, Vol. 38, No. 3/4, July–October 1957.

Devi, Mahasweta. *The Queen of Jhansi*, translated by Mandira and Sagaree Sengupta, Seagull, 2000.

Dhara, Lalitha. *Phules and Women's Question*, Dr Ambedkar College of Commerce and Economics, Mumbai, 2011.

Doniger, Wendy. (trans.). *Rigveda*, Penguin.

Falk, Nancy Auer. 'The Case of the Vanishing Nuns: The Fruits of Ambivalence in Ancient Indian Buddhism,' *Unspoken Words: Women's Religious Lives*, edited by Nancy Auer Falk and Rita M. Gross, Wadsworth, 2001, pp. 196–206.

Farooqui, Amar. 'From Baiza Bai to Lakshmi Bai: The Sindia State in the Early Nineteenth Century and the Roots of 1857', *Issues in Modern Indian History*, edited by Biswamoy Pati, Popular Prakashan, 2000, pp. 45–74.

Forbes-Mitchell, William. *Reminiscences of the Great Mutiny 1857–59 Including the Relief, Siege and Capture of Lucknow*, Echo Library, 2010.

Futehally, Shama. *In the Dark of the Heart: Songs of Meer*, Indus, 1996.

Gabbay, Alyssa. 'In Reality a Man: Sultan Iltutmish, His Daughter, Raziya, and Gender Ambiguity in Thirteenth Century Northern India', *Journal of Persianate Studies*, Vol. 4, No. 1, 2010, pp. 45–63.

George, Anjali. 'Warrior Woman "Unniyarcha": The Kalarippayattu Legend of Kerala', Shaktitva, 8 March2019, https://shaktitva.org/blog/2019/3/8/unniyarcha-the-kalarippayattu-legend-of-kerala.

Goshwami, Hareshwar. *History of the People of Manipur*, Kangla Publications, 2004.

Grose, John Henry. *A Voyage to the East Indies*, S. Hooper, 1766.

Guha, Ramachandra. *Makers of Modern India*, Penguin, 2012.

Gulbadan Begum. *The History of Humayun: Humayun-Nama,* translated by Annette S. Beveridge, LLP, 1902.

Gupta, Archana Garodia. *Women Who Ruled India: Leaders. Warriors. Icons.,* Hachette, 2019

Gupta, Charu. 'Dalit "Virangana" and Reinvention of 1857', *EPW,* Vol. 42, No. 19, 12–18 May 2007, pp. 1739–45.

Haraniya, Krutika. 'Kashmir's "Ruthless" Queen Didda, Live History India, 19 February 2018, https://www.livehistoryindia.com/story/people/kashmirs-ruthless-queen-didda.

Hazra, Nivedita. 'Rudrama Devi: The Queen Who Wore a King's Image', *Feminism in India,* 8 November 2019, https://feminisminindia.com/2019/11/08/rudrama-devi-queen-kings-image/.

Hoskote, Ranjit. *I, Lalla: The Poems of Lal Ded,* Penguin, 2013.

Imam, Syeda. *The Untold Charminar—Writings on Hyderabad*, Penguin, 2008.

Jaffer, Mehru. 'Begum Hazrat Mahal: The Pari Who Became a Revolutionary', *The Citizen,* 30 May 2016.

Jha, Shweta Sachdeva. 'Tawaif as Poet and Patron: Rethinking Women's Self-Representation', *Speaking of the Self: Gender, Performance and Autobiography in South Asia,* edited by Anshu Malhotra and Siobhan Lambert-Hurley, Zubaan, 2017, pp. 141–64.

John Kaye and George Bruce Malleson. *Kaye's and Malleson's History of the Indian Mutiny of 1857–8: Volume 1*, Cambridge University Press, 2010.

Kabui, Gangmumei. *History of Manipur, Vol. 1: Pre-Colonial Period*, National Publishing House, 1991.

Kamal, Kishan. *1857 ki Krantikari Jhalkari Bai*, Raja Pocket Books, Delhi 2015.

Kamat, Jyotsna. 'Abbakka the Brave Queen', Kamat's Potpurri, 31 October 2007, http://www.kamat.com/kalranga/itihas/abbakka.htm.

Kambar, Chandrasekhar. 'Kannada Poetesses', *Our Cultural Fabric—Indian*

Poetesses Past & Present, Part 2, edited by P.N. Chopra, Ministry of Education, Social Welfare and Culture, Government of India, 1977.

Kaur, Lakhpreet. 'Ten Badass Sikh Women in History', *Ms.*, 17 March 2015, https://msmagazine.com/2015/03/17/10-badass-sikh-women-in-history/.

Kavya Phule, translated by Ujjwala Mhatre, edited by Lalitha Dhara, Dr Ambedkar College of Commerce and Economics, Mumbai, 2012.

Keay, Julia. *The Woman Who Saved an Empire*, I.B. Tauris, 2014.

Ketning, M. Whitney. 'Candanbala Embodied' *Jinamanjari*, Vol. 34, No. 2, 2006, pp. 6–17.

Khalid, Haroon. 'How Lahore Came to Claim the Rebellious and Gifted Mughal Princess Zeb-un-nisa as Its Own', *Scroll.in*, 11 August 2017, https://scroll.in/article/846816/how-lahore-came-to-claim-the-rebellious-and-gifted-mughal-princess-zeb-un-nisa-as-its-own.

Khan, Aqsa. 'Remembering Fatima Sheikh: A Woman Lost in History', *Feminism in India,* 22 June 2017, https://feminisminindia.com/2017/06/22/fatima-sheikh-essay/.

Khan, Farha. 'Begum Samru of Sardhana: Socio-Political Interventions and Continuing Legacy', *Proceedings of the Indian History Congress,* Vol. 73, 2012, pp. 707–718.

Khan, Shahryar. *The Begums of Bhopal*, I.B. Tauris, 2000.

Khayal, Ghulam Nabi. 'Kashmiri Poetesses', *Our Cultural Fabric—Indian Poetesses Past & Present, Part 2,* edited by P.N. Chopra, Ministry of Education, Social Welfare and Culture, Government of India, 1977, pp. 33–42.

Khosro Amir of Delhi, *Duval Rāni Khezr Khān* (Persian), edited by M.R.A.S. Ansāri and K.A. Nezāmi, Delhi, 1988.

Kurup, Pushpa. 'What MT did to Unniyarcha', *Deccan Chronicle*, 28 November 2017, https://www.deccanchronicle.com/nation/current-affairs/281117/what-mt-did-to-unniyarcha.html.

Lal, Ruby. 'Historicizing the Harem: The Challenge of a Princess's Memoir', *Feminist Studies*, Vol. 30, No. 3, Fall 2004.

Lall, John. *Begum Samru—Fading Portrait in a Gilded Frame*, Roli Books, 2005.

Leah Verghese, Ranjna and Medha Sundar. *Savitribai: Journey of a Trailblazer*, Azim Premji University Publications, 2014.

Leena, P.K. 'The Rani of Attingal and the English in Travancore', *Proceedings of the Indian History Congress*, Vol. 46, 1985, pp. 364–72.

Llewellyn-Jones, Rosie. *The Last King in India: Wajid Ali Shah*, Random House India, 2014.

M.B. Kamath and V. Kher. *Devi Ahalyabai Holkar: The Philosopher Queen*, Bharatiya Vidya Bhavan, 1995.

Madur. 'Onaka Obavve Kindi—An Epitome of Bravery', 3 October 2017, Karnataka.com, https://www.karnataka.com/personalities/onake-obavva/.

Mah Laqa Chanda, Rekhta, https://www.rekhta.org/poets/mah-laqa-chanda/all.

Mahabharata, Section CCCXXI, pp. 52–72, https://www.sacred-texts.com/hin/m12/m12c020.htm.

Mahanama-Sthavira, Thera, *Mahavamsa: The Great Chronicle of Sri Lanka*, Asian Humanities Press, 2012.

Majumdar, R.C. *Ancient India, Motilal Banarsidas, 2007.*

Malaiya, Yashwant. 'Great Ascetics', Jain History, http://jainhistory.tripod.com/ascetics.html

Marco Polo. 'Chapter 19', *The Travels of Marco Polo: Book 3*.

Martin, Nancy M. 'Mirabai Comes to America: The Translation and Transformation of a Saint',

Mattoo, Neerja. *The Mystic and the Lyric: Four Women Poets from Kashmir*, Zubaan, 2019.

McLoughlin, Margo. 'The Verses of Ambapali', *Parabola*. 2016, https://parabola.org/2016/11/08/the-verses-of-ambapali-by-margo-mcloughlin/.

Minhaj-i-Siraj, Juzjani, *Tabakuat-i-Nasiri, 1260 CE*, Sang-e-Meel Publications, 2006 .

Monserrat, Antonio. *Commentary—On His Journey to the Court of Akbar, Humphrey Mildord*, Oxford University Press, 1922.

More, Leena. *English East India Company and the Local Rulers in Kerala: A Case Study of Attingal and Travancore*, Institute for Research in Social Sciences and Humanities, MESHAR, 2003.

Mubarak, Abul Fazl Ibn. *The Akbarnama of Abul Fazl*, translated from the Persian by H. Beveridge, The Asiatic Society, 1939.

Muddupalani. *The Appeasement of Radhika: Radhika Santwanam*, translated by Sandhya Mulchandani, Penguin, 2011.

Mukherjee, Priyanka. 'How Rani Velu Nachiyar Planned the First Suicide Attack to Disarm the British', INUTH, 9 August 2017, https://www.inuth.com/india/women-freedom-fighters-of-india/how-rani-velu-nachiyar-planned-the-first-suicide-attack-to-disarm-the-british/.

Mukherjee, Soma. *Royal Mughal Ladies: And their Contribution*, Gyan Publishing House, 2011.

Mukhoty, Ira. *Heroines: Powerful Indian Women of Myth and History*, Aleph Book Company, 2017.

———— *Daughters of the Sun: Empresses, Queens and Begums of the Mughal Empire*, Aleph Book Company, 2018.

Mulchandani, Sandhya. *For the Love of God: Women Poet Saints of the Bhakti Movement,* Penguin, 2019.

Murcott, Susan. *First Buddhist Women: Poems and Stories of Awakening*, Parallax Press, 1991.

Naimishrai, Mohan Das. *Veerangana Jhalkari Bai,* Radhakrishna Publications, 2003.

Nayak, Prateeksha. 'Onaka Obavve—An Ordinary Woman who Displayed Extraordinary Courage, HerStory, 15 August 2015, https://yourstory.com/2015/08/herstory-flashback-onake-obavva/amp.

Nyanaponika Thera and Hecker Hellmuth, et al. *Great Disciples of the Buddha: Their Lives, Their Works, Their Legacy,* Wisdom Publications, 2012.

Obeyesekere, Donald. *Outlines of Ceylon History*, Asian Educational Services, 1999, pp. 17–18.

Parita, Mukta. *Upholding the Common Life: the Community of Mirabai,* Oxford University Press, 1994.

Parks, Fanny. *Wanderings of a Pilgrim in Search of the Picturesque During Four-and-Twenty Years in the East; with Revelations of Life in the Zenana*, 2 volumes, Pelham and Richardson, 1850.

Patton, Laurie L. 'The Fate of the Female Rishis: Portraits of Lopamudra', *Myth and Mythmaking—Continuous Evolution in Indian Tradition,* edited by Julai Leslie, Routledge, 1996, pp. 21–38.

Pechilis, Karen. *Interpreting Devotion: The Poetry and Legacy of a Female Bhakti Saint of India*, Routledge, 2012.

Pezarkar, Leora. 'The Story of Raziyat-ud-din', Live History India, 14 October 2017, https://www.livehistoryindia.com/story/people/the-story-of-raziyat-ud-din-razia-sultan.

Pillai, Manu S. 'The Woman Who Cut Off Her Breasts', *The Hindu*, 18 February 2017, https://www.thehindu.com/society/history-and-culture/the-woman-who-cut-off-her-breasts/article17324549.ece.

Pillai, Manu. 'Holding Kings to Ransom—Royal Women in Matrilineal Kerala', *Kafila*, 9 December 2015, https://kafila.online/2015/12/02/holding-kings-to-ransom-royal-women-in-matrilineal-kerala-manu-pillai/.

Pillai, Manu. *The Ivory Throne: Chronicles of the House of Travancore*, HarperCollins, 2016.

Prabha, Shashi. *Rani Durgavati*, Publications Division, Information and Broadcasting Ministry, Government of India, 1990.

Prasad, Shilpa. 'Remembering Tarabai Shinde: Breaking Caste and Patriarchy Glass Ceilings', *Feminism in India,* 1 March 2017, https://feminisminindia.com/2017/03/01/remembering-tarabai-shinde-essay/.

Preckel, Claudia. 'The Roots of Anglo-Muslim Cooperation and Islamic Reformism in Bhopal' *Perspectives of Mutual Encounters in South Asian History: 1760–1860*, edited by Jamal Malik, Brill, 2000.

Priya Sarukkai Chabria and Ravi Shankar. *Andal—The Autobiography of a Goddess,* Zubaan Books, 2016.

Rajagopalachari, C. *Avvaiar a Great Tamil Poetess*, Bharatiya Vidya Bhavan, 1971.

Rajan, Senthil. 'Veera-mangai Velu Nachiar', Live India, https://www.liveindia.com/freedomfighters/veera-mangai-velunachiyar.html.

Raman, Sita Anantha. *Women in India: A Social and Cultural History*, Praeger, 2009.

Ramanujam, A.K. *Speaking of Siva*, Penguin, 1973.

——— *Poems of Love and War: From the Eight Anthologies and Ten Long Poems of Classical Tamil*, Oxford University Press, 2005.

Rangachari, Devika. 'Five Extraordinary Indian Queens Who Have Been Reduced to Footnotes in History', *Scroll.in*, 19 April 2015, https://scroll.in/article/700539/five-extraordinary-indian-queens-who-have-been-reduced-to-mere-footnotes-in-history.

Rekhta Foundation, 'Begum Zeb-u-nissa: A Princess Enchained', https://artsandculture.google.com/exhibit/begum-zeb-un-nissa-rekhta-foundation/PgKihOmfW69MLg?hl=en.

Rekhta Foundation, 'Jahanara the Sufi Princess', https://artsandculture.google.com/exhibit/jahan-ara-rekhta-foundation/AQKSGf9d5enTKA?hl=en.

Rhys-David, Carolyn. *Psalms of the Sisters,* Pali Text Society, 1909.

Russell, William Howard. *My Indian Mutiny Diary,* Cassell, 1957.

S, Lekshmi Priya. 'Velu Nachiyar and Kuyili: The Women Who Took Down the British 85 Years before 1857', *The Better India,* 28 August 2018, https://www.thebetterindia.com/157316/news-india-independence-women-fighters-british-raj/#:~:text=Velu%20Nachiyar%20%26%20Kuyili%3A%20The%20Women,British%20in%20the%20eighteenth%20century.

Safvi, Rana. 'The Forgotten Women of 1847', *The Wire,* 19 November 2018, https://thewire.in/history/the-forgotten-women-of-1857.

Salve, Mukta. *Mang Maharachya Dukhvisayi,* Dalit Web, 23 November 2015, https://www.dalitweb.org/?p=2947.

Sanajaoba, Naorem. *Manipur Past and Present—The Ordeals and Heritage of a Civilisation,* Mittal, 1991.

Sarah Sellergren. 'Janabai and Kanhopatra: A Study of Two Women Sants', *Images of Women in Maharashtrian Literature and Religion,* edited by Anne Feldhaus, SUNY Press, 1996.

Sarna, Jasveen Kaur. 'Five Women in Sikh History You Should Know About', *Feminism in India,* 12 July 2017, https://feminisminindia.com/2017/07/12/5-sikh-women-know/.

Sayyed Ahmed and Farid Ahmed. 'The Maxims of Khona: A Contextual Study of Sustainability over Vernacular Architecture Practices of Bangladesh', *Journal of Modern Science and Technology,* 2015.

Sebastian, Sheryl. 'Kerala's Casteist Breast Tax and the Story of Nangeli', *Feminism in India* 12 September 2016, https://feminisminindia.com/2016/09/12/kerala-breast-tax-nangeli/.

Sellergren, Sarah. 'Janabai and Kanhopatra: A Study of Two Women Saints', *Images of Women in Maharashtrian Literature and Religion,* edited by Anne Feldhause, SUNY Press, 1996, pp. 213–138.

Sen, Nabaneeta Dev. 'Rewriting the Ramayana: Chandrabati and Molla', *India International Quarterly*, Vol. 24, No. 2/3, Crossing Boundaries, 1997, pp. 163–77.

Sengupta, Nandini. 'The British Woman Traveller in India: Cultural Intimacy and Interracial Kinship in Fanny Park's Wanderings in Search of the Picturesque', *New Readings in the Literature of British India, c. 1780–1947*, edited by Towheed Shafquat, Columbia University Press, 2007, pp. 93–118.

Shah Jahan, Begum of Bhopal. *Taj ul Iqbal Tarikh Bhopal, or the History of Bhopal,* translated by H.C. Barstow, Thacker, Spink and Company, 1876.

Shashidhar, Melkunde. *A History of Freedom and Unification Movement in Karnataka*, Laxmi Book Publications, 2016.

Sikandar Begum. *A Pilgrimage to Mecca*, translated by E.I. Willoughby-Osborn and William Wilkinson, W.H. Allen, 1870.

Singh, Balbir. *Maharani Jind Kaur: A Rebellious Queen*, Reader's Paradise, 2018.

Singh, Brijraj. 'The Enigma of Begum Samru: Differing Approaches to Her Life', *India International Centre Quarterly*, Vol. 24, No. 4, Winter 1997, pp. 33–43.

Singh, Upinder. *A History of Ancient and Early Medieval India: From the Stone Age to the 12th Century*, Prentice Hall, 2009.

Sitaram Pandit, Ranjit (trans). *Kalhana's Rajatarangini,* South Asia Books, 1990.

Sri Aurobindo, *Rigveda: Samhita and Padapatha—Translations and Commentaries*, http://sri-aurobindo.in/workings/matherials/rigveda/01/01-179.htm.

Stephanie W. Jamison and Joel P. Brereton. *The Rigveda: 3-Volume Set*, Oxford University Press, 2014, pp. 379–84.

Sultan Jahan Begum. *An Account of My Life,* translated by Abdus Samad Khan, John Murray, 1912.

Sultan Jahan Begum. *Hayat-i-Qudsi: Life of the Nawab Gauhar Begum Alias the Nawab Begum Qudsia of Bhopal,* translated by W.S. Davis, Kegan-Paul, Trench, Trubner and Co. Ltd, 2017.

Sushil Bhati and Mahipal Singh.'1857 ke Svatantrata Sangram mein

Avantibai ki Bhumika', Jan Itihas, 13 February 2013, http://janitihas. blogspot.com/2013/02/1857-avanti-bai-lodhi_19.html.

Susie Tharu and K. Lalita. *Women Writing in India: 600 BC to the Present. Volume 1: 600 BC to the Early Twentieth Century*, Oxford University Press, 1995.

The Telugu Archive. 'A Tale of Two Devadasis', Medium, 22 May 2019, https://medium.com/@theteluguarchive/a-tale-of-two-devadasis-603ee867a172.

Theri, Tathaloka, 'The Amazing Transformations of Arahanta Their Uppalavanna', http://www.bhikkhuni.net/wp-content/uploads/2013/08/Transformations-of-Arahant-Theri-Uppalavanna1.pdf.

Therigatha: Poems of the First Buddhist Women, translated by Charles Hallisey, Murty Classical Library of India, Harvard University Press, 2015.

Thomas, Patricia. *Indian Women through the Ages*, Asia Publishing House, 1964, pp. 94–98.

Valle, Pietro Della. *The Travels of Pietro Della Valle in India, Vol 2*, translated by G. Havers, edited by Edward Grey, Cambridge University Press, 2010.

Vanita, Ruth.'The Self Has No Gender: A Female and a Male Scholar Debate Women's Status in the Mahabharata', *Gandhi's Tiger and Sita's Smile: Essays on Gender, Sexuality and Culture*, Yoda Press, 2005, pp. 14–34.

Varma, Ram Dayal. *San 1857 ki Shaheed Virangana Uda Devi*, Manoj Printers, Hardoi, 2004.

Venkateshwarlu, K. 'Two Sculptures of Rudrama Devi Shed Light on Her Death,' *The Hindu*, 5 December 2017, https://www.thehindu.com/news/two-sculptures-of-rani-rudrama-devi-shed-light-on-her-death/article21268201.ece.

Walters, Jonathan S. 'A Voce from the Silence: The Buddha's Mother's Story', *History of Religions*, Vol. 33, No. 4, May 1994, University of Chicago Press, pp. 358–79.

Wills, C.U. *The Raj-Gond Maharajas of the Satpura Hills: A Local History Based Mainly on Mahomedan Authorities*, Central Provinces Government Press, 1923.

Women Heroes and Dalit Assertion in North India, edited by Badri Narayan, Sage Publications, 2006.

Yadav, Dhirendra. 'Pratham Svatantrata Sangram mein Pramukh Sutradhar Theen Veerangana Avantibai Lodhi', Patrika, 13 August 2017, https://www. patrika.com/agra-news/rani-avanti-bai-lodhi-history-in-hindi-1711469/.

Yashoda Devi. *The History of Andhra Country—1000 to 1500 A.D.*, Gyan Publishing House, 1933.

Zeb-un-nisssa. *The Diwan of Zeb-un-Nissa- The First Fifty Ghazals*, translated by Magan Lal and Jessie Duncan, Westbrook, 1913.

Zelliot, Eleanor. 'Women and Power: Women Saints in Medieval Maharashtra', *Faces of the Feminine in Ancient, Medieval and Modern India*, edited by Mandakranta Bose, Oxford University Press, 2000, p. 197.

Zelliot, Eleanor. 'Ahilyabai Holkar: The Queen of Warriors', *Manushi*, No. 124, May–June 2001.